Advance Responses to

Viable Utopian Id[...]
Shaping a Better Worl[...]

"Art Shostak's editorship of essays on the intriguing concept of Utopia could not be more timely. By providing a forum for promulgating this powerful collection of utopian ideas from noted leaders right now, as the world seems to jolt from crisis to crisis, Shostak and his 47 erudite and creative contributors have offered up some desperately needed hope. This hope itself becomes the very seed for the full flowering of Utopia. Thus, I like to say that optimism is a moral imperative. This book, in addition to being highly instructive, is nothing less than an act of moral courage."
— Dr. Rick Lippin, M.D., FACOEM, Tobyhanna Army Depot-Medical Officer

"It is so refreshing to see the forgotten dream of Utopia resurrected in such a timely and compelling fashion. These thought-provoking essays give voice to the forgotten language of hope, dreams, and possibilities and make even the most jaded cynic take a few minutes to reflect upon 'what might be.'"
— Sharon R. Pinnock, Labor Futurist and Director of Membership and Organization American Federation of Government Employees (AFGE)

"*Viable Utopian Ideas,* a collection of essays written with the perspectives of an entering college student in mind, provides deep intellectual food at a time when we need it most. The tragedies and doubts caused by the terror of 9/11, major corporate betrayals, and intense struggles regarding educational equity are some of the fundamental issues facing us as we venture into this uncertain century. The book's 47 essays should cause us to think more deeply and richly about who we are and where we want to go. Educators, in particular, need to be at the center of efforts to re-think our particular mission as the world's supposed democratic superpower. Bravo for this effort to dream before today's realities claim all of our minds and souls. With effort like this, maybe we can create the future rather than simply react to the present!"
— Terry Furin, Saint Joseph's University

"Creating better futures is a critical task for us as individuals, through our organizations, and in our communities. Art Shostak's collection explores twenty-first century options for creating better futures as seen by a diverse group of academics, futurists, and visionaries. The various articles give much to think about, opportunities for disagreement, and the opportunity to enhance our own sense of utopia—and our role in creating it."
— Clement Bezold, President, Institute for Alternative Futures

"'Utopia' can be an intimidating word, suggesting a state of unattainable perfection. But scholars are coming increasingly to define utopia simply as a much better world, a world that for all we know may lie within our grasp. In *Viable Utopian Ideas,* people of many backgrounds offer their best thoughts on how we can bring utopia nearer, in our own lives, in our nation, on our planet, and even beyond."
—W. Warren Wagar, Distinguished Teaching Professor of History Emeritus, Binghamton University, SUNY

"Drenched as we are with news of corporate corruption, a widening rich-poor gap, church scandals, and fundamentalist fanaticism, it comes as a breath of fresh air to sample the utopian ideas in this book. Remembering that, even fifty years ago, concepts such as a manned landing on the moon, the Internet, and an integrated South Africa seemed utopian visions, we may find that some of the ideas broached here may also not be as remote as they now appear. There is much delicious food for thought in this volume."
— Hal Linstone, Professor Emeritus of Systems Science, Portland State University

"George Bernard Shaw is still remembered for his powerful statement: 'Some men see the way things are and ask, 'Why?' I see the way things could be and ask, 'Why not?' Art Shostak has brought together 47 varied, rich, and inspiring reflections on what could be and why not, touching such topics as ethnic conflict, outer space, poetry, the web, environmental degradation, and overpopulation."
— Earl Babbie, Sociologist and Author

"The faster you go, the more important is vision. When technological, economic, cultural and personal change happens as fast as it does today, we need to have a vision of where we are going, a beacon that guides us through the turbulence of rapid change. *Viable Utopian Ideas: Shaping a Better World* is such a beacon. It presents a wealth of ideas and visions for the future. It points to ideal and not-so-ideal futures (depending on your point of view) that will help us think about our own personal utopias and our own vision of what we want the world to be. As I see it, the concept of 'utopia' is a tool we use for measuring ourselves and our society. It is a definition of success—what the world should look like. This book is a valuable tool for helping us see and measure the health of our society."
— Medard Gabel, CEO, BigPictureSmallWorld.com
Author, *Global Inc. An Atlas of the Multinational Corporation*

"When considering a new idea (or even revisiting one with fresh eyes), it is helpful to sample perspectives that stimulate, challenge, and otherwise develop one's own views. *Viable Utopian Ideas* provides a guided tour through more than a dozen significant lenses of creating a better world, covering the range from a personal future to societal change on a wider scale. This collection of essays is timely, easily accessible, and worthwhile."
— Bill Ringle, Executive Director, LearnWell Institute, Philadelphia

"Capturing and packaging many different perspectives on utopian thinking is a refreshing shift given today's high levels of uncertainty. We all need to have a dream about a utopian environment that propels us through the current struggles and gives us hope and energy to move forward. Such a collection of essays provides the opportunity to leap to the future. This can be particularly valuable in the business world today, which is full of uncertainty and lacks clarity. It permits thinking beyond what 'is' to 'what can be' and enables breaking through current business challenges."
—Dudley P. Cooke, CEO, Liberty Business Strategies, Ltd., Ardmore, PA

"Economists have a saying: In the long run we are all dead. This emphasizes attention only on today's problems—the opposite of any discussion of utopian dreams or planning to forestall future societal concerns. This book is a welcome addition to counterbalance

the prevalent American attitude of focusing on immediate issues. Focusing on a multitude of future issues from diverse vantage points can only be an endeavor of value."
— Edgar Czarnecki, Retired Assistant Education Director, AFL-CIO

"Sanity is inevitable. Human beings will do the right thing—after they've tried everything else. This collection of distinguished essays will play a part in keeping utopian thinking alive, and maybe even making it respectable."
—Dr. Karl Albrecht, Futurist and author of
Minds at Work: Leveraging the Power of Organizational Intelligence

"Think of the varied images in this book as positive futures, hoping to be created. We all need to think beyond the frustrations of the present, to imagine what might be possible. While we cannot predict the future, we can help to create it. This book gives us some important clues about what could be created, and how."
— Bob Johansen, President, Institute for the Future, Menlo Park, CA

"This is an extraordinary and compelling set of essays, which address a range of issues. . . . This book's scope is a dreamer's (in the sense that we should not lose our dream) delight. At a time when optimism is not as high as we would like to see it, this book offers many reasons for older adults (like myself) or young college students to think about how we might address some of the problems that face us as an idealistic nation."
— John A. DeFlaminis, Superintendent, Radnor Township School District, PA

"At the age of twenty, when I challenged many of the ideas my parents and community had given me, I looked for a book like *Viable Utopian Ideas: Shaping a Better World*. I wanted to create a new future for others and myself. I wanted to stretch my thinking. I wanted a book like this to help me envision a different world and develop a commitment to its creating. I hope that others who want to challenge themselves and the world find this book."
— Bill Clinton, Consultant and Director of the Organizational Development and Leadership Master's Program at the Philadelphia College of Osteopathic Medicine

"This is certainly an ambitious and helpful book for anyone who aspires to help make a better future. Forty-seven insightful thinkers open a door to a higher level of accomplishment. Introductions to the essays are very reader-friendly, and I especially commend the book's diversity of material, its hints on how to achieve gains, and its ability to help us reflect anew on our lives. New editions over the years ahead are something to look forward to."
—Rei Kawashima, Tokyo Chapter Coordinator of World Future Society,
Secretary General, University Space Engineering Consortium,
Writer, Translator, Futurist

VIABLE UTOPIAN IDEAS

shaping a better world

Edited by Arthur B. Shostak

M.E.Sharpe
Armonk, New York
London, England

Essays by Stephen Downes, Valarie Fournier, Michael Marien, Stanley Shostak, and Harris
Sokoloff have been shortened and/or revised by the editor with the permission
of the authors. In the case of the Downes material, it previously appeared only on the Internet.
In the other cases, the version in this volume departs substantially in length and significantly
in depth from the original source (acknowledged at the end of each essay). Accordingly,
permission to reprint was sought and received from only two sources: Sarah Warner
(swarner@wfs.org), gave permission on behalf of The World Future for reprinting of an
essay by Michael Marien, "Utopia Revisted: New Thinking on Social Betterment," which
appeared in the March/April, 2002, issue, of *The Futurist*. Sally Banks Zakariya, the Editor,
gave permission to publish an adaptation of an article by Harris Sokoloff, which appeared in
American School Board Journal, September, 2001, pp. 26-29. Both instances of cooperation
are gratefully acknowledged.

Library of Congress Cataloging-in-Publication Data

Viable utopian ideas : shaping a better world / [edited] by Arthur B. Shostak.
    p. cm.
  Includes bibliographical references and index.
    ISBN 0-7656-1104-X (alk. paper) — ISBN 0-7656-1105-8 (pbk.: alk. paper)
     1. Utopias. 2. Idealism. 3. Social change. 4. Social prediction. I. Shostak, Arthur B.

HX806.V49 2003
335'.02—dc21

2002036588

Printed in the United States of America

The paper used in this publication meets the minimum requirements of
American National Standard for Information Sciences
Permanence of Paper for Printed Library Materials,
ANSI Z 39.48-1984.

⊗

BM (c) 10   9   8   7   6   5   4   3   2   1
BM (p) 10   9   8   7   6   5   4   3   2   1

For my two grandsons,
David Milton Shostak and Benjamin Jesse Shostak,
and for grandchildren everywhere,
in the fond hope that
our viable utopian ideas
will inspire, inform, and enable
even better ideas
of their own.

Contents

III. METHODS: EVEN BETTER TOOLS

IV. METHODS: INFORMATION TECHNOLOGY

V. LOOKING INWARD

VI. LOOKING HOMEWARD

XIV. DRAWING IT TOGETHER—AND MOVING ON

Acknowledgments

Thanks are owed to Ted Goertzel, an applied sociologist at Rutgers University, Camden, NJ, for first suggesting use of the term *viable*. He located it in the work of Fernando Henrique Cardoso, a prominent Brazilian sociologist who recently served eight years as the president of that country. The theme of Cardosa's last campaign was "the viable utopia."

Many of the contributors to this volume provided extra help throughout the book-preparation process, especially Douglas Bedell, Wendell Bell, Joseph F. Coates, Sohail Inayatullah, Roger Kaufman, Ross Koppel, Michael Marien, Robert Merikangas, and Thomas Reiner. Many commented insightfully on first drafts, and their feedback often resulted in upgrades by cooperative authors with whom I shared the comments; Wendell Bell, Tsvi Bisk, Joseph F. Coates, Sohail Inayatullah, Roger Kaufman, and Ross Koppel were particularly helpful.

Carol Montgomery, a friend who is the head of the Drexel University Library, referred me to a potential contributor whose story she thought belonged in this book, and in this manner we obtained a fine essay from Diane Mc-Manus. Similarly, Wendell Bell recommended contributor Jesse Rhines, and Robert Merikangas called others to my attention. Several essayists, including Carroy U. Ferguson, Ross Koppel, and Harris Sokoloff, suggested people to write blurbs.

Alison M. Lewis, the Drexel University Information Services Librarian for the Humanities and Social Sciences, located bibliographic material on very short notice, and she walked it in 90° heat to my office: I am very appreciative.

My wife, Lynn Seng, as she has with all of my books since we began our many-faceted collaboration over a quarter century ago, gently made this suggestion and then that one, always seeing more deeply and more clearly than I could in the matter. My loving debt to her, in this and 101 other realms, can only be hinted at here.

Above all, Sharon Gehm, a friend and ally, did yeoman work as the administrative associate on this project. As some of the fifty contributors anxiously made this and that last-minute improvement in what had been the final version of their essay, Sharon stayed on top of the changes and on top of a dizzying array of other mind-boggling details. Working patiently behind the scenes, always with a smile and a word of encouragement, Sharon made all the difference, and there would be no book without her. As with two other recent books of mine she made possible, Sharon earned my heart-felt appreciation for a job exceedingly well done.

Lynn Taylor, Executive Editor, Economics, at M.E. Sharpe, was a model of calm and supportive help, for which she has my lasting gratitude. Likewise, Emma Bailey, the production editor with Westchester Book Services (Danbury, CT), explained complex matters in understandable terms, calmed my upset at critical moments, and in many other ways made the often stressful matter of finalizing a many-faceted publication project a smooth and constructive experience. I wish other editors soon have publishing colleagues as able and cordial as these two.

As always, the responsibility for the book in your hands is mine as its lone editor. Typos that I should have caught, misspellings, etc., along with substantive disagreements you may have with certain ideas or entire essays are just what I welcome learning about, the better to improve later editions. Please send me feedback at shostaka@drexel.edu. Similarly, all of us who worked hard (and enjoyed) bringing this project to closure welcome any compliments or upbeat suggestions . . . along with your offer to write a new essay for the next edition.

VIABLE UTOPIAN IDEAS

Introduction

*"It is not your duty to complete the work, but neither are
you excused from it."*
—Rabbi Tarfon, Talmud: Pirke Avot
(Ethics of the Fathers).

*"Always the beautiful answer who asks a more beautiful
question."*
—E.E. Cummings, *Collected Poems*,
1956 ed., p. iii.

Viable utopian ideas are an energizing resource for helping meet the never-ending challenge to "complete the work," an artful combination of dream, detail, and determination. Our dreams help us focus beyond the present, and they require us to labor at defining just what it is we are *really* seeking. Details keep our feet on the ground and force us to stay pragmatic, to keep our advocacy doable, rather than fanciful. Details also keep us from the hubris of seeking perfection, as if we could agree on it (and then pressure others to agree with us), one of the arch errors of traditional utopianism. Finally, our determination reflects our understanding we will not see "the task" completed in our lifetime, or possibly ever, but at best, seemingly advanced. The task, in any case, is a moving target, not a crisply definable "thing." Each generation must define it and pursue it anew.

Viable utopian ideas are available for just about any and every area of life, a richness that immediately explains why this volume can offer only partial coverage, especially, by our choice, at an introductory level. Fourteen parts of this book, complete with forty-seven essays (forty-two published here for the first time), can only introduce this well-developed, many-faceted, and multi-disciplinary subject.[1] We hope our material will whet your appetite to pursue the matter further, and we therefore cite many print and Web resources throughout. Feel free, as well, to initiate a dialogue with any essayist (or two or more), using the e-mail addresses deliberately included in "Notes on Contributors."

Our opening section—*Part I, Challenges—Personal in Nature*—asks us to consider whether viable utopian ideas are optional—whether, that is, we would advance the Common Good. Furthermore, why is a root source—creative altruism—so poorly regarded, and what might we do about this? In *Part II, Challenges—Conceptual in Nature*, the level of analysis shifts from the individual to the theoretical, although the questions raised are similar. Note that the essayists in this section share some telling and constructive criticisms of the concept—*utopia*—as we require frankness if we are to make gains, not "politically correct" fluff.

We focus in *Part III, Methods: Even Better Tools* on field-proven aids and take special pleasure in including one that is commonly overlooked (poetry); another that is often treated too generally (dialogue options); a third that is pivotal here (sociological practice); and a fourth which is a site for incubating better uses of the first three (a reinvented university). *Part IV, Methods: Information Technology* carries the discussion farther into the realm of "Gee whiz!" info tech possibilities. Essayists appropriately explore both dystopian threats (as in promoting slavish dependency) and utopian rewards (as in aiding direct democracy) posed by these new Internet-based tools.

With *Part V, Looking Inward* we return our focus to the individual and draw on social psychology, humanistic psychology, and the like to suggest new routes to improved mental and spiritual health (our ideas and our person are intimately related; advances in the former often hinge on the health of the latter). *Part VI, Looking Homeward* places the individual in a habitat, and essayists here share viable utopian ideas for soon achieving significant improvement therein.

We move next in *Part VII, Schooling Possibilities* to K-12 reform possibilities, but not of the garden-variety type. Overdue attention is paid to the need to draw black American youths into a quality of hopefulness that makes utopia-building exercises relevant and likely. The same is true for youngsters in trouble with the law and for low-income urban communities too seldom available for such an exercise. To underline the positive possibilities here, *Part VIII, High-Schoolers on Utopia* features a teacher and two of his students who demonstrate the fine capacity of teens for more and better utopian thinking of the viable type.

Part IX, Choices: Very Personal dares to go into those aspects of our private lives that make us uneasy and are therefore all the more important to process on behalf of fresh gains. Abortion, male privilege, and career decision making all receive constructive treatment, and the possibilities for a transformative experience in and from each are well sketched. Similarly, *Part X, Choices: Societal* applies the viable utopian perspective to questions raised by organizational responsibilities, the hopes of labor unionists, and the contribution the Third Sector can and should make.

We shift our concern dramatically with *Part XI, Nation-Building Aids*, and we are usefully reminded of challenges in emerging nations that often respond quite well to viable utopian ideas. Attention is paid to grassroots movements, the struggle to preserve even while modernizing, new social inventions for preventing genocide, and appealing and empowering additions that could soon be made to the United Nations. The level of discussion is raised quite high in *Part XII, The Big Picture: Global Transformation*, in which wonderfully imaginative ideas for sweeping change are shared, along with a useful cautionary note about the tendency of citizens to allow the government to overreach itself.

Our book closes with two parts—*Part XIII, Looking Forward* and *Part XIV, Drawing It Together—and Moving On*—which wrestle helpfully with some of the many fundamental questions that have coursed throughout; for example, what *is* an ideal society? How can we rebut those who scorn the pursuit of viable utopian possibilities? Why should we bother? What are our prospects for making gains soon? Attention is paid to such strategic matters as peace making, transforming the culture of our college courses, recognizing the value of spirituality, anticipating vexing issues raised by life-extension gains, and preparing for life off-planet.

In all, then, our essay collection is an effort to help ourselves—and you—think more positively and do more ably, especially against the backdrop of the Holocaust, the deadly attack on the World Trade Towers, the disease of terrorism, and other evidence of our inherent ability to harm one another grievously. We seek with viable utopian ideas to help keep hope alive, to highlight creative and pragmatic ways to create a better planetary society, and to help assure a twenty-first century world that honors us all.

Note

1. Essays by Stephen Downes, Valarie Fournier, Michael Marien, Stanley Shostak, and Harris Sokoloff were shortened and/or revised by the editor with the permission of the authors. The versions used in this volume often draw on a much longer original source acknowledged at the close of each essay.

References

Bell, Wendell. *Foundations of Futures Studies*. Vol. 1. *History, Purposes, and Knowledge*. New Brunswick, NJ: Transaction, 1997.
———. *Foundations of Futures Studies*. Vol. 2. *Values, Objectivity, and the Good Society*. New Brunswick, NJ: Transaction, 1997. Thoroughgoing reviews of pref-

erable futures, universal human values, objective methods of testing values, and values that ought to be changed.

Brown, Lester R., et al. *State of the World 2001: A Worldwatch Institute Report on Progress Toward a Sustainable Society*. New York: W.W. Norton, 2001. An overview of the livability of planet Earth, now and in the future.

Coates, J.F., J.B. Mahaffie, and A. Hines. *2025*. Akron, NY: Oakhill, 1996. The future of technological revolutions in information, materials, genetics, and energy.

Cooper, Richard N., and Richard Layard, eds. *What the Future Holds: Insights from Social Science*. Cambridge, MA: MIT Press, 2002. Experts in their fields discuss the past and future of population, energy, work, monetary policy, and government.

Dator, James A. *Advancing Futures: Futures Studies in Higher Education*. Westport, CT: Praeger Studies on the 21st Century, 2002. Futurists discuss their challenges, concerns, and methods in teaching futures studies.

Glenn, Jerome C., and Theodore J. Gordon. *2001 State of the Future*. Washington, DC: American Council for the United Nations University, 2001. Reports a survey of futurists' beliefs and attitudes about the future.

Hicks, David, and Richard Slaughter, and eds. *Futures Education, World Yearbook of Education 1998*. London: Kogan Page, 1998. Understanding the futures field, young people's hopes and fears for the future, student responses to learning about the future, and the need for sustainable futures.

Kim, Tae-Chang, and James A. Dator, eds. *Creating a New History for Future Generations*. Kyoto, Japan: Institute for the Integrated Study of Future Generations, 1994. Why and how we must take action on behalf of future generations, what is now being done, and ethical foundations for caring about future generations.

Marien, Michael. "Best Books on the Future." *The Futurist* 35, no. 3 (May-June 2001): 42–49. Perhaps the best-read of all futurists judges books dealing with the future.

Masini, Eleonora Barbieri. *Why Futures Studies?* London: Grey Seal, 1993. Why and how we ought to think about the future; an excellent introduction to the futures field.

Nováky, Erzsébet, Viorica Ramba Varga, and Mária Kalas Köszegi, eds. *Futures Studies in the European Ex-Socialist Countries*. Budapest, Hungary: Futures Studies Centre, 2001. The state of futures thinking in ex-Socialist countries.

Shostak, Arthur B., ed. *Utopian Thinking in Sociology: Creating the Good Society*. Syllabi and Other Instructional Materials. Washington, DC: American Sociological Association, 2001. Aids for teachers who want to plan a course in utopian thinking and the creation of desirable futures.

Slaughter, Richard A., ed. *The Knowledge Base of Futures Studies*. 3 vols. Hawthorn, Victoria, Australia: DDM Media Group, 1996. Comprehensive foundations for studying possible, probable, and preferable futures.

———. *New Thinking for a New Millennium*. London and New York: Routledge, 1996. Futures thinking and creating a better world.

Stevenson, Tony, Eleonora Barbieri Masini, Anita Rubin, and Martin Lehmann-Chadha, eds. *The Quest for the Futures: A Methodology Seminar in Futures Studies*. Turku, Finland: Finland Futures Research Centre, 2000. Theory, method, and policy contributions of futures studies. (Graciously provided by contributor Wendell Bell, sociologist and futurist.)

Web Site Resources

The "Utopia" Web Forum of the World Future Society includes essays on "preferred futuring" and on the relationship between utopian thinking and the study of the future. Its Global Strategies Forum offers ideas and proposals for resolving the complex issues today and in the near-term future. Its Cyber Society Forum explores how life may look in the future as information technology changes our world. Its Social Innovation Forum presents proposals for improving life in the future. Participants in its Opportunity Forum trade ideas about how to improve one's personal and professional life. At its Wisdom of the World Forum, British scholar Bruce Lloyd offers quotes containing wisdom essential for humanity. You can submit your own quotes for possible posting. Valuable futures techniques are discussed in the Methodologies Forum. One can preview and comment on a forthcoming new edition of *The Study of the Future* by World Future Society president Edward Cornish: http://www. wfs.org.

The Society for Utopian Studies was founded in 1975. It holds an annual meeting and publishes a refereed scholarly journal that appears twice a year, *Utopian Studies: Journal of the Society for Utopian Studies*, edited by Lyman Tower Sargent, as well as *Utopus Discovered: A Most Informal Newsletter*. The stated purpose of the society is the study of utopianism. Mailing address: Professor Lyman Tower Sargent, Society for Utopian Studies, Department of Political Science, University of Missouri-St. Louis, St. Louis, MO 63121–4499; Web page: http://www.utoronto.ca/utopia; e-mail: Lyman.Sargent @umsl.edu or utopian_studies@umsl.edu. There is also an electronic forum on H-NET, available at no charge to subscribers and edited by Professor Peter Sands of the University of Wisconsin-Milwaukee. His e-mail address is sands@uwm.edu, and the e-mail address of the forum is H-UTOPIA@H-NET.MSU.EDU.(WW)

Bibliography of Resources for Shaping the Future. A selective list of books and websites for citizens imagining a better world, with categories of intellectual tools and social change agendas. Prepared by Robert Merikangas, a contributor to this book: www.wam.umd.edu/~bobmerik/biblio.htm.

An unusual source for future-shaping ideas: www.globalideasbank.org/.

Imagination Engines. "The World's First Company Dedicated to Producing Neural Networks Capable of Human Level Invention, Discovery, and Artistic Creativity." Sponsored by Dr. Stephen Thaler: www.imagination-engines.com/.

Transhumanism, a loosely defined interdisciplinary approach to understanding and evaluating the ethical, social, and strategic issues raised by current and anticipated future technologies: www.nickbostrom.com/tra/values.html

Additional Web Site Resources

(A small sample, identified by Robert J. Merikangas, a contributor to this book.)

Futures and Education

Hawaii Center for Futures Studies: http://www.futures.hawaii.edu

Swinburne AFI: http://www.aboutforesight.org

University of Arizona: http://ag.arizona.edu/futures

University of Houston, Clear Lake: http://www.cl.uh.edu/futureweb/

Futures Organizations

World Future Society: http://www.wfs.org

World Futures Studies Federation: http://www.wfsf.org

Journals

Futures: http://www.elsevier.nl/locate/futures/

Future Survey: http://www.wfs.org/fsurv.htm

Journal of Futures Studies: http://www.ed.tku.edu.tw/develop/JFS

New Renaissance: http://www.ru.org

Methods and Reports

National Security/21st Century: http://www.rssg.gov/Reports/reports.htm

Future Tool Kit: http://www.futuretoolkit.com/

Futurecasts: http://www.futurecasts.com

Millennium Project: http://www.acunu.org

Northern Arizona University: http://futures.anthro.nau.edu

Other

Open Directory on the Future: http://www.dmoz.org/Society/Future/

Plausible Futures Newsletter: http://www.plausiblefuture.com/

Rio Salado Web Bibliography: http://futures.rio.maricopa.edu/electroniclib.html

Welcome ETI: http://members.aol.com/WelcomeETI/5.html

Yahoo! Futures Studies: http://dir.yahoo.com/Social_Science/Futures_Studies/

I. Challenges—Personal in Nature

We begin this collection of more than forty essays with the irreverent question—Should we? That is, should we even consider being utopians? How might we deal with the concept's seeming implausibility—its stigma in popular culture? Is the problem here a technical one (our seeming inability to help everyone achieve the necessities of life), or something else entirely? Is the problem within other people (their selfishness), or somewhere else? By making an artful comparison of two familiar lifestyles, the essay below helps us craft constructive—and indispensable—answers for ourselves.

1. Private Dreams and Collective Ideals

Douglas Porpora

Should we be utopians: people who long for and struggle toward utopia?

This is a very peculiar question to ask. Today, *utopian* is a word we use dismissively. When we describe someone as utopian, we generally mean that his or her ideas have no chance of realization. As non-starters; those ideas or visions should not even be brought up. When they are brought up, people quickly try to redirect the conversation along more "productive" paths. To be utopian, therefore, seems a prescription for not being taken seriously.

If to be utopian is to pursue an impractical vision, then clearly we should not be utopians. Utopianism sounds like an error to be avoided. We should keep our eyes on what is realistic here and now. All else is unhelpful, even frivolous. Why would anyone counsel anybody differently?

Utopianism is a kind of idealism, and idealism in general has suffered the same fate as utopianism in particular. Thus, we need to back up from utopianism and think first for a while about idealism.

Today, idealism connotes the desire to have everything unrealistically perfect. As such, idealism generally is regarded as folly. There was a time—especially in the 1960s—when young people were encouraged to be idealistic. Today, instead, we encourage people to pursue their "dreams." "Keep dreaming," we tell them. "Don't lose your dreams."

Not only are young people encouraged to pursue their dreams, but they themselves seem fervently to accept this advice. Many take it to heart. They may regard idealism as impractical folly, but not their own dreams. To their own dreams they are intent on staying true as long as possible. When told that their personal dreams are unrealistic, many insist that they must still try to accomplish them. Sometimes they go on to say that with enough will and enough effort, anyone can make one's dreams come true. "Just do it," or "Go for it," as the sneaker commercials say.

So today private dreams are good, whereas idealism is bad or at least silly. Something does not add up here. What is the difference between a dream and an ideal? If it is not silly to nurture our own private dreams—if it is something we actively encourage—then why should it be otherwise with ideal? The inconsistency reveals a cultural shift in norms that we would do well to examine.

The first thing to notice is that we currently hold a degraded notion of idealism. Contrary to the way it is often understood today, idealism is not the unrealistic desire to have everything work out perfectly for us. Idealism does not even concern us personally. Nor is an ideal even a desire. An ideal is a value—like honesty, compassion, justice, or equality. To be idealistic is to be committed to certain values even at the expense of our own advantage or benefit. To be idealistic is to put principles ahead of our own selves. An idealist committed to justice will act justly, even if that means he or she will have to give way to another. If we are committed to honesty as an ideal, then we will behave honestly even when that means we ourselves will suffer.

Here perhaps lies the rub, one way our cultural norms seem to have shifted. Ideals are other-regarding. They concern how things should be independent of any personal benefit to us. In contrast, our dreams are all about us, about what we want or aspire to be. If idealism is considered unrealistic today, perhaps it is because today it is considered impractical or unrealistic to be concerned about anything other than ourselves. Today, perhaps, it is difficult to take anyone seriously who professes to be other than selfish.

Our private dreams, of course, are not always exclusively selfish. Some young people do privately dream to serve humanity in some way, as, for example, a physician, a teacher, or a lawyer. Perhaps some young people even dream of serving humanity—or at least our country—by becoming the first female or black or simply honest president. Perhaps some young people consider it a service to humanity if they become a professional basketball star.

Others express the desire to be as rich as possible, after which, they will "give back" by becoming philanthropists.

Our private dreams are not necessarily exclusively selfish. What is selfish is the cultural shift in the language we use to describe our aspirations—from ideals to dreams. Whereas talk of ideals is other-regarding and oriented toward moral values, talk of dreams focuses on our own, individual selves, and it is morally neutral.

When we are counseled to follow our dreams, we are seldom asked what our dreams are. Perhaps it is taken for granted that no one is dreaming of becoming a serial killer or a stock defrauder. Certainly, some dreams are generally considered immoral to pursue. Beyond clearly immoral pursuits, however, all dreams are considered equal. Unless morally prohibited, everyone's dream is deemed as good as anyone else's. It is in this sense that licit dreams at least are all morally neutral, none favored over any other.

Let us put aside consideration of those dreams that are clearly immoral and confine ourselves to those dreams we all would consider licit. Why should we think that licit dreams are all equally good? One answer is that our dreams express ourselves and we, ourselves, are all equal. Thus, no one can say that anyone's dream is any better or worse than anyone else's.

Such reasoning expresses what sociologists call "individualism." It places all value and, sometimes, even all truth in the individual. America was founded on this ideal, and it remains a strong cultural value even today. In fact, a renewed emphasis on individualism is a second aspect of the cultural shift that has taken place since the 1960s talk of idealism. It shows up in this reasoning about the equality of our dreams.

Such reasoning also expresses a laudable degree of tolerance. Certainly, we should be prepared to accept others whose dreams differ from our own. As intolerance continues to be a problem today, it is commendable that so many young people are so idealistically committed to tolerance as a virtue.

Still, the reasoning expressed is faulty. Not only is the individualism excessive, even the tolerance is overdone to the point where it undermines critical judgment. Yes, it is true that we, ourselves, are all equal. It does not follow that all our dreams are also equal. To suppose that dreams that are not definitely bad are all equally good assumes that it is enough for us just not to be bad. That is a morally weak standard by which to judge ourselves: If we are not bad, we are good.

Important gradations of goodness are overlooked. Suppose Julie dreams of becoming a medical doctor so she can go to Africa to work with children dying from untreated disease. John, meanwhile, dreams of becoming a lawyer so that he can buy a big house, raise a big family, take vacations in France, and never have to worry about money. Neither dream is bad, but are they equally good? Is not Julie's dream at least more noble, more courageous, less self-absorbed than John's?

The young today consider it intolerant to make such distinctions, but they are mistaken. No one is arguing that we should not tolerate John or wish him ill. No one is arguing that we should force John to be different, or that we should even go out of our way to tell John that he fails to measure up to Julie. On the other hand, if John is entitled to dream what he wants, we are equally entitled to assess morally John's dreams for ourselves. By that reckoning, we might evaluate John's dreams perhaps not as bad, but possibly as shallow or materialistic or inattentive to the state of the world.

These assessments do not make John a bad person. Today we encourage personal ambition, and John's dreams certainly exhibit that. From a moral point of view, however, John's ambitions, if not bad, are conventional, unremarkable, even banal. From a moral point of view, John's dreams make him an average Joe. In contrast, Julie is an idealist. Today we may refuse to see the moral difference in the dreams dreamt by John and Julie, but it is nevertheless still objectively there.

If we cannot objectively assess the dreams of others, how can we ever objectively assess our own dreams? Suppose Julie was once like John. Suppose before she dreamt of being a physician, but for the same reasons John wants to be a lawyer. She dreamt of making a lot of money. Then, one day, Julie happened to see a PBS special on untreated disease among children in Africa. Being a smart, driven, premedical student, she investigated further. Given the unalleviated suffering in the world, Julie came to regard her own dream of personal financial security as self-absorbed.

Perhaps Julie is Jewish. Thus, she is familiar with the ethical wisdom of Hillel, a rabbi who lived around the second century B.C.E. Hillel famously used to say, "If I am not for myself, who will be?" So far so good. Julie's original dream showed due consideration for herself. But Hillel's follow-up question began to haunt Julie: "If I am only for myself, what am I?" Julie asked herself, "What am I if I just continue down this path toward personal fulfillment, if I just ignore the state of the world?"

At first, Julie decided that when she became a rich doctor, she could give some money to Doctors without Borders. Would that be enough? Hillel also used to say—he evidently used to say a lot—"If not me, who?" This question especially haunted Julie. She concluded that she could not responsibly live a life of private affluence while children are dying, especially not when she was given the resources to help them. Julie then reflected on what it means to be a physician, how it is less an avenue to wealth than a noble calling. To be true to that calling, she had to reorder her priorities. As a result, Julie changed her dream to help the untreated children in Africa.

Julie put a lot of deep thought and moral reasoning into revising her aspirations. Now, suppose she and John meet and begin discussing their individual dreams. For the sake of argument, let us imagine that, unlike Julie, John has engaged in no thought at all about his dream. He is not very inclined to introspection and, whenever he is alone, immediately reaches for his cell phone. He more or less has just found his dream in his head, probably because he is smart, because his financially struggling parents have always stressed economic security, and because from childhood on, he has loved television shows about lawyers.

Is Julie supposed to assess her new dream as morally no better than John's? Remember that John's current dream is the same as the old one Julie discarded. What many people today—especially young people—want to say is that Julie's new dream is better for her, whereas John's dream is better for him. But Julie decided her new dream was better for her because she judged it to be morally better for anybody. It was precisely because she judged it morally better for anybody that she decided it was better for her. If that is the reasoning, then Julie's new dream must be morally better for John, too.

Julie's new dream comes at considerable personal cost in comparison with her old dream. If objectively her new dream is morally no better than her old dream, then she would be foolish to abandon the old one. She might just as well do as she wanted to in the first place. All that time and energy Julie spent thinking about personal responsibility and what one owes the world was just a waste. Without any thought at all on the matter, John arrives at the same moral place. Are we really prepared to say all this?

The point here is that we cannot apply objective, moral reasoning to our own case without also applying it to everyone else's case. The point of denying that all dreams are equally good is not to make us intolerant of others' dreams, but to make us intolerant of those dreams of our own that are morally less than they could be.

If we really think that our dreams are immune to objective criticism—even from ourselves—then we have allowed individualism to collapse into utter subjectivism. There are no objective or independent grounds for thinking anything other than what we want. The world, society, fellow human beings, even the earth—none imposes any obligations on us beyond what we prefer to accept. Such subjectivism becomes a radical selfishness which makes each of us the creator of his or her own private world. A common world to which we all belong is totally lost. Lost with it is any value to moral reasoning. We should just decide what we want and "go for it."

Culturally, this is where the moral shift in our language has taken us—to a kind of radical selfishness. Perhaps the real reason idealism is disparaged is not because it is unrealistic, but because it is culturally dangerous. It is dangerous to our complacency, to our own selfish plans. If so, then the disparagement of idealism turns out to be a kind of cultural defense mechanism. We disparage idealism so that we need not feel the moral demands it imposes on us, so that we do not have to engage in rigorous moral reasoning and can go on "just doing" whatever pleases us personally.

Of the two dreams, it is actually Julie's that is the more realistic. From a practical point of view, Julie's idealistic dream is no less likely to be realized than John's more materialistic dream. Julie's has costs that John's does not, but if Julie is prepared to accept those costs, she is no less likely to succeed than John.

On the other hand, in two important senses, Julie's idealistic dream is more realistic than John's. First, from a social point of view, John's dream reflects a life lived in a cocoon. It totally ignores, even blocks out, the wider world as it actually is. Julie's dream, in contrast, actively confronts larger social reality.

Second, John's dream is totally subjectivistic in that it originates entirely from within him. No wider understanding of the world informs it. In contrast, Julie's dream originates not from within, but from the world itself. Julie, remember, once had the same dream as John. What changed her was an encounter with the world. That encounter left Julie feeling called by the world to something larger, something higher, something deeper than she was planning to pursue.

Idealism thus takes us out of ourselves and into the world. It interrupts our private plans and calls us down a public path. Ideals call us by moving us emotionally, by awakening in us feelings we had never before experienced and, once experienced, do not go away. We do not choose our ideals. They choose us. An ideal impacts us as a call we hear. If we respond, we leave the pack of conventionality. What we become is an idealist.

Utopianism is not only a kind of idealism; it is also a kind of dream. Rather than a private dream, utopianism involves a collective dream. A utopian vision is a dream not of what we might achieve individually, but a dream of what we might achieve together. Although like idealism in general, utopianism has been disparaged as unrealistic, we may now be more skeptical of that assessment. Utopianism, we might begin to suspect, is disparaged not because it is unrealistic, but because, like idealism generally, it too is dangerous.

Skipping ahead twenty years, we find that John and Julie both have realized their dreams. John is rich, has a beautiful wife, and lives in a beautiful house, through which run five beautiful kids. Through it all, John has remained a decent person. He has started to "give back" by making donations to charity. Among those donations, in fond memory of Julie, is a yearly check to Doctors without Borders.

In Africa, working with Doctors without Borders, we find Julie, gaunt and still unmarried. Unlike John, Julie is dissatisfied—not particularly because she is unmarried, although it bothers her a little that she is gaunt. What is really troubling Julie? Through all these years, she has been laboring to save children's lives, and she has saved more than a few. Yet there are still so many to be saved. Her clinic lacks supplies, and the world lacks concern.

What really troubles Julie is that after all these years, she has come to realize that what she and her fellow physicians are doing is just a palliative. For the past few years, she has begun to ask herself how things were allowed to get this way—allowed by whom? Allowed by us collectively. Julie reflects that the richest hundred people in the world possess more wealth than the poorest forty countries combined. From thinking in terms of her own charitable work, Julie has begun to think in terms of global social justice. How is it just for some people to be so rich, while others are so poor?

Through such reflection, Julie comes to dream yet a new dream. This time, it is not a dream about herself, but a dream about the world, about what the world could be. Julie dreams about a world in which no one lives in affluence until everyone lives with sufficiency. Julie knows that unless this collective dream is realized, all the work she is doing is just a drop in the bucket. With this dream, Julie becomes not just an idealist, but now also a utopian. Utopia does not mean impractical. It means "nowhere" because it does not anywhere yet exist. Julie firmly believes that her utopia could exist if only we all work toward it. She resolves to begin spreading the word.

She does so at her high school reunion, where she once again meets John and his beautiful wife, resplendent in all her jewelry. John is mightily glad to see Julie again, but he scoffs at her idea for the world. "That is so utopian," he laughs. "Have you tasted the quiche?"

Julie is not about to be diverted. "Why do you say my idea is utopian?"

"It will never work," John tells her, and John's beautiful wife nods with adoring approval at her husband. "It's not viable." John likes this word, viable. He keeps using it, each time proud to see that his wife likes it too. To prove his point, John, now a devout Christian, quotes Jesus at her. "The poor you will have always with you." Of course, Jesus also counseled those who have two coats to give one to those who have none, but as Julie is unfamiliar with the Christian texts, she is without retort.

Back in her hotel room, Julie realizes she was shaken by this encounter and annoyed, especially when she thinks of the nodding head of John's beautiful, but vapid wife. Vapid, Julie thinks, do they know that word?

It is not that Julie herself has never doubted the viability of her idea, but John just seems so glibly sure it is not viable. She wonders what gives John his certainty. Is it based on John's extensive research on the subject? No, Julie, reminds herself, apart perhaps from tax law, John has never extensively re-searched any social issue. More fundamentally, Julie wonders what John even means by not viable.

What do we mean when we dismiss utopian visions like Julie's as not viable? Do we mean it is technically impossible to give everyone the neces-sities of life? In terms of food, the world produces enough to provide everyone with over 3,000 calories a day. So at least in the case of food, it cannot be a technical problem of production. Is it then a technical problem of distribution? Given our current ability to communicate and distribute across the globe, this hardly seems plausible either.

The real problem is not technical at all. It is social. The problem is a matter of collective will. When people dismiss ideas like Julie's as utopian, they most likely mean that it is not viable to get enough people to agree to anything like it.

Put this way, those who despise utopian ideas make it sound as if the problem is other people, not themselves. It is other people, not they, who cannot be counted on to overcome selfishness.

There is a good question to put to such despisers. If we could get enough people to go along with this utopian idea, would you go along with it too? If the despisers say *no*, then we and they themselves know where they stand. If they say *yes*, then they have already taken the first step along the road to a viable utopianism. The next question is then, "Would you work to get enough other people to dream this collective dream?" If the answer is *yes* again, then they are all the way there.

Should we be utopians—people who dream of and struggle toward a viable utopia?

The greater our understanding of what we are up against in our effort to get a fair trial of viable utopian ideas, the greater is the likelihood of our success. Why, for example, do so many Americans seem to place so low a valuation on creative altruism? What are the root sources of neglect, even of antagonism toward the concept? What part is played by our relationship to our families? To our self-advancement needs? To the market? Guided by the mind stretching essay below we can see deeper into the matter and better understand how strategic is altruism to our utopian prospects.

2. Why Altruism Is Considered Deviant Behavior: Obstacles on the Path to a Viable Utopia

Jay Weinstein

According to sociology's leading theorist of altruism, P. A. Sorokin (1950: 208), we are living today in a "late sensate" world, one in which egoism, materialism, and greed dominate our beliefs and values. In this world, "Good neighbors and saints are deviants." Contemporary culture, especially in the United States, reinforces this negative view of altruism. The important thing to note is that the attitudes portrayed here are all learned and sustained through socialization and experience. If they are learned, then, as difficult as it may be, they can be unlearned.

Real Men Are Selfish

Deeply rooted in late sensate ideology is the belief that generosity and concern for the welfare of others is immature, unrealistic, and unintelligent. "Real men," so the implication goes, have a sound understanding of how the game is played: Every man for himself, and let the others take care of their own interests. "Real men" put this perception into practice whenever possible.

Notions such as creative altruism are simply ridiculous from this perspective, and they generate a range of responses from scorn to outright hostility. The very possibility of altruistic behavior poses a real threat to the foundations upon which the late sensate personality are constructed. Of course, most of these real men fail to see the similarity between their so-designated mature outlook and the ranting of a child who wants what he or she wants when he or she wants it, and will get it no matter what.

Popular culture, rather than exposing this attitude as "unmanly" (that is, inhumane), nurtures and reinforces it. Consumer products and the advertising promoting them routinely appeal to the selfish side of the consumer. They encourage getting one's very own, whatever it is, and they harp on your choice, your rewards, your way (while, ironically, everything becomes increasingly standardized).

In a disturbingly similar approach in a different context, politicians win elections and approval points by offering reductions of public-sector revenues disguised as tax rebates (invariably labeled tax cuts) so that "you" can have "your own money" to do "whatever you want with it." Sharing and working in the interests of others have no place in this scheme of things. Instead, they are viewed as evidence of weakness and—ultimately—a lack of patriotism.

I Love My Family (So Don't Bother Me about Other People)

Certain values and behavior that ought to be considered routine, indeed among the most natural responses in the world, are now viewed as praiseworthy, if not heroic.

The most obvious among these is expressing and showing concern for the well-being of one's immediate family. One would imagine little needs to be said about such an orientation, in part because it is widely expected and nearly universally practiced. But in America today, the claim—made by self or others—that a person loves his or her spouse, children, mother, or father resonates deeply.

This complex trait can be traced to several sources. Most obvious perhaps, but probably least pervasive, is that self-directed praise for caring about one's own family hides an unpleasant reality. That is, some people who emphatically proclaim that they (or those whom they admire) are very good to their families may be anything but that. Understanding the expectations of others, they attempt to avoid scrutiny by making it obvious what good parents or spouses they are.

Another possibility is that in publicly celebrating the performance of what might otherwise be viewed as routine role obligations, the speaker is implicitly—though not necessarily subtly—making an invidious comparison. When one announces that "I (or you or she or he) really love my family," one assumes that the listener will understand that we are not discussing those kinds of people who do not feel this way. In this scenario, racism is often an unspoken assumption.

Of most direct relevance to the sources of resistance to altruism, the elevation of concern for family from a necessity to a virtue carries an important implication: Caring for one's own immediate relatives fully satisfies the need to reach out to others.

Kristin Monroe (2001) has shown that many interviewees at the less altruistic end of her continuum establish a sharp boundary between themselves and family, on one hand, and the rest of humanity, on the other. Within their inner circle, these people are willing to act on behalf of the other, to perform selflessly, and to sacrifice their own well-being. However, beyond this circle, the well-being of others is "not their business." In contrast, Monroe's more altruistic subjects—including Holocaust rescuers—do not perceive such a sharp difference between thine and mine. They care just as much for strangers in need because they too are part of a common humanity.

At least part of the reason Americans these days are so publicly proud of loving their children, etc., is that they thereby excuse themselves from caring about anyone else. When confronted with the possibly of reaching out beyond the immediate family to help others, many citizens react angrily: "I would never place my children at risk to help a stranger." Since this is rarely asked, it seems clear such a response is not the result of measured calculations, but an assertion that they are justified (indeed virtuously so) in not being altruistic.

I Worked Hard for What I Have (and No One Is Going to Take It from Me)

Another antialtruistic strain in late sensate ideology is the myth of self-reliance. From this perspective, one's material accomplishments and worldly possessions have come as the result of concerted, personally unassisted effort and sacrifice. As the account goes, if one has achieved what one has on one's own, then others are expected to follow suit. Furthermore, I won't help anyone because no one helped me. Moreover, because I worked so hard for what I have, I am not prepared to waste it on strangers who are less deserving. If other people have needs, let them satisfy their needs as I did mine—through hard work.

The myth of self-reliance (see Hsu 1983; 1990) more or less denies everything sociologists know about achievement, success, and indeed how human relationships operate. No one has ever experienced material accomplishments or accumulated worldly possessions on their own. Every action we perform presupposes socialization agents (parents, peers, teachers, etc.) and the presence of other actors.

The myth of self-reliance is so patently false it is difficult not to wonder how it can ever be sustained. Certainly, we all experience times when much needed assistance is not forthcoming—that is the grain of truth in the myth— but how can anyone seriously assert that he or she is entirely self-reliant?

The answer obviously lies not in the truth of the claim, but in the functions it performs. Like the assertion that one loves one's family, the statement to the effect that one has achieved one's station in life on one's own is a signal to others to expect nothing by way of gratuitous help. It is a rationalization for selfishness: No one ever did anything for me (this is untrue) and I don't need to do anything for anyone else. As with all ideological claims, a premise that is false by virtue of excluding important facts is used to justify a self-serving conclusion

The Ideology Called "Market Economics"

As with the assertions that "I love my family" and "I made it on my own," the success of rational choice theory is derived not from its veracity, but from its function of justifying selfishness and discrediting altruism. By asserting a priori that rational people are selfish people, it follows that there is something wrong with the way unselfish people think and behave. In this case, however, the outcome is considerably more insidious, in two ways.

First, economic theory has developed an elaborate scenario of the dire consequences that would follow if people do not behave in their own self-interests. Second, because of the power wielded by economics and economists in late sensate society, rational choice theory has become a self-fulfilling prophecy.

In the first case, the analysis/warning has been repeated time and again for more than 200 years that many small acts of individual greed "add up" (through the operation of invisible hands and the like) to benefit all, whereas acts designed to help others create chaos and suffering. If one cannot succeed, one cannot breed. Thus, the weak are weeded out of the system to the benefit of all. Social Darwinism has many faces.

When we consider this revered claim from a sociological perspective, it is simply absurd. Who can presume to know what the relationship between greed and the common good is in every case—especially when the perfect markets assumed by Adam Smith to support this transformation "from private vice to public virtue" do not now (and probably never did) exist? And who is to determine which mental and social traits deserve to be sustained, and which ought to be eliminated?

Clearly, every moment of operation of any existing market is unique in ways that affect the outcome of self-interested acts. Complexities are ordinarily so great as to defy the kind of analysis that could reveal which acts do and which do not benefit "all." And the entire notion that (in human affairs) only the strong survive is merely a circular claim: Those most fit to survive will survive—and, equally enlightening, an object following a downward trajectory will come down.

Who knows whether selfishness or selflessness is better on the whole, in the long run, and in relation to the common good? If I am in need and someone who can help me is available, I'm willing to accept the help and hope the "general welfare" does not suffer overly much. Like the psychological premise associated with it, the argument that selfishness is best for all concerned simply rationalizes selfishness—no more and no less.

With regard to self-fulfilling prophecy, it is clear that rational choice theory is not so much a description of how people do behave as an instruction about how they should behave. If people wish to gain the most out of the economic side of their lives (or, as the sociological rational choice theorists would prefer, all sides of their lives), they should 1.) look to maximize their own benefits; 2.) be unconcerned about every one else; 3.) assume everyone else is out for himself or herself and expect no help from others.

Now, if enough people take this advice, in part because to behave otherwise is "irrational" and in part because any other kind of behavior would lead to general disaster, the economic system will work in this fashion. Then rational choice theorists can "discover" that people behave selfishly. Unfortunately, this is not merely a "what if" account. It is the way things work in late sensate economies, as if there were simply no choice (at least any rational choice) other than self-gratification.

Reciprocity with Corporate Capitalism

There is a close, functional reciprocity between the kinds of beliefs and attitudes identified above and corporate capitalism. No ideology can be sustained unless it is supported by a system of effective sanctions. In the case of late sensate ideology, these sanctions come in the form of the rewards and punishments dispensed by the "corporation nation" (Derber 2000).

Most people in contemporary U.S. society truly believe that real men are selfish, that the main goals of life are the accumulation of "stuff" and the gratification of the senses, and that rational behavior is that which maximizes material benefits for self, or, at most, for "my family."

Fortunately for the corporations, these attitudes happen to coincide perfectly with the corporate ideal of the consumer mentality. The self-serving "stuff," the endless gratification, and the material benefits that the huge corporations produce in gross excess are precisely what these people "need." "It's my money, I'll spend it as I like," warns the good consumer. Well, not quite: You'll spend it as the producers and advertisers dictate.

To ensure demand never drops below the point at which corporate profits are threatened, the corporations dedicate an enormous amount of resources to marketing, including advertising. Much if not most of this time and money are spent not to inform potential consumers about what is a available, but to make them feel incomplete and unappealing if they fail to buy the product of concern. Similarly, products are identified with attractive people or settings, with the skillfully manipulated impression that attractiveness follows from the appropriate purchase.

The message is simply "buy and be beautiful" and "don't buy, and be left out and be ugly." Because they prefer the "rewards"—a relatively new marketing term that applies to promotional stuff, discounts, and the like and which suggests that consuming is a heroic act—they buy. Thus the circle is completed. Selfishness is rewarded with approval. Things that gratify are consumed. Gratification justifies selfishness. Failure to consume leads to disapproval, and those who fail are shamed into consuming.

Conclusion: Applying Our Understanding

Why are creative altruism and related behavioral orientations incompatible with contemporary values and styles? The general answer has already been suggested: In late sensate culture, materialism, egoism, and self-gratification are considered fundamental aspects of human nature.

By examining the kinds of beliefs identified here, sociologists can provide more specific and more useful answers to the question. With such knowledge, we can begin to identify the day-to-day mechanisms that sustain what amounts to an all-out attack on altruistic ways of thinking and acting. This is important because these mechanisms are the very mechanisms that need to be altered or eliminated if a serious turn toward idealism is to occur.

References

Derber, Charles. *Corporation Nation: How Corporations Are Taking Over Our Lives and What We Can Do about It*. New York: St. Martins Griffin, 2000.

Hsu, Francis L.K. *Psychological Anthropology: Approaches to Culture and Personality*. Homewood, IL: Dorsey, 1990.

Hsu, Francis L.K., ed. *Rugged Individualism Reconsidered: Essays in Psychological Anthropology*. Knoxville: University of Tennessee Press, 1983.

Monroe, Kristen Renwick. *The Heart of Altruism: Perceptions of a Common Humanity*. Princeton, NJ: Princeton University Press, 1996.

———. "Morality and a Sense of Self: The Importance of Identity and Categorization for Moral Action." *American Journal of Political Science* 45, no. 3 (2001):491–507.

Sorokin, Pitirim A. *Altruistic Love: A Study of American "Good Neighbors" and Christian Saints*. Boston: Beacon, 1950.

II. Challenges—
Conceptual in Nature

Few students of futuristics, and thereby also of utopian thinking, know the literature as well as Michael Marien, the creator and editor of the invaluable monthly abstract journal Future Survey. *He shares below his reservations about the concept of* utopia *and offers alternative terms. He identifies three broad trends in social-betterment thinking, fifteen outstanding new books of a "social-betterment" bent, and a list of current social-betterment terms. The essay provides much of worth to ponder, as does every issue of* Future Survey.

3. Utopia Revisited: New Thinking on Social Betterment*

Michael Marien

Thousands of scholars have devoted their careers to making careful studies of urban designs, plants, animals, languages, and other subjects. However, they have made little or no effort to record and analyze schemes for social betterment: the improvement of institutions and culture at the local, national, and global levels.

---

*This essay, reprinted with permission from the magazine of the World Future Society, *The Futurist*, March–April 2002, draws in turn on a chapter written by Michael Marien appearing in *Utopian Thinking in Sociology: Creating the Good Society. Syllabi and Other Instructional Materials*, compiled and edited by Arthur B. Shostak, Washington, DC: American Sociological Association, 2001, 225 pages. Paperback. Available from the World Future Society Bookstore.

The multidisciplinary character of social-betterment thinking is one reason for its neglect. It does not fit neatly into any academic category, although sociologists are probably more involved in it than members of other disciplines. Instead, the best thinking about social betterment draws on the ideas of many academic disciplines and professions.

A second reason is the burdensome legacy of idealistic utopian thinking, embraced by some academics because it is appropriate to ivory towers and is not practical. Exclusive focus on utopias, however, distracts attention from agendas and proposals that do have some chance of being realized to some degree. Indeed, political opponents of many betterment agendas often attack them as "utopian" and "pie-in-the-sky," and thus otherworldly and incapable of realization. To prevent this tarnishing, savvy proposers of ambitious betterment schemes avoid the word *utopia* and stress that their ideas are practical, reasonable, and cost effective.

What Pure Utopias Miss

Utopia: The Search for the Ideal Society in the Western World, a lushly illustrated coffee-table book, was recently copublished by the New York Public Library and Oxford University Press. Although it gives a splendid overview of the history of utopian thought, the book is very weak on addressing utopian developments in the last few decades. Only one chapter covers recent thinking, and it is devoted to communes.

It is all well and good to follow the progress of these small, progressive communities, which typically seek self-sufficiency, community, equality, and attunement to nature. But the New York Public Library's utopia book makes no mention of contemporary right-wing utopias, which would typically be an offshore tax haven with minimal government.

Another recent book, *Impossible Worlds: The Architecture of Perfection* (Princeton Architectural Press, 2000), presents a far wider ideological spectrum of recent proposals, including a sketch of the Ayn Rand–inspired nation of New Utopia, an artificial island in the Caribbean where residents live in luxury and an absence of taxation, and the Freedom Ship, a tax-free floating city of 40,000 people, over a mile long and twenty-five stories high. Both projects are seeking funds to begin building their libertarian dream.

Together, these two books provide a good introduction to the classic, purely utopian, completely new community or society, viewed in all of its dimensions. But there is certainly far more to "good society" thinking than these books provide. Beyond pure utopia, a wide range of thinking on human betterment can be seen, from the highly idealistic to the reasonably pragmatic. Some of this thinking feeds into the political process and gets translated into platforms and legislation. However, by considering the whole spectrum of betterment thinking, futurists, scholars, and activists could explore a new realm of possibilities.

Such processes as "future search" and "strategizing" evoke conscious actions to shape preferred futures. Also, the use of scenarios to articulate a range of possible futures often includes an ideal or preferred scenario, in addition to a dystopian or dark scenario and the business-as-usual continuation of the status quo.

Betterment thinking might be critically important in the war on terrorism. To win the "war," a strategy will be needed to win the peace. Betterment thinking would be helpful in providing a full menu of possibilities for a better world from which to choose.

Trends in Betterment Thinking

Three broad trends have emerged in betterment thinking over the past few decades:

1. *From fiction to nonfiction forms.* The classic utopian novel, such as Edward Bellamy's *Looking Backwards* (1888), is seldom seen anymore, since betterment thinking has taken an increasingly pragmatic approach, informed with scientific findings. With the shift from the pure to the pragmatic, utopia now appears not as fiction, but as the serious business of scholars and activists, especially those housed in think tanks and interest groups.
2. *From whole society to sectoral proposals.* As befits an increasingly complex and fragmented society, proposals for reform are now largely made in a single sector, such as the economy, health, education, welfare, defense, cities, energy, and so on. An across-the-board exception to this trend was former House Speaker Newt Gingrich's "Contract with America" reform package, which inspired conservatives and terrified liberals in 1995.
3. *From public-sector to private-sector action.* One of the most profound trends of recent years has been the marked shift from the public to the private sector as the locus for human activity, including idealized action. Many crypto-utopian views of the good corporation have been published in the last decade, as well as proposals for public and private collaboration on various matters heretofore considered the concern of government.

To illustrate the variety and nature of contemporary normative thinking, fifteen books are described below. These are just a few of the hundreds, perhaps thousands, of attractive, research-backed ideas for social, economic, political, and environmental betterment, written by individuals, small teams, nongovernmental organizations, and commissions, and scattered widely in books from many publishers and articles in many periodicals. None of the authors calls his or her proposal *utopian* nor should we. *Practical utopianism* or *effective dreams* are more apt terms, even for the most idealistic of these proposals.

Social-betterment literature encompassing many political points of view should become an academic specialty as common as literary criticism. Stimulating courses on social betterment, alternative futures, global futuribles, and general public affairs should be available at every college and university. The plethora of ideas for betterment should be mixed and matched, compared and contrasted, debated and discussed, with new ones constantly being added and older ones being placed in the historical file, but not forgotten.

Enhanced attention to social betterment could very well accelerate and upgrade the process of creating improved, if not ideal, societies of the twenty-first century. Our survival may depend on it.

Some Recent Social-Betterment Proposals

None of these books uses the term *utopia*, although opponents might stigmatize them as such. Rather, the idealistic authors present these proposals as practical. Many more books of this sort can be found in *Future Survey*, which I edit every month (www.wfs.org).

1. Global society. *The World Ahead: Our Future in the Making*, by Federico Mayor with Jérome Bindé (UNESCO and Zed Books/Palgrave, 2001), presents a broad-ranging view from UNESCO calling for humane globalization based on four pillars of a new international democracy: a new social contract, a natural contract, a cultural contract, and a new ethical contract.

2. Global economy. *Eco-Economy: Building an Economy for the Earth*, by Lester R. Brown (W. W. Norton, 2001), seeks to provide a vision of an ecologically sustainable economy and how to realize it. It updates and expands many of Brown's previous ideas.

3. Global economy. *Beyond Globalization: Shaping a Sustainable Global Economy*, by futurist Hazel Henderson (Kumarian Press, 1999), sketches the many reforms needed to reshape the global economy on seven levels: the global system, the international financial system, the nation-state, the corporate system, local systems, civic society, and family lifestyles.

4. Global governance. *The Capacity to Govern: A Report to the Club of Rome*, by Israeli political scientist Yehezkel Dror (Frank Cass, 2001), offers a sweeping agenda for facilitating high-quality gover-

nance, raising the morality of politicians, deepening policy reflection, and improving the central minds of government with special units devoted to the moral imperative of *raison d'humanité* as a decision criterion.

5. Global peace. *Cultures of Peace: The Hidden Side of History*, by Elise Boulding (Syracuse, 2000), proposes cultures that promote "peaceable diversity." She reflects on humanity's continuing passion for the good society and on macrolevel utopian experiments of the twentieth century, such as Russia, Spain, Cuba, China, and Israel.

6. U.S. society. *Next: The Road to the Good Society*, by Amitai Etzioni (Basic Books, 2001), applies communitarian principles to policy proposals, taking us from merely asking what we should be doing for our communities to creating a cabinet-level Community Development Agency.

7. U.S. society. *Building a Healthy Culture: Strategies for an American Renaissance*, edited by Don Eberly (Eerdmans, 2001), includes thirty-four largely right-of-center essays on why culture is important, models for cultural transformation, strategies for cultural renewal and reforming academia and the professions.

8. U.S. society. *Racist America: Roots, Current Realities, and Future Reparations*, by Joe R. Feagin (Routledge, 2000), a recent president of the American Sociological Association, calls for "antiracist strategies and solutions" including a new Constitutional Convention and large-scale restitution to eliminate the effects of past discrimination.

9. U.S. economy. *The Future of Success*, by former U.S. Secretary of Labor Robert B. Reich (Knopf, 2001), promotes a more balanced culture and outlines policies to support it, such as widening the circle of prosperity by providing every eighteen-year-old with a nest egg to be reinvested in further education or a business venture.

10. U.S. economy. *The Missing Middle: Working Families and the Future of American Social Policy*, by Harvard sociologist Theda Skocpol (W. W. Norton, 2000), advocates a "family-friendly America" by turning Social Security into a "generational allowance" which could channel fund surpluses into education programs.

11. Corporations. *A Spiritual Audit of Corporate America*, by Ian I. Mitroff and Elizabeth A. Denton (Jossey-Bass, 1999), reviews models for fostering spirituality and values in the workplace, so that people can have meaningful lives and improve the human condition.

12. Unions. *CyberUnion: Empowering Labor through Computer Technology*, by Arthur B. Shostak (M. E. Sharpe, 1999), provides a passionate vision of how Organized Labor can benefit from comput-

erization and form "cyberunions" to counter growing corporate power.

13. Cities. *e-topia: "Urban Life, Jim, But Not As We Know It,"* by William J. Mitchell, the dean of architecture and planning at MIT (MIT Press, 1999), envisions how we can create "lean and green" cities that work smarter.

14. Cities. *Carfree Cities*, by J. H. Crawford (International Books/Paul & Company, 2000), offers detailed ideas on restricting motor-vehicle traffic for a more sustainable, healthier, and happier future.

15. Neighborhoods. *Restoring America's Neighborhoods: How Local People Make a Difference*, by Michael R. Greenberg, director of the National Center for Neighborhood and Brownfields Redevelopment at Rutgers University (Rutgers University Press, 1999), has useful insights on developing poor urban areas.

A Betterment Vocabulary

The following terms have been used to identify social-betterment thinking, which ranges from the highly idealistic (utopian) to the modestly pragmatic and incremental: advocating, agenda making, better futures, blueprints for action, changing, designing, desired futures, development, enspiriting, future search process, futuring, goal setting, hoping, idealizing, imaging, imagining, improving, inventing, leading/leadership, manifestos, moral discourse, normative futures, planning, policy proposals, positive futures, preferred futures, prescriptions, proactive futures, proposals, recommending, reforming, self-fulfilling prophecy, shaping the future, strategizing, utopian thinking, visioning, wayfinding, willed futures, and wishful futures.

Constructive critics of the concept—utopia—have much to teach us. The essay below traces problems in the concept from its original formulation. It examines what is required "if there is [to be] any hope of utopian thinking. . . ." It identifies reasons for the absence of positive thinking. It locates in brain technology a new source of hope for the securement soon of viable utopian ideas. And it is quite clear about what current utopian thinking lacks—this, a provocative challenge accepted and addressed by others in this volume.

4.   Utopia—An Obsolete Concept*

Joseph F. Coates

If Utopia is taken to be a future ideal state or some imagined general condition of perfection of social, political, institutional, and personal life, then it has no place in contemporary thinking. The conditions for imagining a utopia do not exist today in the general Western world and, to the best of my knowledge, never have existed in the non-Western traditions.

Utopian thinking ultimately comes from the recognition that the world does not have to be the way it is. When one looks at the conditions of the world at any particular time, the human condition is fighting evil, meeting the challenges and stresses of daily life, and anticipating and planning for disasters or misfortunes. Utopias, which recognize people as social animals, have usually drawn attention to our shortcomings, to unfairness, threats, inequities, risks, and the hazards of simply living. Utopias, therefore, are usually visions of what the world might be like if those threats, risks, and stresses were removed.

Background

In the Western tradition, it would be hard to imagine any utopia for the Greeks. Their gods populated a heaven which provided great entertainment and interest and an explanation of events, but it hardly presented the world as an ideal existence, even for the gods. The population of Mount Olympus was anthropomorphous to an extent that super humans, with capabilities humans could envy, primarily reflected arbitrariness, impetuosity, jealousy, greed, and vindictiveness.

Christianity in the West carried an entirely different religious message, namely, that there is a purpose to human life. If one behaved according to certain precepts one was gloriously rewarded; if one failed to follow them, one was severely punished. Going beyond its antecedent Jewish roots, which are unclear about any afterlife, the Christian tradition established an afterlife with God in Heaven or in Hell.

One can see the difficulties experienced by artists through the second millennium in picturing life in Heaven. God is surrounded by fluttering angels and risen people in some position of adoration. None of it has any concrete reality in defining and illustrating happiness. For most people, Heaven is a utopian afterlife free from problems. The sterility of the Christian Heaven leads to jokes about rejecting Heaven: "Send me to Hell, that's where the interesting

*For related information on this topic, see essay by Joseph Coates in *Technological Forecasting and Social Change*. Vol. 69 (5) (June 2002): 507–509.

people are!" The tradition of a place of punishment leads to great creative energy in the numerous paintings of life in Hell, in sharp contrast to the vacuity of images of existence in Heaven.

Muslims in a post-Christian religion do better in populating their afterlife, even aside from the free-flowing milk and honey with houris (voluptuous, alluring women). The Muslim Heaven is a step ahead of the Christian Heaven, which took a hostile view of sexuality and other physical pleasures. Incidentally, modern criticism of the Koran by at least some scholars suggests that the houris in heaven is a misinterpretation of the proper symbol for white raisins, which were a widely appreciated delicacy at the time of writing.

The development of democratic institutions and the concept of progress and the steady unfolding of tangible benefits from technology, and later in the modern era from science as well, caused these perceptions to change. The post-Renaissance period stimulated looks to the future in which the religious elements remained strong, but the secularization of society and a more nonreligious orientation to issues and concerns led to an expansion of eschatology, from being a solely religious concept to outcomes that might be terrestrial.

During the transition era from the modern into the contemporary world, there has been a fading of ideology, hence a fading concept of utopia. Without some eschatological goal, usually formed around religion, it is difficult to conjecture positively about any future ideal state. In the contemporary period, Karl Marx and his disciples, notably V. I. Lenin, who had the power to bring about drastic change, did little by way of presenting images of the utopia. Socialist slogans were abundant, but the images were scarce and vague.

The various religious groups so common in America in the eighteenth and nineteenth centuries, which set out to found ideal new societies, all failed or withered away when the strongest adherents died. Each of them that had any modest success had a religious base while the members attempted to found a real utopia.

The prominent benefits delivered by technological developments in the eighteenth and nineteenth centuries led to the explication of a relatively new concept—progress. Unlike the religiously based eschatologies with a fixed end state, the concept of progress does not comfortably lend itself to an end state, only to continued improvements. At the same time, economic and industrial changes demolished social and family life for a large percent of people. The new visions of society emphasized a future free of elementary threats to survival and well-being, marked by equality in which people engaged in democratic practices. But the prophecies and outcomes were obscure or, at best, cartoonish.

Nineteenth-century technological successes led to science fiction. H. G. Wells, Jules Verne, and others presented interesting and entertaining outcomes of a new technology—carried to extremes. The social elements of life in the future were not the focus of thought. Current science fiction concerns futuristic cowboys and Indians or knights in armor in some fantasy world. The most recent attempt in film to give some imagery to utopia was Arthur C. Clarke's *2001*. When all is said and done, what can the response be to that last scene other than, "Huh?" The content is no more interesting than a medieval heaven.

Dystopian Thought

Meanwhile, the potential troublesome outcomes of science and technology create a new type of image of the future for which the word "dystopian" had to be coined. Almost all the imagery in recent stories and film is dystopian. Whether it is Los Angeles in the twenty-first century, or stories of the perpetual and ancient matters of conflict, disease, evils and stresses, modern movies remain virtually free of positive imagery about the future.

The dystopian images in films have made it almost impossible for us, or for our most talented thinkers, to conceptualize in positive imagery about the future with clarity and details comparable to those of dystopian imagery. Consequently, the possibilities of pictures of any positive future are harder and harder to swallow.

What Is Necessary?

If there is any hope of utopian thinking, there must be a broad-based change in thinking about long-term futures, in ways that go beyond relief of the current problems. Would-be utopians must supply complex detailed images of the social, economic, political, and personal lives of all people if they are to have any creditability or have any value in directing the evolution of society. Utopian visions must be at least as grainy and engaging as their dystopian competitors.

Numerous things underline the absence of positive thinking about the future, but at its core is a fundamental lapse in education, in thinking positively, in thinking systemically, and in thinking optimistically. A recent issue of the *New Scientist* reported on a contest looking merely to 2050; none of the contestants dealt well with the social and personal aspects of life.

My own experience, reported elsewhere, in conducting 250 people at a World Future Society meeting through a three-hour exercise on the next thousand-year future, was disappointing. People were asked as a wrap-up to create a picture or an image of some tiny piece of life in the world 3000. The responses could have been drawn from situations found in the previous six months of the *New York Times*.

A further difficulty is the epidemic of political correctness which is infecting the nation. Perhaps it is peaking, but political correctness inhibits thinking and not only fails to reward but actually punishes people who generate visions radically different from the way the world is today. Yet utopian thinking implies a future far different then the world today, unless in some perverse way one thinks that the world today is ideal or already close to perfect.

Reading and enjoying the accumulated utopian literature is fun, and it has important and strong historic value. But it will increasingly become like being fluent in Sanskrit, interesting and entertaining as an avocation, but with little or no significant payoff.

Limits on Utopia

Don't forget the Morlocks. Bad behavior, misbehavior, destructive behavior, murderous behavior all have a history coeval with humankind. One of the greatest social discoveries in history is Original Sin, namely, the idea that we are born with a burden which leaves us open to committing, not merely being vulnerable to, evil. The concept is continually rediscovered and reformatted. In the modern era the most interesting example is found in the idea of Sigmund Freud, especially his concept of the id, the dark force in our tripartite mind.

More recently, science has offered trauma, damage, and lesions as the causes of bad behavior. It was recently discovered that kleptomania originates at a specific site in the brain as a result of what amounts to a brain lesion. Psychopharmacology is leading us to recognize that chemical imbalances of several different origins lie at the core of much misbehavior. The rapidly unfolding research in genetics is identifying more and more defects, modifications, alterations, or differences, whatever is the most appropriate term, in specific genes, which influence our behavior in undesirable ways.

In his great novel *The Time Machine*, H. G. Wells carries the hero into a nearly idyllic world, the world of Elysian Fields. Below those fields are the terrible people, the Morlocks, who represent competence and skill and keep the machinery of the world going, but at a terrible cost to those living in Elysian bliss. The Morlocks are like Freud's id, but with a conscious evil role.

The harsh reality is that for any projectable future, we will have our Morlocks. They are not necessarily the leaders and the thugs of the mafia, or of any specific social or ethnic origin. They run through the whole spectrum of society, from Morlocks such as Jack Welch, the former head of General Electric, and Bill Gates, the president of Microsoft. They are men in positions of high responsibility, who are driven by unidimensional objectives to be the biggest, best, most powerful, most influential, and most dominant in the field, at whatever cost, to the uncounted scores, thousands, or hundreds of thousands affected by their behavior.

No utopia can exist so long as we have Morlocks. It is difficult to see any effective way of controlling them, particularly as the socioeconomic unit of society grows to the big city, the metropolitan area, and the continuing megalopolis.

If we assume that half of 1 percent of the population are Morlocks, in a community of 100 people, there is a fifty-fifty chance there would be one. If he or she shows up, the social pressures and the sources of observation and intervention will keep him or her under control. In a community of 50,000, that half percent is 250 people who can find each other and organize. As we know from experience with organized crime, a small consolidated group is capable of intimidating large portions of the population totally out of proportion to their number.

In populations of a million, which in the near future will be relatively common in a hundred or more such cities throughout the world, that half percent gives us 5,000 Morlocks. We must anticipate a world of organized private and public evil over which society must exercise vigorous control—hardly a utopian situation.

In the long run, there almost surely will be developments in brain technology coming out of the combination of genetics research and mental- and brain-specific research now going on, which will open up the possibilities of radical change in people's behavior, thought patterns, and other mental functions. Whether the Morlocks will be subject to those potential controls is certainly an open question. But the imposition of those controls hardly sounds like an ideal society, certainly not in terms of the current political thinking in any of the advanced nations.

Summary

Utopia as a goal makes no sense. What we lack is a detailed discussion of what an ideal society would be like and how we could move incrementally toward approaching that ideal.

Adopting a term given some currency by Michael Marien [see his essay in this volume], perhaps we should think about *betterment* and the associated notion of *incremental improvement* in promoting the good and constraining the bad.

Viable utopian ideas suffer unduly from contagion—they are hurt by the low regard in which the general public holds the basic concept of utopianism. Many social scientists have caught this mental "virus," and far too many students have been steered away from the subject by miseducating faculty. Why does the prejudice exist? Why is there a rejection of "the current vision of the innate possibilities of the human being?" How vital is it to live as a realistic visionary? What can we learn from post-modernism about power? How can utopian thought profit from a post-reductionist view of American life? Can the "death" of utopianism be reversed? What part can futurism play in any such resurrection? Tsvi Bisk tackles all of these questions and explains a new role we might elect—that of "neo-utopians," pragmatic visionaries who embrace a "realistic Romanticism."

Although the concepts may at first seem strange, Bisk helps make them clear, even as his mind-expanding argument gains conviction and sets the pulse racing. His prescription for "utopianism come of age" empowers a reader in a very exciting way.

5. Utopianism Comes of Age*

Tsvi Bisk

The dismal record of the twentieth century made utopianism unfashionable. It seemed silly and infantile. One was not a serious social scientist if one engaged in such frivolity. Ice cold, valueless, statistical social science became de rigueur.

Some interesting exceptions, including C. Wright Mills and Ernest Becker, were around, but they were always on the margins of serious social science. To get ahead in academia, one talked statistics, not values. Statistics are useful analytical tools, but they are not fertile soil for nurturing utopian thought or anything approaching a science of man.

The concrete examples of various twentieth-century utopian pretensions— such as collectivization in the Soviet Union and China, the pathetic self-indulgent communes of the 1960s and 1970s dropouts, or such bizarre religious communes as Jonestown and the Branch Davidians—have done little to improve the reputation of utopian speculations and experiments.

On the Rehabilitation of Utopian Thought

Why should we preoccupy ourselves with utopianism at all, given its sad record? Because, quite simply, we require concrete visions of our possible future in order to live as human beings on this earth.

As the early Enlightenment modernists so rightly understood, what separates the human from the animal is the rational mind. The rational, volitional mind is the chief survival tool of the human species. When we use it, we prosper; when we fail to use it, we endanger our own survival. War and the human suffering it causes are irrational; peace and the human fulfillment it makes

*Editor's Note: See also "Toward a Practical Utopianism," by Tsvi Bisk, *The Futurist*, May–June 2002; 22–25; "How Should Utopianism be Taught?," in A. Shostak, ed., *Utopian Thinking in Sociology: Creating the Good Society*, Washington, DC: American Sociological Society, 2001; 93–95.

possible are rational. A polluted environment is irrational; a clean environment is rational.

1. *The Value of Values.* Can we have a rational social science that is not based on a social philosophy possessed of a coherent vision of the innate possibilities of the human being? How can we have a rational social science (a true science of man) without social values? Just as the physical sciences must be valueless in order to be scientific, so must the social sciences be value laden in order to be scientific.

Science is a rational, volitional, intentional activity that must say *yes* or *no* to the data it gathers. The physical sciences make the decision based upon the quantitative coherence of the data itself after experimentation and translation into mathematical language. If the social sciences are to be relevant to the survival of humanity (i.e., rational), they must base their *yes* or *no* on non-quantifiable values.

Values cannot be perceived by way of statistics; they can be perceived by way of pictures or visions or scenarios. Indeed, scenarios are kinds of mini-utopias. Futurist methodologies will probably be a basic functional tool by which we might construct a neo-utopianism.

Human society cannot conduct itself rationally without a clear idea of where it wants to go. Clear ideas would be a better term because "neo-utopianism" should be pluralistic in order to avoid the totalitarian know-it-all temptation that has doomed utopian experiments in the past. The horrific consequences of a single-minded (as opposed to an open-minded) utopian instinct are well documented in Yaacov Talmon's classic work *Totalitarian Democracy* (2002). Whatever the case, we must have a vision of the kind of future we want in order to make rational decisions on a daily basis.

2. *The Value of Vision.* Having a vision and being a *realistic* visionary are absolute necessities for functioning as a rational human being. This is contrary to popular prejudice, which equates visionary with unrealistic fantasy, but it is nonetheless self-evidently true.

Human beings make practical judgments and value judgments every day of their lives. We must do this in order to survive, as the primary human survival tool is not instinct, but the reasoning mind evaluating the human environment. Human beings who are better at this usually have much more successful lives. Societies and cultures that encourage this kind of thinking are usually much more developed.

Modernism was simplistically optimistic about the possible planned perfectibility of human society. The postmodernist critique identified the simplistic hubris of modernism and showed how this hubris resulted in catastrophe in ecology, politics, economy, and so on. Postmodernism gave us wisdom about the limitations of power.

Today we have graduated to an even higher wisdom—that criticism of simplistic visions is not enough; that human society absolutely requires visions of where it wants to go; that without such visions, it is impossible to conduct society in a rational way. These visions might be vague, but exist they must if a culture is to be vigorous and healthy.

The question is on the basis of what do we make our judgments? If we do not have a clear vision, or several alternative visions, then how do we make rational decisions? If we do not know where we want to go, if we do not have a future ideal of the kind of life we want, how can we judge the practicality or the value of any judgment we must make in the course of our daily lives?

A plurality of visions might be necessary for practical reasons in such a rapidly changing world, and not only to avoid the totalitarian temptation. Utopianism must avoid becoming a finalistic one-dimensional picture. It must reflect a "new view of the cosmos (and) be progressively evolutionary, infinite in its capacity and comprehensible both qualitatively and quantitatively," as Eric J. Lerner asserted in his brilliantly original book *The Big Bang Never Happened* (1991, 327).

Stephen Jay Gould, commenting on the ramifications of the human genome project in the *New York Times*, wrote "only humility (and a plurality of strategies for explanation) can locate the Holy Grail" (February 19, 2001). Gould hinted at the infinite human potentialities offered by a post-reductionist view of human life.

3. *The Value of Utopian Thought.* There is a sociopsychological price to be paid for the death of utopianism. Observe the number of people in the modern world who seem to float through life rudderless without a clear view of their own value as human beings. They are so confused about the complexities of modern life that they have shut off their cognitive rational faculties. They are trying to fill the subsequent spiritual vacuum by going shopping, taking drugs, getting involved in cults, becoming "saved" religiously, adopting New Age fads, and so on.

The inability to construct rational, realistic, alternative future visions leads people to create fantastic ones (benevolent aliens will come in their spaceships to take us away to eternal bliss; in preparation, we must castrate ourselves and then commit collective suicide).

Human beings are the only species that can conceive of the future, the only species truly cognizant of its own mortality. The resultant angst leads us into the future-conceiving business. Religions had a monopoly on this business for the longest time (the End of Days, the Coming of the Messiah, eternal life, eventual human salvation, life after death, reincarnation, and so on). Science began to replace religion in areas amenable to quantitative measurement. The profession of futurism has attempted to make this process more comprehensive and as rational and as realistic (i.e., connected to reality) as possible.

4. *The Value of Futurism.* Utopianism was one of the foundational building blocks upon which futurism was built. Now, futurism must serve as one of the foundational building blocks of a neo-utopianism.

Modern utopianism coincided with the secularizing process of the Renaissance. People were beginning to shed the certainty about the future provided by religion. This uncertainty was reflected in the plays of William Shakespeare, the first truly modern writer who anticipated the angst of modern man: "To be or not to be, that *is* the question!" Utopian speculations, such as those of Thomas More and Francis Bacon, in all likelihood responding to this incipient angst, offered secularized versions of a possible "end of days" as it pertained to human society on this earth.

One of the positive aims of the postmodernist project was to attack human certitude (moral, scientific, or political) as insufferable hubris. While this project has performed a valuable service in critiquing modernist ideology, it is essentially nihilistic. It offers no coherent alternative to modernism. Indeed, it would view the very search for coherence as a modernist pretension.

But if humanity is to survive and have a meaningful existence, then the intellectual project of the twenty-first century must be to move from postmodernism to a neomodernism. We must reinstate the Enlightenment ambition to create a science of man. We must become neo-utopians.

Perhaps we can find support for a new utopianism based upon a new science of man based on new developments and insights in the biological and cosmological sciences. Just as the social sciences, dominated by a reductionist mechanical science, destroyed the value-laden science of man, so might a new value-laden science of man find its justification in philosophical insights drawn from new developments in evolutionary theory (physical and biological) based upon plasma physics, genetic research, and ever-increasing knowledge about life itself. Edward O. Wilson has made a heroic attempt at a synthesis which reintroduces objectivity and meaning into the discussion in his book, *Consilience* (1998).

5. *Recognizing the Threat.* Secular humanism, an outgrowth of the Renaissance, scientific revolution, and Enlightenment, has been one of the foundation blocks of modernist ideology. But its growing spiritual inadequacies (based in part on the uncertainties of the new physics) has led to the radical moral relativism of new age postmodernism, on the one hand, and a return to the bedrock certainties of religious fundamentalism, on the other hand.

Both these extremes feed off one another, and both, together and separately, are very dangerous for the future of human society. Only a neo-utopianism can offset this double trend and reinvigorate secular humanism, which is the necessary meta-ideological underpinning of constitutional democracy.

Is the United States better off because academic research has "proven" that the American Dream was a manipulated myth? Is Israel better off because intellectuals have "proven" that the Zionist idea was flawed at its very inception? Is Europe better off because the Enlightenment dream of a more rational and just society has become unfashionable, replaced by dubious theories of false consciousness and the inherent alienation of the human being? Are any of us better off because radical Greens have "demonstrated" that human beings are basically pests infecting Mother Nature?

Neither individuals nor societies can function efficiently and flourish in an atmosphere of declining self-esteem. Human beings are not just economic beings, or cultural beings, or social beings. They are first of all heroic beings, who require a heroic image of their own future in order to stimulate and sustain the energy capable of bringing out the best of their human *being*.

This is the task of utopianism—not a blueprint, but a vision of what things could be like and should be like.

6. *The Value of Neo-Romanticism.* Let us define this mood as neo-Romanticism. A neo-utopianism would want to change the tense of Romanticism. It would want us to be romantic about the future, not about the past.

I use the term *Romanticism* in its most precise sense (not in its popularized perversion). Romanticism is the literary genre that sees the human being as a heroic creation and deals with human life as it ought to be, in light of heroic human nature, and not as it is. It is appositive to naturalism, which deals with life as it is and even celebrates life as it is.

Futurism is, in a way, a realistic Romanticism. It does not deal in fantasy or wishful thinking, but in the rational organization of empirical fact in order to assist us in constructing positive alternative visions of our future.

Rather than an idealized nostalgic attachment to the past, let us cultivate a Romantic attachment to the possibilities of the future. We live in the future, not in the past. Therefore the future is more important then the past, and if we are to love our own lives we must learn to fall in love with the future.

The call for vague visions and Romantic attachment in no way justifies mushy and impractical thinking. The challenge must be clearly and precisely formulated, and it must reflect reality, not wishful thinking.

It must deal primarily with the "objective" life of the human being as a *social animal*, not with the "subjective" life of a so-called alienated individual whose "false consciousness" malevolent forces are manipulating. The challenge must be long term, but not so long term as to be inconceivable. Any vision that transcends 100 years in the future usually turns into the fantasy genre of science fiction—interesting, but essentially useless.

7. *Getting There from Here.* I will formulate a possible neo-utopian challenge as a question, hoping by doing so to avoid the totalitarian tendency of positivist utopianism. The question is, "How can we create, by the year 2100, a planetary human society composed of 12 billion people with an American standard of living, and with one tenth the negative environmental impact present human society has on nature?"

What research and development policies, international trade policies, tax policies, and space exploration policies must we pursue in order to achieve such a vision? This is a practical question *given to rational treatment* that will engender *numerous* alternative possible answers. The debate, therefore, will be utopian, but *pluralistic and nontotalitarian.*

By clearly defining the challenge, we will avoid the imprecise, wishful thinking of New Age postmodernism reflected, for example, in calls to lower the world's population from 6 billion to 2 billion within the next century, and to educate the remaining 2 billion to adopt the way of life of a European village before Charlemagne.

This is neither clear nor moral thinking; its immorality is a direct consequence of its lack of clarity. To attain such a goal we would have to exterminate a few billion people, forcibly sterilize a few billion more people, and reeducate the remainder in the Rosseau/Robespierre tradition of "forcing people to be free," a chilling oxymoron that began with the guillotine and ended with the gulag.

People do not require a grand theory of global warming to support a clean environment. They are for a clean environment because they do not want to breathe, drink, or eat poison.

Whether the theory of human-induced global warming is correct is beyond the point. Any future vision of society that envisions a clean environment must argue its case on the basis of the interests of real human beings, living real lives in a sophisticated technological society.

Most human beings have no intention of giving up their technological lifestyle, and billions more aspire to a technological lifestyle. Frantic self-righteous calls by neurotic dropouts to give up soap and hot water and live in teepees are not likely to have wide appeal.

8. *Neo-Modernism: A Better Approach.* A practical utopianism would not present a vision of the future that would require people to give up modern dentistry in order to save the environment.

Indeed, modern dentistry might be the greatest justification for the inherent human morality of the Industrial Revolution. When you go to a dentist you are giving sanction to the metallurgy industry, the chemical industry, the electronics industry, and the pharmaceutical industry, as well as to industrial civilization in general which has provided both the technical means and the surplus wealth to train the dentist.

The Modernists were right: The Industrial Revolution was the greatest event in the history of humanity. In 1750 in France 70 percent of children died before the age of five, the life span was less than forty, most women were toothless by their late teens, and only a minority of the population could read and write. How many sane people would want to return to such an era? Yet it is this very gloomy "utopianism" that we are being offered in some antimodernist quarters.

A practical utopianism would be based upon a neomodernism that accepts the postmodern critique of the hubris of modernism, but rejects postmodernism's radical relativism and lack of coherent vision. It would have a good chance at being relevant and offering positive direction for human civilization. It would enable us to once again instill human society with purpose, rejuvenating human culture around a coherent, yet pluralistic, framework of ideals and values. This would be *Utopianism Come of Age!*

References

Becker, Ernest. *The Structure of Evil.* New York: Free Press, 1976.
Bury, John. *The Idea of Progress.* Westport, CT: Greenwood, 1982.
Capra, Fritjf. *The Turning Point.* New York: Simon and Schuster, 1982.
Cornish, Edward. *The Study of the Future.* New York: World Future Society, 1977.
Lerner, Eric. *The Big Bang Never Happened.* Carmarthen, UK: Crown Publishers, 1991.
Popper, Carl. *The Poverty of Historicism.* Boston, MA: Beacon Press, 1957.
Talmon, Jacob. *The Origins of Totalitarian Democracy.* Portland, OR: Frank Cass, 2002.
Wilson, Edward. *Consilience.* New York: Random House, 1999.

Progress in advancing viable utopian ideas hinges in part on our achieving a reformulation of the challenge. Plainly, many of our tired and worn ways of "seeing" the matter have spent their force and now serve us poorly. Too many of us spend too much of the time relying too heavily on the appeal of vague word pictures. Our audience silently wonders what it is all about. Many privately think, "The devil is in the details." When pressed for specifics, for a clearer-than-ever notion of destination, too many utopians hem and haw, coming up only with more pieties or pie-in-the-sky homilies.

All the more welcome, therefore, is the call below for a fresh approach, one which highlights our ability to get specific and compels more rigor. Concrete examples are offered of the power of clarity about our overarching goals. Careful not to misrepresent itself as a "magic bullet," the approach makes a sound contribution to the reformulation already under way. Written by an applied social scientist with decades of successful fieldwork to his credit, it warrants careful consideration as an alternative to the "same old, same old."

6. Utopia and the Attempted Flow of Useful Ideas: Why Being Able to Define and Measure a Clear Vision Matters

Roger Kaufman

Utopia as an idea has given us a lot. It was initially intended to define a civil society in which everything worked. It was to be an ideal process that would benefit everyone. Over the years the concept has been both pursued and derided. Clerics, for example, have defined their own versions of utopias, which have varied from seventy-two virgins for the new male arrival for simply blowing up themselves and some others, to playing harps sitting on a cloud of happiness as the reward for living a good life.

Many variations of definitions of utopia have been offered by dictators, well-doers, kings and queens, and politicians. Most of these definitions were based on processes, often best described as an ism, such as Marxism, capitalism, socialism, communism, fascism, pluralism, pacifism, and a host of others. Most isms have failed to bring about an ideal state for citizens, but temporarily they have lined the pockets of a few.

All isms have been temporary triumphs of processes in search of useful results, but all have been quite prescriptive of the processes to be used. The critical flaw for each, including the original concept of utopia, is that they did not define the end state, but rather confused the means with the ends.

Confusing means with ends has been a popular sport over the years. We see it daily when we talk with politicians, listen to news broadcasters, and relate with friends and coworkers. We hear a steady flow of ideas about means (or solutions, or programs, or projects, or activities, or laws, or policies): welfare, work fare, income redistribution, tough love, campaign finance reform, arms buildups, unilateral disarmament, banning insecticides, diversity, ethnic cleansing, rapid transit, smaller class sizes, tougher tests.

Everyone seems to have a solution, while usually well-meaning, is at best a part of the total situation. We tend to look at parts of the whole, instead of the whole, before selecting the parts. In our rush to make things better, we often fail to relate means with ends, but rather select a logical sounding means, and assume that useful ends will flow directly. Disappointment occurs again.

Just as many concepts of utopia have talked more to means and resources, any means should be selected based only on the ends to be accomplished. This definition of the results of utopia has been elusive, if nonexistent. But we keep trying, for the inspiration of utopia is seductive. Every year brings a new ism for us to apply to make our world better. And try we do, as we flit from one "flat earth" idea to another.

Solutions in Search of Problems

Our planet is littered with the wreckage of means that did not bring useful ends to all of our fellow earthlings. Wars rage, crime hits innocents, terrorism expands, people are manipulated. Oracles—be they occupying pulpits, professorships, public offices, or lofty industrial perches—pronounce sure-fire means and solutions. And hope springs eternal while we seek utopia. The consequences are: disappointment, disillusionment, frustration, apathy, hostility, and depression.

There is, nevertheless, much to be learned from the intentions of utopians and the failed attempts to bring one about. What we can learn is that it continues to be folly to confuse means (perfectly functioning government, socialism, etc.) with ends (the survival of the species). Each hopeful attempt at creating a utopia seems to have suffered one fatal flaw: Utopia has never been defined in measurable terms.

To be sure, utopias have been described as a "perfect world" and "universal happiness." Those intentions, while honorable and laudable, are not precise enough for anyone to select the processes—the means—to get from here to there. A very fuzzy roadmap might enthuse our creativity, but it certainly does not make for a sure-fire successful trip. And since we are talking about the lives and survival of our planet and all on it, creativity must be tempered by practicality—we ought to do no harm. We require a compass based on a destination that benefits all stakeholders.

At this juncture, I can picture the frowns and rolling eyes of the academic or politician (and they often are the same) as they throw up their hands and claim that such a compass and a defined destination are not possible. I disagree with this self-defeatist, old-paradigm thinking. I think it can be done if we follow a few simple and shared ground rules:

1. We focus only on ends (or "whats"), not on means (the "hows)
2. We define, in measurable terms, the kind of world we want to help create for tomorrow's child
3. We include criteria so all can determine if we have arrived at where we want to be
4. All statements of purpose will identify the results of anything we use, do, produce, and deliver for our shared society
5. All statements of results will benefit all
6. We realize that our progress toward this agreed-upon end state (or results-referenced utopia) will be steady and relentless. We will use our progress to improve continuously what we use, do, produce, and deliver.

Over many more years than I care to admit, I have been working with others—very diverse others from almost around the globe—to define what I call an ideal vision. You might call it a next evolution of the concept of utopia, in that it speaks to ends, not means. It talks to results and consequences; and it is made possible by employing the rules above.

The hallmark of useful strategic thinking and planning is the singular focus on the ideal vision—the planning level I call "mega" because the primary client and beneficiary is tomorrow's child—and measurably delivering safety, survival, and a positive quality of life. It is this mega level of thinking and planning that defines a results-focused utopia.

Here is what my research provides by way of an ideal vision—the mega level of strategic thinking and planning:

1. Every woman, man, and child will feel secure and move around the globe safely without regard to time or place.
2. Their communities and countries will be free of infectious diseases and the consequences that limit survival, self-sufficiency, and quality of life.
3. The world will be at peace, with no deaths or disabilities from combat or terrorism, and there will be no murders, rapes, or starvation. There will be no crimes, no disabling substance abuse.
4. Every child brought into the world will be a wanted child, and thus none will suffer physical or psychological abuse, starvation, malnutrition, or incapacity for becoming self-sufficient and contributing people.
5. Food and water will be available, pure, and wholesome, and no one will die or become disabled from them or lack of them.
6. Poverty will not exist, and every woman and man will be self-sufficient and self-reliant so that they will earn as much as it costs them to live, unless they are moving (such as going to school) toward preparing themselves to be self-sufficient and self-reliant. No one will be under the care, custody, or control of another person, agency, or substance.
7. All citizens will be assisted to help themselves so that they are self-sufficient and self-reliant. People will take charge of their lives and be responsible for what they use, do, and contribute. They will revise what they do and produce based on their contributions to self and others.
8. Personal, intimate, and loving partnerships will form and sustain themselves, and abuse will not occur.
9. No species will become extinct as a result of unintended human intervention, pollution, or action. Accidents will reach zero, and thus there will not be any accidental death, disability, or impairment of daily living.
10. Government's contribution will be assisting people to be happy and self-sustaining. It will reinforce independence and mutual contribution, and it will be organized and funded to the extent to which it meets its objectives.
11. Business will earn a profit without bringing harm to its clients and our mutual world.
12. All people will themselves decide how they will contribute to this ideal vision.

Some might argue, and they will, that things like greed, prejudice, and avarice will always exist, and thus this ideal vision is not realistic. But is this current widespread tendency a reason for not taking our first collective steps toward achievement of this ideal vision? Would they rather curse the darkness than light a match?

If one never intends to reach perfection, then certainly they never will. They will not even know where to head and what to change or what to continue. An ideal vision is practical, pragmatic, and hopeful.

Let us examine some current cases in point where the ideal vision was not part of the decision criteria:

1. The procedures for checking on foster children in Florida were tight, solid, and published. However, a child was not physically checked in more than fifteen months and turned up missing. Did the caseworkers and their supervisors use mega to guide their everyday actions, or did they look after their own well-being? What would have happened if each and every person, including the foster parents, focused first and foremost on the survival, self-sufficiency, and quality of life of the dependent child?

2. A huge accounting firm faces extinction because of allegations that it put its billable hours before making public audit reports on the true financial condition of clients. Did the executives focus on mega—the survival and self-sufficiency of all shareholders and employees? Or did they instead look only at the financial condition of a few organizational members?

3. Killing is being conducted around the world by self-professed freedom fighters who feel that anyone who does not believe and act the way they feel is correct should be eliminated. If killing such infidel people includes women and children, that is of no concern. Are the murderers focusing on mega—the survival, self-sufficiency, and quality of life of everyone (utopia measurably defined), or are they only looking after their own power and image?

4. The Congress of the United States does budgeting on an agency-by-agency basis. Since money is tight, agencies—often with similar missions, such as the FBI and CIA—compete with each other for scarce resources. This competition often results in withholding from fiscal rivals critical information that might make the other look good, and thus be in line for monies they themselves are seeking. Are the players in this drama, including the politicians, focused on mega—the survival, self-sufficiency, and quality of life for all—or are they looking after their own power and position?

Those who decide, for whatever reasons, not to move continuously toward mega and the ideal vision limit all of us. If we are not headed toward the ideal vision, where are we headed? If we are not going there, how do we decide the moral and ethical choices concerning what we—individually and collectively—use, do, produce, and deliver? What will be the compass with which they would replace this one?

I see a hopeful life where everyone moves toward the shared ideal vision, moves in ways and uses means they decide are useful to themselves and to our shared future. We can and must learn from past attempts at defining utopia. We can and must dare to define and assess the ends toward which we would advance.

III. Methods:
Even Better Tools

Having spent over forty years as an applied sociologist, I am especially pleased to have a longtime friend, collaborator, and mentor explain below some of the many imaginative and rewarding uses we make of this discipline. Created at the start of the nineteenth century to help humankind employ the scientific method where social challenges are concerned, sociology is employed by 101 occupations and professions in 101 different ways. Steadily advancing in its power to employ both quantitative and qualitative tools, the discipline, at its best, directs our attention to the fundamental (viable utopian) question— knowledge for what?

7. Modest Steps toward an Ideal World: Sociological Practice and Utopia

Ross Koppel

Most of us would welcome the opportunity to live in a paradise or in a utopia. But we must realize that there is a difference between the two ideals. Paradise is a great place to hang out; you need do nothing to improve it. Utopia, in contrast, must be earned. Utopia is usually a kind of place where good work and humane values will be rewarded justly and fairly for individuals and for society. Paradise is generally passive; utopia is our chance to *make* a better world. It is an active ideal—a setting where virtue and effort will create the kind of society not achievable in whatever is the current political and social system.

Sociology, from its very beginnings, was about *making* a better society, perhaps a perfect society. Most of its founders expected to *use* sociology while they were developing the discipline.[1] The apparent leap from trying to create a more perfect society to the daily work of sociological practitioners is largely illusory. Applied sociologists, like myself, are typically called upon by organizations, groups, governments, and societies to help improve our understanding of problems and to suggest ways of fixing them. The goals and even the basic methods of sociological practice and the founders' vision are not really divergent.

This sociological work may be a grand effort, such as making Social Security more responsive to the needs of the elderly or ill. Or it may be at the organizational level, such as improving the use of information to serve clients better. Or it may be at a municipal level, such as helping to resolve conflicts in communities or designing a transportation system that makes sense. The ideal is always to improve the lives of people.

The process (what we do) and the underlying rationale are products of the eighteenth century's great intellectual contribution: a belief in the perfectibility of society and the power of human kind's reason and ability. In this sense, we are very much children of the Enlightenment, although we are now armed with fancy statistical techniques, sophisticated questionnaire designs, elaborate computer models, and theories honed (although always still developing) over our discipline's almost 200-year-old history.

Examples of Sociological Practice

The volume's editor asked me to discuss two of many projects I have directed in my almost thirty years as a promoter of viable utopian ideas.

1) *Addressing Race- and Ethnicity-based Differences in the Teaneck, NJ, School System.* About seven years ago, I was asked by the Teaneck School System to help explain and address race- and ethnicity-based differences in the academic outcomes of its students. Minority students were not doing as well as expected, even though Teaneck, NJ, was a model community of proactive integration (including introducing busing five years before the federal government mandated it for school systems) with a solid African American professional class, very limited poverty, and a community focused on educational achievement. Minority students were not graduating with the same grades as the white students.

To help find out why, I assembled all of the school system's many datasets into one large database so that I could compare the students across demographic categories, grades, course history, subjects, and behaviors. This enabled me to ask such questions as did students who recently moved to the community, or students with poor attendance records, or students who lived in particular parts of town do significantly better or worse than other students? Were there race- or ethnicity-based links to such patterns?

- I developed and administered a questionnaire on students' expectations and aspirations, TV watching, time spent on homework, and on students' attitudes toward school, grades, homework, teachers, and so on. The data enabled me to examine the importance of these factors on grades and allowed me to observe any other patterns and trends.
- I conducted focus groups with teachers, parents, students, special education teachers, guidance counselors, and administrators. These interviews, in addition to providing invaluable insights about school and family, helped me write the questionnaire and helped me interpret the findings.
- I geocoded every house, inserting the exact longitude and latitude of every home in the community to link each family's location to databases on income and housing costs. This enabled me to examine income/race patterns to determine to what extent differentials in academic outcome were related to parental earnings rather than to race or ethnicity.

At the completion of the research I issued a series of reports and gave several presentations. The community and the school system came together to explore many of the findings, some quite surprising, and to develop programs that addressed those disparities that could be ameliorated with school-based and community-based programs.

Changes included a new focus on remedial programs (African American teachers and parents were previously so concerned with stigmatizing students that many students who could benefit from help were never referred to the program). New emphasis was placed on homework and homework follow-up programs. School administrators began active recruitment into an honors programs and advanced placement classes. The community gained a new awareness that a large Latino population of students was experiencing difficulties and not receiving special services. In all, Teaneck took a major step toward achieving better and broader educational goals—a bit of a viable utopian victory.

2 *Determining the Cost of Alzheimer's Disease to U.S. Businesses.* In 1998 I was approached by the Alzheimer's Association to see if I could estimate the cost of Alzheimer's disease to U.S. businesses.

We knew then about four million people had the disease, and a series of studies had estimated the annual cost to society to be about $100 billion. My task was to determine the cost to *businesses* alone. My job was to determine what part of $100 billion was paid by businesses.

Upon investigation, I realized that most of the costs to businesses had never been analyzed. Why? Most people with Alzheimer's have already retired from the labor force. The costs, therefore, were assumed to be borne by their families, by the medical system or medical insurance, and by the government via Medicare and Medicaid.

There are two fallacies in these assumptions, one rather obvious and one not so. First, it is obvious that businesses pay a share of all taxes and contribute directly to health care insurance. Second, it is less obvious that people with Alzheimer's disease are often cared for by relatives who are in the labor force. The loss of their time and productivity, the replacement costs for workers who leave, and the related distractions and constant crises results in a serious economic burden to businesses.

In 1998, using data from the Bureau of Labor Statistics, the Commerce Department, the Healthcare Financing Administration, and research from scholars in human resources management, sociology, social work, and economics, I estimated that Alzheimer's disease cost American businesses alone more than $33 billion a year. More surprising, most of those costs were over and above the usually stated $100 billion. My new research four years later reveals the cost to businesses in 2002 is $61 billion, nearly twice the amount I calculated in 1998. This $61 billion is the equivalent of total profits of the top eight *Fortune* 500 companies.

In 1998 my report helped influence Congress to allocate an additional $50 million to Alzheimer's research. I hope my new report will also be effective in spurring additional attention to the need for research and for adequate policies to address the needs of caregivers. I was proud of the original outcome, and I will continue to work to inform Congress and the public of the recent research.

Please note that my calculations were based on four million people with Alzheimer's disease. Within the decade, baby boomers will enter their retirement years, and the numbers with Alzheimer's will begin to explode, reaching as high as 14 million by the middle of the century. The related costs here will be unbearable—and dystopian in the extreme—unless we act now to address the causes and treatment of this disease . . . unless we work hard now at activating relevant viable utopian ideas.

Aiding the Utopian Impulse

From its beginnings almost 200 years ago, sociology has focused on overcoming the limitations of an existing society. Although many in and outside the discipline undervalue its utopian impulse, it is strong and pervasive, and my specialty, sociological practice, exemplifies its most noble ideals. Utopia, in its own way, remains an idea and an ideal. While it may not be fully achievable, certainly not in our lifetime, we can and routinely do employ sociological practice to take modest steps in its direction. If you are to help promote utopian-like gains, you would do well to include applied sociology in your tool kit.

Note

1. Auguste Comte (1798–1857) wanted sociologist-priests to guide society and policy. Emile Durkheim (1858–1917) argued that it was "vain and sterile" to do nothing when so many are suffering, and when polices are so ineffective. He was involved in dozens of policy councils and applied research projects. He wrote seventy-five articles for general magazines and popular journals. Max Weber (1864–1920) helped write the German Constitution after World War I, served as an advisor to the Versailles Conference, and was briefly a candidate for president. Karl Marx (1818–1883), although not trained as a sociologist (there were no academic departments with that name), exerted an extraordinary influence on the discipline, and he was more than a little concerned about social action and creating a better society.

Reference

Koppel, Ross. "American Public Policy: Formation and Implementation." In *Using Sociology: An Introduction from the Applied and Clinical Perspectives*, ed. Roger A. Straus. Lanham, MD: Rowman and Littlefield, 2002.

Fortunately, we have many dreamers who can help us imagine both ever-finer social systems—and their obverse. In addition to prose writers of both fact and fiction, we get creative help from artists, cartoonists, choreographers, composers, critics, dancers, musicians, performance artists, playwrights, poets, reviewers, singers, sculptors, street performers, and many other explorers of novel realms.

Poets, in particular, have much to offer. Their artistry with words, their capacity to layer multiple meanings, and their ability to draw us into mindscapes otherwise unavailable to us warrants our special attention . . . and appreciation. Grasping what viable utopian ideas are about—always a challenging task—is made a bit more manageable when we share ourselves with this ancient and wondrous art form.

8. Utopian Poetry: A Medium for the Message

Lane Jennings

Poetry has fallen out of favor as a popular mode of expression since the days (less than fifty years ago) when newspapers routinely featured a poem every day on their editorial page. Some readers will remember when a poem last appeared on the front page of the *New York Times*. It was July 21, 1969, and the poem, by Archibald MacLeish, ran beside photos of the first astronauts on the moon.[1]

What *is* poetry, anyway? I like to call it "language doing more than what is legally required."[2] In this sense poetry is all around us still even if sometimes hidden from plain view. We find poetry in advertisements, greeting cards, song lyrics, political slogans, and soundbites. Writers in all these forms use words for what they suggest, look, and sound like—above and beyond their dictionary meanings.

Poetry—like all art—arises to fill a need. I believe that active futurists, and the vastly larger group of men and women who find desirable futures hard to imagine in detail, need poetry now.

We all think hard about the future sometimes. Unfortunately, the futures we visualize most clearly tend to be the ones we would prefer to avoid. We daydream in general about wealth and success. But we pre-experience with all our senses what we fear will happen when we bring a poor report card home; what the dentist is about to do to us as we squirm in his waiting room; and the awful possibilities attending life's big problems: love, money, accidents, crime, war, and death.

Sadly, worry over worst-case futures is largely wasted. Most never happen; and those that do bring opportunity as well as pain. We would do better to think more, and more clearly, about desirable futures, then plan actions designed to bring those futures to reality.

Some years ago, I started looking for better ways to envision positive futures—not futures that *had* no heroes, but futures that did not absolutely *require* a hero to make life endurable.

Stories and scenarios show us future time in motion. Why not zero in on a static image, one particular future moment—produce a snapshot, not a feature film? And the word-art closest in form to a photograph or painting is . . . a poem.

Readers approach poetry with different expectations than they bring to prose. Prose is ordinary, everyday; poetry is special. Odd-looking on the page, different sounding to the ear, poetry announces from the start that something extraordinary lies ahead. Children turn instinctively to nursery rhymes, nonsense verse, and word games for enjoyment, but rhymes and rhythms are also teaching tools making words and information easy to remember.

Readers expect prose (especially nonfiction) to proceed with care, fill every page completely, stick to business, appeal to reason not emotion, and leave no doubt by the end what the author wishes readers to believe. Poems, by contrast, can take many shapes, and they are often tightly compact. Poets are free to use intense, often emotionally charged words, place them in ways that heighten their impact, and frequently suggest more than they say. Occasionally, prose writers use words this way too (advertising copy and public speeches offer examples), but a poetry reader can expect to meet words freighted with more meanings than their strict prose definitions would convey.

So how does poetry relate to futures and particularly those best, or most-desired, futures we call utopias?

Well, there have always been poets who have written about the good life. The tradition of pastoral verse-poems describing in more or less realistic detail the joys of ideal country living goes back thousands of years.[3] Beautiful and moving scenes of ordinary people at peace with each other and their surroundings appear in poems and songs from every time and country. In the English language alone we find examples from the Middle Ages, from William Shakespeare and other Elizabethans, through John Milton, Robert Browning, Alfred, Lord Tennyson, Gerard Hopkins, Emily Dickinson, and on to twentieth-century poets, such as Robert Frost and Gary Snyder.

Like other writers, poets tend to focus on the present and the past. However, some have ventured to describe life in the future. For example, there are anthologies and magazines devoted entirely to science fiction poetry.[4] These poems, however, often are examples of storytelling carried on by other means.

Instead of relying solely on other writers for poems that portray attractive, sustainable futures, I began writing my own. The result was *Virtual Futures*, published in 1996, and still available from the World Future Society, Washington, D.C., bookstore.

Like many science fiction stories, each poem, or "word-view," has some basis in reality and draws on concepts that have been explored to some extent by scientists and technicians. As in many scenarios, there is little emphasis on characters in conflict or dramatic action. Instead, title and year date (in brackets) evoke a theme and designate a specific future time. Then a scene is sketched or a process briefly described. Readers are invited to look, absorb the details, and react as critical observers—to ask, "Does this future make sense to me, or not?"

As published, each poem was followed by a brief comment and several questions to spark discussion. Here are three examples.

INHERITANCE [2350]

In clearness, thirty feet below you,
lake trout circle lazily.
Old scars are healing in a ground
no longer overrun. Those cities
not recycled, carted off for souvenirs,
grow slowly picturesque.
Through stillness, you can hear
the play of water, press of wind in leaves,
animals and birds on the instruments they know.

Let the scramblers go starward!
We who remain have no regrets.

Home is best. Our ancestors
knew this. Others pushed westward,
trundled wagons over stone and snow
toward shimmering mirages.
We are the brood of stayers—
and of some who turned again,
in time, still whole and thankful.

Generations passed us by.
We stood aside, content
to let them pass.
Now at last we hold secure
this domain that was always ours
because we watched and tended
what the scramblers
only clutched
and left behind.

"Inheritance," *Virtual Futures*, pp. 84–85.

The utopian concept here is not simply humankind's dream of roaming the
universe, but what might happen when the meek DO inherit the earth. Few
physicists today concede that humans will ever escape to the stars, but it is
interesting to consider that two (or more) coexisting utopias might be required
to accommodate the wide differences in human temperament.

FOOD FOR THOUGHT [2060]

Tide foam
a hem of lace
along our hull, until
we slow and settle
riding the swell
like a clump of ocean weed.

At sonar signal
probes school out,
a dozen
skewer one silver
mackerel-strike home
their needle-thin pipettes
then pull away
with all its gene-encoded knowledge
safe aboard.

Moments pass.
The fish,
stunned but unhurt,
swims off
to feed and spawn
the old true way,
Oblivious of us,
his former hunters, now
his copyists—
contented
cloning only the cells we need
to steaks and slices,
natural filets
shaped to our taste
but free of pain-guilt
or the taint of murder.

Vegans and carnivores
unite
to feast on all creation,
knowing now
we need not live
by death alone.

"Food for Thought ["Omnivore Lib"]," Virtual Futures,
pp. 63–64.

This poem offers a utopia nearer in time, but more narrowly focused. It offers a tech-fix for the moral dilemma posed by raising and killing living things for human use, especially food. Great practical problems are involved in trying to clone only selected tissue-raising beefsteaks instead of cows, growing board lumber instead of trees.

A verbal snapshot such as this is designed only to prod readers into asking themselves what is—or may be—possible. A poem need not foresee and answer objections in advance, much less imply that its writer knows what the future will (or ought to) be.

RETIREMENT [2025]

At 81, his fortune made,
and legacy assured, our poet
took his final vows—gave up
identity, possessions, rights,
for tenure
in the Avalon Pleasure-Hospice.

There, in a twilife haze
of drug-euphoria
and self-selected
virtual realities,
he lay for years: indulging
wicked fancies harmlessly,

Boring no one
with stale memories,
consuming his own produce, till
his inner eye went blind,
and sleep
rolled down around him.

His component chemicals
helped fertilize
an onion field that season.
And today, his works
are still encountered widely
and admired.

"Retirement," *Virtual Futures*, pp. 40–41.

Death is the one future we can all be certain of—so far. [See Stanley Shostak's paper on immortality as utopia elsewhere in this book.] Still, assuming that we must die sometime, is there a way to make death more good than bad?

A utopian death ought to come with no pain, no regrets, and no avoidable impact on those left behind. There are many precedents in history for entering a monastery or similar closed community to renounce officially active involvement in the world's affairs. Tomorrow's equivalent act might supplement the joys of living simply with technologically induced delights from electronic brain stimulation and psychoactive drugs. Indeed, society's drug problem might be greatly eased if there were "mind-resorts" where pleasure-giving techniques and substances could be legally enjoyed, studied, tested, and their effects refined and made safer under medical supervision.

Taking time off from life's responsibilities to drop out at such resorts could become a regular routine—an escape valve for the strains and pressures of society. But the fullest use of dream vacationing might come toward the end of life when possibilities for other forms of pleasure were diminished by physical frailty and mental confusion. Once the mental line dividing reality from fantasy is crossed, physical death may matter very little.

This particular utopia could be realized today, if the laws allowed it. But one man's heaven can become another's hell; and it is easy to imagine how greedy, careless, or malicious staff could turn a psychedelic dream resort into a death camp.

Whether the utopian visions in these poems strike readers as practical or even desirable, they may at least suggest the range of possibilities that poetry opens for exploring alternative futures—particularly those that resist depiction in stories or scenarios.

Billy Collins, a poet of the United States, describes poetry as

> a kind of travel writing . . . [that] provides not only a change of scenery, but a change of consciousness. The poem's music and its rhythms combine to form the soundtrack to these mental excursions which carry us in two directions at once: out into the world and back into ourselves. . . . No wonder John Keats thought of poems as journeys into "realms of gold."[5]

"Realms of gold" . . . could that be poet-speak for utopias?

Notes

1. "Voyage to the Moon," MacLeish's poem (*New York Times*, July 21, 1969, page 1, column 1). The complete text is printed in *New and Selected Poems of Archibald MacLeish* (Boston, MA: Houghton Mifflin, 1969). Poets, by the way, themselves are much to blame for poetry's decline as daily reading. Like many studio artists and composers of the mid-twentieth century, poets became content to win praise from critics and scholars, convinced that popularity and artistic quality do not mix. Blame also falls on the way in which poetry has long been taught in schools—as if each poem were a locked box or secret code to be cracked for its "true" meaning, which the poet might just as easily have spelled out in simple prose.

2. Lane Jennings, "Six Approaches to Defining Poetry," in *Fabrications* (Fredericksburg, VA: Black Buzzard Press, 1998); pp. 78–79. For other definitions, see *The New Princeton Encyclopedia of Poetry and Poetics*, ed. Alex Preminger et al. (Princeton, NJ: Princeton University Press, 1993).

3. Besides Hesiod's *Works and Days* and Virgil's *Georgics*, see *The Penguin Book of English Pastoral Verse*, eds. John Barrell and John Bull (New York: Penguin Books, 1982) for examples of how poetry can make "the good life" appealing to read about.

4. For more on science fiction poetry, check the Ultimate Science Fiction Poetry Guide online at <www.magicdragon.com/UltimateSF/sfpo.html>. Two interesting print anthologies of futures-related and science fiction verse are *Inside Outer Space*, ed. Robert Vas Dias (New York: Anchor Books, 1970); and *Lower Than the Angels*, ed. Vonnie Winslow Crist and David W. Kriebel (Baltimore, MD: Lite Circle Books, 1999).

5. From a two-minute radio talk by Billy Collins, aired June 4, 2002, as a paid advertisement by the Boeing Corporation. Text and audio are available online at <www.boeing.com/companyoffices/aboutus/advertising/radiospot/index.html>.

Improving the quality of dialogue in the public arena is a strategic, if under-recognized goal. While the Internet is a remarkable new resource here (see the essays in Part IV), other communication options remain popular and are in need of improvement. We cannot expect to increase the number of participants in public discussions of utopian ideas until we first upgrade forms of "engagement." Several pragmatic reform ideas are offered below, and all would seem to warrant our support.

9. Building Common Ground: Rethinking Rules of Engagement*

Harris Sokoloff

> *He drew a circle that shut me out—*
> *Heretic, rebel, a thing to flout.*
> *But Love and I had the wit to win:*
> *We drew a circle that took him in!*
> —"Outwitted," by Edwin Markham

Often, when we think of a better world (utopia), we imagine a world that has what we lack—so we imagine a world in which we have more leisure time or time to ourselves and with friends, more and easier access to materials that will make our work easier, a world in which what we think and say can make a difference. If that is so, then in a utopia we will have more voice—a world in which we have time and opportunity to talk and be heard, really heard, and in being heard, to make a difference.

To be sure, we already have lots of opportunities to voice an opinion—from telephone and Internet polls, to web-based discussion groups. Time-Warner-AOL, the Roper Group, and other organizations daily publish reports on public opinion culled from polls of ordinary citizens. And each day Web-based opportunities to talk with others multiply.

But voicing an opinion is different than having a voice. We voice many opinions daily, most of which evaporate into the ethers without any impact. And there is little reason to believe that the daily opinion polls conducted by professional organizations have much more impact. Thus, voicing an opinion is not the same as having a voice. Having a voice involves both speaking and listening, and then speaking again, having considered what was heard and

---

*Adapted by the author from "Engaging the Public: How School Boards Can Call for Community Involvement in Important School Decisions," by Harris Sokoloff, which originally appeared in *American School Board Journal* 188, no. 9 (September 2001), 26–29. Used with permission of the *American School Board Journal*.

taking it into account in subsequent speaking. In short, having a voice is a form of being engaged with others about some issue.

Unfortunately, far too many forms of so-called engagement are actually a way of drawing a circle to shut us out, to limit citizen engagement with the organization, with others who are interested in the issues being addressed by that organization. Is it any wonder then that every index of public engagement shows a decline of citizen participation for the last forty years?

Imagine, instead, forms of public engagement which draw a circle to pull us in. Conjuring up such an image, or creating it in our lives, requires that we ask two questions as we interact with different organizations: "What kind of relationship do we really want to have with that organization?" and "Which practices will really enable us to have that relationship—that form of engagement? Which kind support excellence in that organization and create the kind of world we would like to live in?"

If the answer to the first question is "adversarial" or "supplicant" or "spectator," then it is clear that our current forms of engagement are quite sufficient—the current rules of engagement or mechanisms of engaging already produce those kinds of relationships. But if we want productive, mutually respectful relationships between citizens and public bodies, then we need some viable utopian ideas to help us develop different forms of public engagement. What might those forms look like?

At one end, we can imagine organizational newsletters which actively solicit, not just donations, but feedback, comments, and alternative ways of looking at things. They might do this by providing a contact person for each article, or by linking each article to a discussion board on the Internet.

At the other end, we might begin to imagine public meetings which include, or are dedicated to, community deliberation or dialogue. Such discussions would be focused on a single topic per meeting, with a moderator and a clear structure and time limit for the discussion. The topics selected would not require special expertise (or at least not a great deal of it), and they would be topics community members can legitimately address with officeholders.

Public schools, for example, might include the role of the arts in education, or the pressures on children. There is, of course, some tension between what parents know and what experts know, and educators have legitimate concerns about parental interference. However, schools cannot succeed without parental and community support and involvement—economic, political, educational, and social.

On high school and college campuses, students might work with student and university organizations to create opportunities for public deliberation (not debate). Topics could be as local as school relationships with the surrounding community, or as national as how a democratic society might best respond to terrorism. Topics might range from the simple (grading policies) to the fundamental (intergroup relations/race relations).

In between the two ends, we can and must rapidly develop a variety of ways to promote interactive public engagement. You can help reassess current activities in an organization's public engagement portfolio and foster modifications or expansions to bolster a relationship of mutuality.

Two key principles are clear. First, only the public can adequately and fully define the public interest. Second, only the public interest can serve as the common ground for public action. Our input, the input of an activist segment of the public, is essential if public boards are to know what policies and parameters we will and will not support and why, as well as what might be done to improve matters. Then, with a smile and a voice, we can participate more fully in the creative making of a finer world.

Recommended Web Sites

Web site of the National Issues Forums Institute (NIFI). NIFI is a agglomeration of people and organizations across the country who are engaged in conducting deliberative public forums using a model developed by the Kettering Foundation: http://www.nifi.org.

Web site of the Kettering Foundation: http://www.kettering.org/.

Web site for the Public Agenda Foundation, founded by Daniel Yankelovich and Cyrus Vance to help leaders better understand the public's point of view on major policy issues, and to help citizens better understand critical policy issues so they can make their own more informed and thoughtful decisions: http://www.publicagenda.org.

Web site of the Study Circles Resources Center, which is dedicated to finding ways for all kinds of people to engage in dialogue and problem solving on critical social and political issues: http://www.studycircles.org.

"Physician, heal thyself" remains today as sound an adage as when formulated very long ago. A look at the nation's campuses demonstrates that today's students, faculty, and staffers must help reinvent higher education to resemble more closely our utopian hopes for it. Valuable clues are offered in the pragmatic essay below, an imaginative guide for steadily and ceaselessly building the sort of schools that incubate viable utopian ideas, put them into practice, and thereby honor us all.

10. The Utopian University of the People: A Story That Is Not Too Good to Be True

Robert J. Merikangas

Utopias often sound great and they might excite us, but we often are given no clue about how to get from here to there. In the trajectory offered here, we start with what we could do tomorrow if we were to engage in shaping universities that aid and abet our desire to help create more utopian lives for us all.

The Trajectory Begins

It could all start with a local problem many campus citizens feel strongly about, such as the parking problem and the need for better provision for bicycles. As a student group explores this problem, they will find connections to transportation planning, environmental impact studies, campus budget issues, and studies being done in the engineering school on alternative vehicles. The student group will stop at some point and ask, "How can we connect our education here to these kinds of issues, and also connect to those in the local communities working on them?" They wonder how to even get a discussion going.

After some desultory meetings, it will become clear that a small group of students, no matter how committed, trying to work with scattered faculty, no matter how erudite, will not succeed. This leadership from the margins will need some structure. Any number of structures might have emerged out of the apparent chaos, but what is called the "partnership" is formed, and it works.

The first partner is the student parking group and the student government association itself, which had existed but without any clear mission for change. The second partner is a new entity, the Council of Senior Scholars, based on the ideas of a senior scholar at Stanford University, Stephen Jay Kline:

> We senior faculty will . . . present to our students worldviews that are simultaneously understandable, realistic, forward-looking, and whole, only if we construct and maintain a multidisciplinary discourse as an addition to the discourses in our separate disciplines.[1]

Once this kind of group is in place, it could also open up the questions of education for citizen action as well as education in multidisciplinary knowledge. The two will be seen to be closely connected, once the new partnership sees that citizens need to form judgments on complex public issues.

The basic assumption is that there has to be leadership to bring about utopia, but leadership, in a democracy, means depending on more democracy, not more control by the elite at the top. Change would have to come from the grassroots, and the place to start is the university, where there is enough free-dom to begin, and the resources exist for creating the symbols of pain and hope that will energize everyone and engage people to work on change with passion. The partnership will realize that its great challenge is to create an education portfolio for democratic leadership. One way is to involve the many students who are already active in a variety of protests and so stimulate their ideas and energy. Students engaged in protests, whether about globalization, sweatshops, debt relief, wages paid to campus workers, all want to learn how to make a difference.

The partnership will soon mobilize enough people and funds to create a new school on campus, the School of Social Movements (SSM). It immediately will become a catalyst for many developments, of which the most influential will be the Citizen Portfolio Project (CPP).

The CCP builds on electronic portfolios already begun on campus, designed to help students integrate their majors and general education courses, their career preparation and plans, and their extracurricular activities.[2] By including a vision of social change, and a wide perspective on all possible roles which might be played in society, the CPP will open up opportunities to move beyond personal resumés to collective skill building. Participation and moves to dem-ocratic governance will become the key, and they will allow what is being done in the SSM to be generalized to all students. People around the country will start to pay attention and come to visit.

The essential ingredient is *imagination*, really a social imagination. The partnership will soon find another magic word for their project, *design*. The campus systems people were already giving attention not just to technical sys-tems, such as space flight and weapons, but also to the design of social systems.

Voila! The link between portfolios, imagination, social movements, and all the intellectual tools would be the design of new social systems, namely, viable utopias.[3] The campus web will be useful for the social system design projects as well as for the portfolios. Web guides for citizens soon will be set up, with links to resources and organizations in relation to a complete political and social agenda.

The idea is to imagine and to develop what could be thought of as a citizens' think tank, which would add to all the current resources on policy issues, such as the Congressional Research Service, General Accounting Office, Public Cit-izen, and the many policy-related think tanks and websites. Individual citizens would monitor all of these and assemble action plans from their resources, and the university would develop policy information brokers for each area. They would help synthesize and integrate the issue alternatives, unrestricted by the ideological commitments of the sources.

The next step will be to identify design projects and to create teams to develop specific websites of resources and frameworks for creative develop-ment. Many proposals for social changes are already in the literature, so it is only a matter of finding them and highlighting their proposed moves. Areas to be covered include the prison system, the education system, the health-care system, the systems of corporate law and accountability, and alternatives to war.

The move to action takes emotional energy, especially when the social movements are competing with each other and with the state power for the attention and allegiance of the people. The partnership will see that emotions are needed along with imagination, and so will have to work on ways to promote and steer this development.[4]

Because the use of service learning across campus is indispensable, the partnership will promote it tirelessly by helping participants reflect on their experiences and connect them to the big picture. All departments will be constantly challenged to take up their responsibility to use service learning.

The partnership must next relate faculty research to civic education. How could service learning, for example, be integrated with the highly important research role? The partnership will seek priority (and funding) for action research that tries to answer the essential question—What works best in a democracy?[5] Moving up to the next level will involve faculty and students with local and regional governance practices and issues, and beyond, even to translational concerns.

Conclusion

How do we then imagine viable utopias and put them into practice? One way is to write scenarios outlining pro-utopian practices, develop our democratic rhetoric for dialogue and deliberation about the scenarios, make our plans, and agree on how to put them into practice. We can then undertake research on the projects and move on to newer and better scenarios. While doing this we also look for viable utopias being put into practice and reported elsewhere and learn from their examples.

It is best to do all of this with imagination and emotion, as well as with the finest knowledge available. We need to be flexible and resilient as we redesign our universities, for they can do a far better job than at present to help us become more active utopia-building citizens.

Notes

1. Stephen Jay Kline, *Conceptual Foundations for Multidisciplinary Thinking* (Stanford, CA: Stanford University Press, 1995), p. 292.

2. For a good overview of the development of electronic portfolios, see the report by Barbara L. Cambridge and others, *Electronic Portfolios: Emerging Practices in Student, Faculty, and Institutional Learning* (Washington, DC: American Association for Higher Education, 2001).

3. For a good example of designing a context for engaging in designing social

systems, see Bela H. Banathy, *Designing Social Systems in a Changing World* (New York: Plenum, 1996).

4. For a good introduction to the literature on social movements, with particular attention to the role of emotions, see Jeff Goodwin, James M. Jasper, and Francesca Polletta, eds., *Passionate Politics: Emotions and Social Movements* (Chicago: University of Chicago Press, 2001).

5. Service learning has become widely known, but action research is yet to be effectively made available on campuses. See Peter Reason and Hilary Bradbury, eds., *Handbook of Action Research: Participative Inquiry and Practice* (Thousand Oaks, CA: Sage Publications, 2001).

References

Banathy, Bela H. *Designing Social Systems in a Changing World*. New York: Plenum, 1996.

Cambridge, Barbara L., et al., eds. *Electronic Portfolios: Emerging Practices in Student, Faculty, and Institutional Learning*. Washington, DC: American Association for Higher Education, 2001.

Goodwin Jeff, James M. Jasper, and Francesca Polletta, eds. *Passionate Politics: Emotions and Social Movements*. Chicago: University of Chicago Press, 2001.

Kline, Stephen Jay. *Conceptual Foundations for Multidisciplinary Thinking*. Stanford, CA: Stanford University Press, 1995.

Reason, Peter, and Hilary Bradbury, eds. *Handbook of Action Research: Participative Inquiry and Practice*. Thousand Oaks, CA: Sage Publications, 2001.

IV. Methods: Information Technology

Enthusiasts ask us to join in hailing a history-making "Web-olution," while detractors prefer to spotlight the dot.com burnout, the unexpected and very costly burst of the balloon. Too many of us, the detractors maintain, expect too much soon at too little cost from the Information Revolution. What are the possibilities here? In the essay below, a leading student of the Information Revolution explores how the Web and the concept of utopia resemble and differ from one another. He notes the dangers inherent in the "cult of perfection" and explains why it is valuable for us to remain imperfect. He discusses five requisites of a genuine utopia and makes clear the pivotal importance here of our capacity to hope.

11. The Human Utopia and the Web

David Weinberger

Traditionally, a utopia isn't a perfect place; rather, it is a place whose properties enable us to perfect our human nature. But our experience of the Web suggests a different type of utopia, one that accepts imperfection as our lot and rejects perfectionism as an inhumane, oppressive ideal.

To see perfectionism at its worst, one need only look at religion, science, and—most of all—business. The use some religions have made of perfectionism is well-known, going beyond teaching us the important lesson of humility, and instead teaching us to despise our bodies and regard sexuality as degraded and degrading. In science, the new possibility of genetic manipulation tempts us to "perfect" plants and animals in ways that may unleash disastrous, un-

65

foreseen consequences. Indeed, we are on the threshold of being able to unkink DNA, so that no one need be born with crippling disabilities, a poor memory, or the shame of not having perfectly blue eyes.

Nevertheless, it is in business that we see our most unblinking acceptance of the cult of perfection. Every brochure shows products pristine and shiny beyond mortal ken. Every press release chisels an image of a company unsullied by failure or uncertainty. Every company meeting rallies the troops to march boldly down a path that can only end in perfect victory. Of course, none of us believe this. We expect the product to have some fingerprints on them and when they don't perform at a godly level, we're not disappointed. We apply a 40 percent discount to the self-image proclaimed by business.

We don't even want to be perfect. Perfection is homogenizing. Perfect humans would have nothing to talk about. In fact, they wouldn't even be able to converse, for talking entails listening and thus possibly learning and thus admitting that one may not have all the answers already. The perfect person might be able to lecture or might even condescend to explain things patiently, but he or she is not going to see any point in sitting around and shooting the breeze. Just as the price of free will is the existence of evil in the world, the price of the world's being interesting is that we are imperfect creatures. A perfect utopia would strike us as boring beyond belief, as we can learn from any child whining about the standard view of the harp-filled heaven.

A real human utopia would have other characteristics. First, a utopia is a fresh start, a break from what was. Second, a utopia is a place. Third, a human utopia has to be highly social, since it is a place where we can perfect our human nature (insofar as it can be perfected), and we are at our best when we are engaged with others. Fourth, the social relationships have to be free of what is perceived to be irrelevant and unfair by the participants. That is, if being fat or poor is an impediment to having genuine social relationships in the normal world, being fat or poor has to be irrelevant in a human utopia. Fifth, since humans are not going to become perfect, the utopia has to be forgiving of our inevitable errors and failings.

Now, we can argue over exactly what form the utopian society should take, and that might be a fruitful discussion, but I am not going to delve into it here because the five basic characteristics I've listed strike me as pertaining to every human utopia, no matter if it's being imagined by Libertarians, Luddites, or Stalinists.

The odd claim I want to make is that the Web shares these characteristics of a human utopia. First, the Web is definitely a fresh page. This is one reason it has so excited the world. And it's also, I believe, one reason people are willing to be more personal in the Web's public than in the real world's. The anonymity of the Web means that we can make a fresh start in showing who we are, and this liberates us to say more about who we are, what we believe, and what we feel than we can on a real-world street corner.

Second, the Web is a place; in fact, it's a world. It is not a medium. A medium is something we send messages through, and while we can do that with the Web, I believe the excitement about the Web hasn't happened because it's a messaging medium. Rather, our language says that we move through the Web—we, not our messages. This is very weird. While the Web consists of pages, we go to them, enter them, and leave them. We don't do that with real-world pages or documents. We experience the Web as a navigable space.

Third, the Web is hugely social. Although purveyors of content present it as if it were a giant library or jukebox, it has achieved its importance in our world culture because it is a conversation. We're connecting with one another by the most basic social act: talking.

The Web's social nature isn't an accident; it wouldn't be a web if the pages weren't linked. But every hyperlink is an expression of interest. I link to your page because I think my visitors might find your page enlightening or amusingly wrong. The real world is shaped by a geography of rocks and water. The Web geography is shaped by links of human interest and conversation.

Compare this to the real world we're born into. None of us asked to be born. Even if God gave us the world as a gift, it's still the given, the datum. And fundamentally this world is indifferent to us. We get buried in it, our atoms dissolve, the worms are happy, and the atoms don't care.

We make of this world what we will, but it's damn hard. You can't move the mountains, and it takes a lot of work to make the desert bloom. It fundamentally isn't our world. The Web, however, is a world we're making for ourselves, and we're making it by connecting to one another in conversation and by linking to one another out of human passion and caring.

Fourth, the Web's social relationships are largely free of influences considered irrelevant or unfair by the participants for the simple reason that the participants get to write themselves into existence on the Web. I am the arbiter of my presentation.

Now, this isn't entirely true. The "digital divide" favors the wealthy over the poor, the educated over the unschooled. Because the Web is mainly mediated through keyboards, it favors good writers. It even favors fast typists. Nevertheless, compared to the real world, the Web's blindness to factors the participants themselves don't choose to reveal is utopian, if not perfect.

Fifth, the Web revels in human imperfection. In fact, sometimes it prefers it to the detriment of all. Homemade sites feel better than the slick, alienating sites typical of almost all businesses. Jokes and parodies spread like gossip, and gossip spreads at the speed of light. At its worst, the Web's love of fallibility cruelly mocks the weak; at its best, it skewers the powerful and self-absorbed . . . those who haven't figured out how to play with others.

Formally, then, the Web embodies the key characteristics of a human utopia. We are headed toward a profoundly stupid conclusion: the Web is a utopia.

A weaker version of that conclusion is, I believe not only defensible, but correct.

Obviously the Web is not a utopia—just check your child's inbox if you have any doubts about that. Our eleven-year-old, for example, every day receives spam offering to show him hot coeds, to enlarge his penis, and to make $15,000,000 just by sending a few thousand dollars to an address in Nigeria.

Every piece of spam we receive raises the question: Is the Web merely an amplifier of human nature, or does it move us toward a better nature? This, of course, isn't an empirical question. And it is unlikely to be any more answerable than "Is human nature good or bad?" Nevertheless, I think we should lean toward the latter. The Web overall is helping us move toward our better nature.

First, it is a general lesson that technologies are not neutral. Our interactions with them almost always change who we are and how we live to some degree. The Web's very architecture, as linked, is social. It is also nonelitist, self-organizing, tolerant of error, and broadly connective.

Of course, that doesn't mean everyone on the Web shares those properties. But the excitement about the Web attracts people who do share those values, who have stories they want to tell, and who want to connect with others. So, it is not merely an amplifier; it is an amplifier particularly sensitive to certain sound waves.

Second, since the question is not an empirical one, and since our beliefs here have consequences, we ought to decide on the side of optimism. If we view the Web as fundamentally a new public space where we can join with others and be our best, we will work toward making that utopian view come true. If we view the Web with fear and wariness, we will pass the laws and put up the sites that make that vision come true. We have a political and moral obligation, in my view, to choose hope.

No, the Web isn't utopia. But it is teaching us to cherish the values that can lead us toward a genuine utopia.

Viable utopian ideas go far beyond pouring new wine into old bottles, or old wine into new containers: Nothing less than new/new will suffice. A sound example is offered below of the Internet's ability to help us perform more ably than ever in our vital old role as voter. At issue is a viable utopian idea for helping us "revise our democracy from the inside out." We are increasingly able to use information technology advances to upgrade access to candidates, voting paraphernalia, and voting results. Accordingly, viable utopian ideas have better prospects now than perhaps at any previous period in human history—provided we control "Big Brother" dystopian threats that also grow greater with every new computer advance. Improved voting, any one?

12. Toward a New Democracy

Stephen Downes

There has been a lot of talk about how the Internet will revitalize democracy, and more than a few sites have been established to promote that concept. With a few exceptions, however, these sites have dedicated themselves to politics as usual, focusing on candidates, leaders, and parties.

There seems to be an unstated consensus among digital democracy advocates that the Internet will simplify, but not radically revise, the democratic system of government. Online voting, political campaign websites, special interest group websites, e-mail your representative websites—these form the bulk of democracy online.

If the Internet has taught us anything over the last few years, however, it has certainly taught us this: To obtain the best of the new technology, we should think not of new ways to do old things, but rather, of ways to do new things entirely.

Internet democracy should be the same. The potential of online technology affords us an opportunity to revise our democracy from the inside out. In what follows, we will take a look at one way in which new technologies may move us toward a new democracy.

Why Should We Do This?

Today's government suffers from many of the complaints that have plagued other pre-Internet enterprises: It is too large, it is too slow, it never reacts to my concerns, it never reacts at all.

The signs of voter malaise are evident. Voter turnout—especially in regional and local elections—is low. Public meetings are sparsely attended. Politicians are viewed as opportunistic and self-serving, bent more on their own interests than the public good.

Some critics argue this is the essential nature of government, and, consequently, government should be reduced or eliminated where possible. Others argue government has been taken over by special interests, and lobbying or election funding should be restricted or limited.

None of these concerns will be changed through online voting or even through a wider range of online government services. The fact that I can vote online will not change the candidate for whom I vote. The fact that I can pay my taxes online will not ensure that these taxes will be lower or spent more effectively.

Today's politicians are already overwhelmed by telephone calls and mail, particularly when a hot issue rises to the surface. Do we really believe these same politicians will be moved by even more contact through mass e-mail campaigns?

Proponents of an Internet Age democracy often point to the virtues of direct democracy, and then suggest that online voting and political processes will enable each citizen to have a hand in the shaping of policy. But direct democracy so envisioned simply replaces one large dinosaur with another; it replaces mass election campaigns with mass referendum campaigns.

No, the Internet will revolutionize democracy only by making government smaller and more localized.

Smaller Government

By smaller I do not mean that government services will be shut down or privatized—there is a role for public policy in everything from roads to schools to health care, and the simple elimination of government departments will not lead to better services.

Rather, by smaller, I mean the breaking up of the government monolith itself. Why should a single public entity control every aspect of government? A voter's interest in housing policy may be very different from that same voter's interest in the environment.

The form of government envisioned here is perhaps best described as distributed government; that is to say, the functions of government are distributed across a number of independent public entities.

We already practice distributed government to some extent. In Alberta, for example, civic affairs are managed by municipal governments, schools are run by school boards, and health care is managed by regional health care boards.

There is no reason why we could not envision a further distribution of government on a wider scale. Why not, for example, create independent parks and recreation boards to oversee our public lands—or transportation boards to manage highways, railways, and airports?

Natural divisions already exist and are defined in contemporary government as "ministries" or "departments." The idea here is that these entities would be disassociated from the central government, and that their membership would be directly elected by the public at large.

The creation of autonomous entities allows the voter to be more selective when electing board members. An elected official's credentials count for more in such votes. For example, we would be more likely to elect doctors to run the health board, teachers and principles to run the school board, park rangers to run the parks board, and civil engineers to run the transportation board.

Moreover, because they are smaller, such entities would be more responsive and more accountable directly to the voter. They are less likely to be swayed by conflicting interests originating elsewhere in government.

And finally, smaller entities are more conducive to localized government.

Localized Government

Think of localized government and you probably think of regions, cities, and towns, even neighborhoods. While these are all important components of localized government, they are not the only components.

Generally, localized government is government restricted to a limited constituency. A town government, for example, is elected only by the citizens of a particular town and, in turn, governs only those affairs particular to that town.

Localized government is effective because it is able to focus on the specialized needs of a particular community. One town's desire for a revitalized Main Street may contrast with another town's desire to clean up the riverbank.

Localized government needs to operate within a broad set of parameters— local governments should not be able to suspend someone's civil rights, for example, or to declare itself an autonomous republic. Within these constraints, a wide range of autonomy is both possible and desirable.

There is no need to restrict our thinking of localized government to geographic entities. The rise of the Internet has contributed to the rise of sectoral communities based on subject area rather than proximity.

For example, the religious community has been able to establish itself as a distinct community on the Internet (see *The Soul of Cyberspace* [1997, HarperCollins], for example). True, the community of pastors and priests has always had a distinct identity, but online communications have made increased cooperation and collaboration possible.

Today's online sectoral communities encompass professional associations, industry groups, service agencies, and more. Such groups already have at least some sort of distinct identity, and online communications are melding them into entities in their own right.

The distribution of government departments and the rise of sectoral communities complement each other. The creation of an autonomous public sector transportation agency would draw together those people involved or interested in transportation policy, creating the dynamics of a small, self-governing virtual city.

The Internet itself points to how a distributed system of democracy would work. Independent bodies, such as the World Wide Web Consortium (W3C) and the International Standards Organization (ISO), already exist to influence and, in some cases, control the development of policies and procedures.

A system of distributed government is an extension of this model—an extension that moves the authority of government from a centralized body to one that reflects the interests and concerns of those directly impacted by such policies.

From Here to There

No fundamental change is easy or sudden, and such also would be the case in the transition to distributed government. The transition of power from a centralized authority would be incremental, with the mechanisms for governance established before a transfer of power would take place.

Because power is being transferred from a central government to a distributed entity, the central government must establish the framework for the creation of distributed entities. Such a framework would mirror the creation of town or city charters. Certain things, such as an established population base, a constitution, and founding officers, must be in place before an entity is recognized.

Once the mechanism is in place, the initiative for the creation of communities of interest would originate within that community itself. It would be up to parks and recreation societies, for example, to become sufficiently self-organized to present themselves as capable of assuming governmental responsibilities.

Upon the creation and recognition of a community of interest, a gradual transfer of powers and responsibilities would occur. In the first instance, authority for managing relevant legislation would be passed to the new body, then the power to propose new legislation, and finally the right to approve legislation in certain selected areas.

In order for these to occur, such units would be required to create mechanisms for self-government. A wide variety of models is possible, and it is likely no two entities would adopt the exact same mechanism.

In many cases, such communities of interest would themselves fragment into international, national, and regional entities. Legislative authority would tend to devolve to the lowest possible stratum, while issues of wide-ranging concern would remain under the mandate of the larger umbrella bodies.

Funding Distributed Government

Under our current system, no matter how much legislative authority is devolved, power remains with the large central government because it controls the allocation of resources. The final stage of a transfer of authority from a centralized government to a distributed government, therefore, would be the transfer of funding mechanisms.

Today, funding flows from taxation through the central authority—which sets priorities—down to the individual department. In a distributed government, the allocation of funding—and therefore of priorities—would be set by individual taxpayers.

Many mechanisms are possible, but perhaps the easiest and most obvious is to define these priorities at the point of payment. As our taxation system moves online, individuals may determine not only how much they pay but also where it will be spent.

The "how much" question is the stickiest because people will want to pay the least possible for the most services. Some people, inevitably, would elect to pay nothing at all, but others would opt to pay a certain percentage of their income, or a certain percentage of sales, in order to pay for government services.

In a distributed government model, the mechanism for setting and collecting taxes would be managed by a taxation authority. Such an authority would probably draw a wide range of interest and participation, and it would endeavor to balance between the citizens' desire to pay low taxes and their desire to obtain government services.

Funding would be divided into two components: internal and external to the distributed authority. Internal funding mechanisms would vary from authority to authority and would often resemble dues, association fees, or fees for services. Money collected by the authority would be used to fund programs intended only for members of that authority.

External funding is, in essence, the tax money received by that authority. Such funding is, in the first instance, intended to cover the cost of services provided by that authority to the general public. The roads authority, for example, would collect external funding in order to build and maintain roads.

Individual and corporate taxpayers would determine at source how much money to allocate to each authority. When paying taxes, an individual could decide to allocate 10 percent to the military, 30 percent to schools, and so on. Another individual, with different priorities, could elect different percentages.

Anarchy

The resulting system of government is to a large degree a system of no government. Government—viewed as the entity which tells us what to do—is replaced by a set of entities which perform publicly funded services for the public good.

As such a system matures, the different branches of government will compete for our attention, our participation, and our tax dollars. While preserving the intent of government—that of pooling our resources for the common good—such a system to a large degree removes the involuntary nature of government.

True, zero-government advocates will find even this minimal form of government unsatisfying, but no system of public enterprise would satisfy them.

On the other hand, advocates of a centralized and paternalistic system would be unsatisfied, because such a system is much more difficult for self-appointed guardians of the public good to control.

By devolving into what is essentially an anarchy of public goods and services, we obtain as much as we can of both worlds, offering choice and freedom to participate (or not), while offering the range and nature of government services needed in an advanced society.

We need far more research reports from the field, far more data-based accounts of ongoing tests of pro-utopian aids. All the more valuable, therefore, is the cogent account below of a four-year study of Internet use—a study that tests the prospects and peril of Internet use aimed at helping to create a productive "community" from an aggregate of far-flung strangers. If we are to soon achieve our goal of exchanging viable utopian ideas worldwide, we must make sage use of the Internet. We have much to learn beforehand, however, about its best use. The study discussed below helps show the way.

13. Internet Dreaming: Investigating Online Community at the Math Forum*

Wesley Shumar

We anthropologists study groups of people over time using a method we call participant observation—essentially, a long-term "hanging out" with a tribe, group, or culture, etc.—while we systematically take notes. For four years now I have had the privilege (and pleasure) of studying a "tribe" known as the Math Forum (http://mathforum.com/). One of its main components, known as the ESCOT (Educational Software Components of Tomorrow) Project (http://mathforum.com/escot), bears directly on the utopian potentials of online educational environments.

A large, unique, and complex online educational environment, the Math Forum includes interactional services, moderated and unmoderated discussion lists, and math resources. It uses new technology to help us get past static, boring traditional classroom interactions. The Math Forum seeks, instead, to

---

*The material for this article is based on an ongoing analysis of the ESCOT project and other work at the Math Forum. For a more in-depth paper, on which this article was based, go to http://www.pages.drexel.edu/admin/ls39/lecture/Shumar.htm.

create dynamic learning environments within which we can all better express ourselves and learn far more mathematics far more readily (Lave 1993; Lave and Wenger 1991).

ESCOT brings together teachers, educational technologists, and programmers. They are asked to develop software tools to enhance math teaching and take advantage of the Web's potential for student learning. One of its underlying principles is the belief that new advances in math learning and mathematical thinking are most likely to come from communities of people who care about each other and share similar goals (Lave and Wenger 1991; Wenger 1999).

My research focused on how we can foster such communities among ESCOT members. How are we to negotiate the different worldviews of the members of each ESCOT group? How are we to assess effective ways to communicate, both face to face and on line? How, in short, are we to boost the ESCOT mission . . . one I have always regarded as a viable utopian idea.

Developing a Community of Practice

To make a long and complicated story short and clear, my four years of field research with this "tribe" helped me find useful evidence of what supports Internet-based community building . . . and what might also support an effort of yours:

1. A small group size was regarded as advantageous.
2. A clear vision in (total) project meetings promoted smoother interaction over the year.
3. Small size, clear leadership, and a clear vision all contributed to well-defined roles and the smooth development of the work.
4. Communication technologies were considered very helpful to the group process, although occasionally they were regarded as a problem.
5. Negotiation across boundaries and "meaning" conflicts showed that the worldview differences were significant, and this situation brought out the need for good leadership.

To consider just one of these five findings, the one concerned with communication technologies, we are seeing that the Internet, if used appropriately, can allow social interaction and social groups to develop organically and also meet the interests of individual members. They are not tied to much constraint, and they can develop new interests together. (Interestingly, instant messaging is one of the virtual channels that seems to help foster desired emotional attachments, as well as help get work done, and do so more than e-mail and other chat online environments.)

Conclusion

The Math Forum's ESCOT Project is a kind of experimental utopia. It asks if groups of people from different professional backgrounds can be brought together and supported primarily through virtual (Internet) interaction. Can they learn to have a sense of attachment and belonging to each other? Can that community feeling allow them to do good work together, even if there are significant professional and cultural differences and a great geographic spread among them?

The answer to these far-reaching questions is *yes*. What is even more, Internet technologies have been found to promote creative crafting that aids both group members and the group alike. This is something quite unique and valuable . . . good news for activists now or soon building communities that would advance viable utopian ideas.

References

Lave, J. "The Practice of Learning." In *Understanding Practice: Perspectives on Activity and Context*, edited by S. Chaiklin and J. Lave. New York: Cambridge University Press, 1993.

Lave J., and E. Wenger. *Situated Learning: Legitimate Peripheral Participation*. New York: Cambridge University Press, 1991.

Wenger, E. *Communities of Practice*. New York: Cambridge University Press, 1999.

Think of the Borg in the Star Trek *series, and, by our contemporary standards, you are thinking about a dystopian possibility few take seriously where we are concerned. This might be a mistake, as this chilling prospect may be more plausible, and all the more threatening for being hard to detect. What is the relevance here of our increasing acceptance of, and reliance on, wireless 24/7 connectivity? Are we really clear about where we want the "Web-olution" to help take us? What about this matter amounts to a viable utopian idea—its promotion, alteration, or our fervid opposition? These and related questions are wrestled with below, the better to help us clarify what is utopian or dystopian about "the Collective."*

14. Welcome to "the Collective": New Meaning to a Meeting of Minds

Allan Stegeman

Like it or not, our individual cognitive existence is electronically becoming slowly, but unceasingly, wed to a disembodied social collective. With the advent of cell phones, we can nearly forget about any physical realities and commune with anyone, almost anywhere on the face of the earth. The only psychic anchor back to our actual spatial placement now is the time differential when calling between different time zones.

Just look around you when you walk down any city street: At least half the people you pass are wending through the crowds on auto-pilot, while they remain focused on communing through the little pieces of plastic they are holding up to their faces. It is as if they were operating, to a limited degree, like the Borg on *Star Trek*, whose minds are all electronically integrated with one another.

Hyperbole? Perhaps, but then again, perhaps not. Cell phones are just a small part of our current phase in this transformation of thought and space, and just the vanguard of things to come . . . things that we might early judge viable utopian, or possibly even dystopian, ideas.

For most of us today, our computers are primarily communication devices. They are becoming both smaller and untethered. Laptops are now outselling desktop PCs. Personal data assistants (PDAs), like the Palm Pilot, are becoming commonplace.

The next phase in the evolution of the personal computer, Pocket PCs (literally scaled down Win/Tel computers that can fit in a pocket), are already in the marketplace, poised to become ubiquitous as well. Not only can you carry these computers around with you, like a cell phone, you can tie them into the Internet via wireless transmitters. Now, regardless of where you are, you need never be without access to the collective information on the Internet, your e-mails, or multiple simultaneous conversations with your Instant-Messenger.

But this is just the beginning. Digital cell phones and computers are converging. If your cell phone is anything but a dinosaur, it already has some of the functions found on PDAs, such as an electronic address book or e-mail access. For around $400 (as I write this), you can get PDAs that have all the typical functions of a Palm Pilot, can send and receive e-mail wirelessly, and work as a fully functional cell phone—all in one nice small package that you can stick neatly in your shirt pocket. In another year, these "communicators" will be even cheaper, smaller, and less cumbersome in their operation.

In the laboratories, not just today, but over the last thirty years, researchers have been developing something called "augmented reality," which is wonderfully frank in its nomination. It refers to visual, or other sensory, interfaces which integrate computer data output with direct, real-world experience. Most commonly today, these take the form of optical see-through displays which superimpose graphic information on the lenses of a pair of glasses.

So, instead of having to look at a computer screen to interface with the information housed within a computer, the information would seem to appear right in front of you. Text, pictures, video, illustrations, all are available anywhere, any time, and in any situation, without having to take your eyes off of "the real world." A computer would synthetically blend the two different sources of information into one seamless sensory experience.

Taking augmented reality glasses and visors one step further is the work being done with electronic sight implants. Now just an experimental tool to help bring sight back to the blind, these implants literally "wire" computers and cameras to the recipient's brain, generating dot-matrix images in the patient's mind. Similar, more refined systems, with more complex imaging systems, operating like current augmented reality systems, integrating computer data, perhaps directly from the Web, may not be too far down the road.

Again, to aid the physically disabled, scientists are at work on utilizing brain waves for inputting information into computers. This technological corollary to sight implants has already been implanted in a rhesus monkey's brain, allowing the monkey to move a cursor precisely about a computer screen, just by thinking. Still in its early stages, this technology offers hope for the handicapped to operate computers, write e-mails, and interact with other human beings in ways which only dreams offered until now. Similar work on reading the brain waves on the language centers of the brain may not be far behind. Then we will be able to send messages to one another, anywhere, electronically, by merely thinking.

We are not at the point where we will all be wired up to our communication machines—at least not yet. But if someday we do reach that stage, basic human experience will make a quantum shift. We will essentially become electronically assisted telepaths. If you want to talk to another person, or a hundred people for that matter, all you will need to do is think it. When you want information on something, be it research for a school project (if we still would need schools) or the price of a new pair of jeans, it will just come to you. Such is life when you have joined "the Collective."

We are now crudely able to exchange ideas with others around the globe. It is a given that the transmission of ideas will become more seamless and natural. We can incorporate this more and more into our daily lives and, in so doing, progressively alter the ways in which we interact with each other.

As we allow exotic new forms of electronic social communion to replace physical communion, we grow closer to joining "the Collective." Our awareness of physical realities can be displaced by those of mediated ones. The question then is whether this optional move is just a different way of experiencing society? Is it actually for the worse? Is it really for the better? Is this a viable utopian idea?

V. Looking Inward

In the mass culture of America at this time, there would seem to be two major claimants on our souls: a narrow, defensive worldview that operates primarily from fear of "the Other" and helps explain our wariness, hesitancy, and loneliness; and a broad, adventurous worldview that operates primarily from trust of "the Other" and helps explain our savoir faire, eagerness, and comradery. Most of us live uneasily between the two systems, leaning first this way, and then that, depending on circumstance.

When we are in the grips of the "Me, first!" mind-set, we have little psychic, emotional, or intellectual tolerance for giving viable utopian ideas a fair hearing. We can manage that only when we are in a better mind space, one rich in self-esteem, mature trust of the unknown, and deep-set confidence in our ability to manage what lies ahead—both in our power to change and beyond our power to change.

Only as we increase the percent of our waking lives spent in the "good" space can we really make progress in operationalizing the best of the viable utopian ideas that appeal to us from the pages of this book.

All the more valuable, therefore, are the guidelines below for learning more about "the Other," that awesome malleable construct that can endlessly come between you and me. As carefully explained in the essay, we can practice talking the role of "the Other" and thereby defang the construct, turn it to peace-making advantage, and help us better connect, care, and commit. When we adopt the field-tested advice offered here, we significantly increase the likely success of our viable utopian projects.

15. Understanding Opposing Viewpoints: Placing Yourself in the Shoes of the Other

R. Dean Wright

Individualism is the first and foremost value encompassing American life. While opposing viewpoints, such as it takes a village to raise a child, are occasionally heard, such notions are talked about politically, but their consideration is shallow. We have disengaged from those institutions that brought us together as a society and community in the past: the extended family living close by, the multigenerational family living in one household, the ethnic urban enclave, the neighborhood parish, the walk-to primary school, and so on. Individualism, or "Me First!," remains the quintessential value of nearly all who regard themselves as true Americans.

What has come to be known as 9/11 offers us an excellent example of how the United States, and especially its government, defines critical issues within the context of individualism, seldom addressing major national or international issues as a collective matter. Indeed, far too many elements of government operate increasingly as a modern bully, punishing those who oppose being bullied and being violent toward those who dare to oppose its mandates.

All of this notwithstanding, we *can* help make this a better world. Ireland, for example, offers a new and pragmatic way to move toward viable utopian values. In their 2002 article, "A More Civil Society; NGOs at Work for Peace in Northern Ireland," Linda Kaboolian and Barbara J. Nelson claim political leadership has waned, and the everyday citizen is skeptical of the abilities of traditional politicians to lead. Nongovernmental organizations (NGOs) have stepped in to occupy the void left by political leadership.

These numerous organizations, which usually have ties to faith communities (commonly referred to as Concord Organizations), have one goal in common: to build "common worldviews and skills necessary to work effectively across communities." This involves forming basic community groups, each based on commonality, and having groups sit down together and talk about the things that are of importance to each person.

Disagreements and agreements arise; the others hear and come to realize the nature of the position of those in opposite groups. The goals and approaches are simple: Achieve a closer connection among conflicting groups. Whereas politics usually gets nowhere in modern society and often creates further fragmentation, the approach here is to organize thousands of small groups that can talk with other groups . . . can communicate across diverse lines.

Regardless of their histories, cross-community groups have common needs, values, and principles. These are characterized by such things as a better future for their children and families, living in peace, and making the world a better place in which they can live today and tomorrow. The simple process of talking through issues that are central to everyone may not convert foes to the cause of the other; instead, each person talks honestly about his or her feelings, while the other listens, and then takes a turn to do the talking.

Each side comes to know the other and, by such a simple medium as talking, helps see tensions melt away. Politicians are adversial, trying to destroy the other by talk, while the common person is the antithesis, seeking to arrive at a peace that can surround his or her life.

The applicability of what Kaboolian and Nelson found that appears to be producing positive change in Northern Ireland is elementary when we reconsider earlier sociological thinkers, especially George Herbert Mead. Reading the works of Mead, and thinking about his work in relation to modern conflict in society and the loss of fundamental social capital, makes one realize that what is being found in Northern Ireland essentially are fundamental sociological principles addressed by Mead.

In *Mind, Self, and Society* (1934), Mead tells us that through "taking the role of the other," a human "becomes not only self-conscious, but also self-critical . . . self-criticism is essentially social criticism, and behavior controlled by self-criticism is essentially behavior controlled socially." Mead tells us that any time we confront or interact with another human being we essentially take that person's role in order to better understand and ground our own role(s).

Through "taking the role of the other," a human fundamentally comes to better understand the role of the other as well as his or her own role, as well as how the role of the other and the self come together. What is more fundamental in making this happen than simply meeting with, on common grounds, those whom one historically ignores, distrusts, and defines as the enemy?

Taking the role of the other: How simple and common this concept is to the fundamental life of the human and toward the continued development and expansion of the self. Through this process one comes to realize that the life and role of that single other (for instance, a Catholic talking with a Protestant in Northern Ireland) is little more than a manifestation of the group represented by that person (Catholics and Protestants as a community) rather than the single individual. The ultimate result is the creation of a "self-conscious" community and, finally, what Mead termed the "generalized other."

The generalized other evolves when one comes to realize that others are individuals with goals and ambitions, just as we are individuals with goals and ambitions. They are little more than manifestations of the community to which they are attached and from which they come. Mead explained this process:

> The very organization of the self-conscious community is dependent upon individuals taking the attitude of the other individuals. The devel-

opment of this process . . . is dependent upon getting the attitude of the group as distinct from that of a separate individual—getting what I have termed a "generalized other."

The most elementary ideas have significant impact, and if Mead is correct, then simple, everyday communication may be *the* key to the reduction and perhaps elimination of cultural and community conflicts. Taking the role of the other may be nothing more than sitting and talking with, listening to, the other. One does not have to agree. One may disagree completely, but at least the image of what the other represents is brought to the front. One listens and one understands, knowing that when it is his or her turn to talk, the same rules of reciprocity apply. Opposing viewpoints are stated, and the other listens; the rules of conduct require this simple courtesy.

With time, logic tells you that the extreme positions will fade into less extremes. Common points will be understood and, if not accepted, at least tolerated. This is fundamental to human conversation, fundamental to the way in which the self goes about defining the self—knowing who we are and knowing who "they are." Everyday life operates that way; it is not especially complex.

As a matter of fact, it is elementary. Even a child can do it. Actually, this is the process by which, we are informed by followers of Mead, the child goes about defining who he or she is, carving out his or her concepts of self, defining the expectations of the roles of themselves as well as others.

What does this tell us in light of continued or accelerated dislikes, if not hatreds of immigrant and community groups within the United States, toward those thought to be related to the disaster of September 11, 2001? As groups pull back into themselves, we have witnessed an increase of hatred in areas of race, ethnicity, religion, and other areas of life marked by personal belief and acceptance. We have struggled for years in an effort to reduce tensions and solve social problems, but there appears to be little change. If anything, there is a reduction of moving toward a utopian concept of living in common accord.

Example after example of social splintering could be provided, but one case stands above all others: race. *Locked in the Poorhouse: Cities, Race and Poverty in the United States*, edited by Fred R. Harris and Lynn A. Curtis, illustrates what has happened since the Kerner Commission identified race as the quintessential problem plaguing American society and called for remedies. We have experienced literally no progress during the three decades since the findings were released. In almost all of the areas they identified, research suggested we have, in fact, lost ground. One could continue to enumerate how little progress has been made in social problem area after social problem area. The line between groups is more pronounced today than it was during past years. Each group has withdrawn into its own community or each of us individually into his and her own living room.

The solution may indeed rest in large part on revitalizing simple conversations: simple encounters among members of groups that have a history of dislike, hatred, and violence, in an attempt to provide an opportunity for members to take the role of the other and, for a short period of time, live in the shoes of the enemy.

We cannot ignore the success of such an effort in Northern Ireland, a country in which legend and tradition fired the flames of hatred and bitterness to the point that an internal civil war brewed for years. Today, by removing the politician from dealing with personal and community morality, and by placing the responsibility in the hands of the common person, empowering changes are being made. Faith communities, as well as secular community groups, along with caring individuals who exist within the context of explicit moral frameworks, assist the process of coming together and sharing ideas.

In our society far too many politicians cannot exist without being adversarial, spin doctoring, lying to protect each other, and refusing to go against party lines. We have to rid ourselves of this if we are to develop a society that is morally just, one that is striving toward some appealing form of viable utopian existence. Most politicians cannot be trusted to help here. Many community groups, especially those that have our best interests at heart, *can* advance this difficult, but worthy task.

References

Harris, Fred R., and Lynn A. Curtis. *Locked in the Poorhouse; Cities, Race, and Poverty in the United States*. New York: Rowman & Littlefield, 1998.

Kaboolian, Linda, and Barbara J. Nelson. "A More Civilized Society: NGOs at Work for Peace in Northern Ireland." *American Prospect* (February 11, 2002): 14–15.

Mead, George Herbert. *Mind, Self, and Society*. Chicago: The University of Chicago Press, 1934 [especially chapter IV, "Society," pp. 227–336].

Given your interest in exploring, assessing, and possibly championing one or another of the viable utopian ideas in this book, you undoubtedly recognize the strategic importance of your own well-being: Our advocacy is conditioned by our own personal health—physical, mental, and spiritual. Accordingly, many of us welcome sage advice on how to assess and improve our inner being, especially as it also enables us to strengthen our interpersonal relationships. The essay below offers twenty-four hallmarks of any who would help advance viable utopian ideas (a "conscious co-creator" of society). Creative and sustained efforts we might make to measure up would seem highly advisable.

16. The Conscious Use of the "Mirror Effect": Co-Creating a Utopian World

Carroy U. Ferguson

The time has come to entertain the possibility of transforming or evolving to another level of consciousness, to the realization we create our own realities according to the nature of our beliefs. We are *co-creators* of our world, not merely robots reacting to a world we have unconsciously created. Outward conditions are the reflections of inner states of mind or inner states of consciousness.

I call this the *mirror effect*. Theoretically, through its conscious use, humanity, at individual and collective levels, may create visions and conditions for a remarkably appealing world. This art of self-creation and reality creation is the underlying framework for consciously evolving or co-creating a utopian world.

Through the media, other sources, and interactions with others we may have attracted, we begin to see and focus on the world as being made up of haves and have-nots, of takers and those being taken. The data seem to validate our condition. We can lose sight then of our essence, our meaning, our higher purpose(s) or focus (foci). We reinforce an either/or way of thinking, and this method of thinking becomes habitual. Scarcity consciousness seems more real and practical than the possibility of prosperity consciousness.

Scenarios can be developed for emotionally backed demands for sensation and for power. For example, reasoning that "I have to compete for my space in life in order to be successful and have status" can lead to nations or groups battling over the correct and most powerful way to experience and practice religion, and to have a proper and powerful sense of a Higher Being or God.

Out of fear, then, we distort meaning, value, and power. The ideas of sharing and collaboration can become distorted. Too many of us are caught up in such a dilemma of consciousness, which is constricted and fueled by fear. We distort the *love principle*, which when genuinely employed, creates the experience that we get more in return when we give. The love principle can set the tone for collaborative enterprises in a utopian world where win-win notions may serve as guidelines for action and as principles for common individual and societal practices.

To change the outward conditions, then, we must first change our beliefs and shift the focus of our inner states of consciousness toward more expansive energies. These tend to have an archetypal nature to them and involve (1) creative imagination derived from understanding and the desire for self-expression, (2) inspiration fueled by love, wisdom, compassion, and the desire to serve others, and (3) intuition that validates the spiritual aspects of the self and the desire for unity.

For example, we, individually and collectively, have significant economic power as consumers if we would harness and channel it. Politically, the urge to validate the individual's voice through democratic processes and to have more representative forms of government have increased in the world, notwithstanding many human rights violations and issues.

In addition to diagnosing our problems, therefore, we need to begin to embrace an expanded level of consciousness. It can make conscious the tools of self-creation and reality creation so that we may build upon our positives and consciously create the kind of reality that works for us, individually and collectively.

I realize that, on the surface, such a suggestion sounds overly simplistic and impractical, and to some it may appear to sidestep the real problems. I suggest, however, that the opposite is true. Indeed, the mirror effect cries out for us to *see* and *transform* destructive and unproductive aspects of a reality we are now *unconsciously* co-creating. I also realize it is difficult to embrace a recommendation that we focus on consciousness when many people are scared, hungry, unemployed, or dealing with basic survival issues. And yet, what is more practical and survival oriented than seeking to grow and to improve one's conditions *consciously* and also *consciously* seeking to assist others in their growth and in the conditions of their lives?

Consciousness precedes outward conditions. This is the lesson of the mirror effect. Practically, then, each individual needs to ask himself or herself, "What do I see in my *personal life space* directly or indirectly as I look out onto my world? What is working and what is not?" Each person then needs to listen to his or her more *intuitively heroic impulses*, then consciously take action in accord with these impulses as well as alter conditions that he or she does not like. Each person must do this in his or her own way, or join forces with like-minded persons in a supportive network. This is an act of self-trust, an act of consciously using the mirror effect to assist us in self-creation and reality creation. It is through such efforts that we may begin the co-creation of a utopian world in practical ways.

How to Know If You Are Being a Conscious Co-Creator

How do we know if we are being *conscious co-creators* of our realities, or are instead only continuing to react in robotlike fashion to ourselves and to others? One method is to use the mirror effect to determine whether our lives reflect some or all of the following twenty-four characteristics of conscious co-creators.

1. You have released the old programming and beliefs that no longer serve you.
2. You have drawn into your life supportive, positive people.
3. You empower yourself and others in all you do and say.
4. You know who you are, why you are here, and what is your higher purpose.
5. Your lifestyle and environment support your life purpose and greater work in the world.
6. You explore new possibilities and choices and continually expand your vision of what is possible.
7. You have the tools to draw to yourself the opportunities, people, and events you need to create your life's work.
8. You operate from your heart, and you trust your inner messages and take action upon them.
9. You are conscious of the energy around you, deciding when to be transparent to it, harmonize with it, or transmute it to a higher order.
10. You are aware of your energy and the effects other people have upon it.
11. You are present in the moment—alert, aware, and at a high level of observation all the time.
12. Your increasing aliveness, enthusiasm, and growth spark growth in everyone around you.
13. You create with energy before you take physical action.
14. You know you can create whatever you want by working with the higher forces and directing your thoughts, emotions, and intent toward your goals.
15. You create change by working at the highest spiritual level rather than at the personality level.
16. You stop before you take action, go within, and receive guidance from your higher self about what action to take.
17. You know that anything is possible.
18. You know that through your understanding of how energy works you can consciously create what seemed like miracles when you had less understanding of the way in which energy works.
19. You are able to create what you want at a speed that seemed impossible at earlier levels of growth.
20. You are able to handle easily and joyfully the things that used to challenge you.
21. Your lessons come faster, but you will also have the tools to move through them more quickly and easily.
22. You have a clearer sense of direction, a greater feeling of being in control, and a deeper understanding of why things are happening.

23. There is an increasing calm that comes as you begin to enjoy and understand your life.
24. You can truly live a life that is joyful and loving to yourself.

As we develop the above characteristics for becoming conscious co-creators, and consciously use the mirror effect to assess our worlds and engage in the art of self-creation and reality creation, we will be evolving or co-creating a utopian world.

Conclusion

We cannot legislate that people use the mirror effect to shift the focus of the inner states of consciousness and to expand to another level of consciousness, but one policy implication of this discussion can be directed toward educational objectives. I would recommend that at local levels our school systems develop a curriculum that helps students learn the tools of self-creation and reality creation, and that such a curriculum be introduced in the early grades. I would also recommend that in various communities appropriate organizations and churches develop what I would call empowerment and consciousness courses for adults, as well as after-school empowerment and consciousness courses and activities for youth.

The mirror effect appears to be showing us that we need to quiet the ego chatter in our minds that focuses on emotionally backed demands for security, sensation, and power. We need to focus on more expansive energies, which will allow our higher intuitive knowledge to take root. When this kind of knowledge takes root, we will know that genuine security, balanced emotions, and the power to act and to create stem from inside us, not from outside us.

We also begin to understand that the tools for self-creation and reality creation flow from our dreams. We begin to understand what it means to be a conscious co-creator, and we begin to understand the nature of what I call our ever-evolving self. We must dare to dream of better realities and then choose to create them.

Note

A much fuller version of this very thoughtful essay can be obtained from the author.

References

Cross, W. "Toward a Psychology of Black Liberation." In *Black Experience: Analysis and Synthesis*, edited by C. Young. San Rafael, CA: Leswing Press, 1972.

Ferguson, C. *A New Perspective on Race and Color: Research on an Outer vs Inner Orientation to Anti-Black Disposition.* Lewiston, NY: Edwin Mellen, 1997.

Ferguson, C., and J. Kamara. *Innovative Approaches to Education and Community*

Service: Models and Strategies for Change and Empowerment. Boston: University of Massachusetts, 1993.

Gershon, D., and G. Straub. *Empowerment: The Art of Creating Your Life As You Want It.* New York: Dell, 1989.

Heideman, C. *Searching for Light: Michael's Information for a Time of Change.* Jefferson, MD: Twelve Star, 1994.

Keyes, K. *A Handbook to Higher Consciousness.* Coos Bay, OR: Love Line Books, 1975.

Roberts, J. *The Nature of Personal Reality: A Seth Book.* Englewood Cliffs, NJ: Prentice-Hall, 1974.

————. *Seth Speaks: The Eternal Validity of the Soul.* New York: Bantam Books, 1972.

Roman, S. *Creating Money: Keys to Abundance.* Tiburon, CA: HJ Kramer, 1988.

————. *Personal Power through Awareness: A Guidebook for Sensitive People.* Tiburon, CA: HJ Kramer, 1986.

Small, J. *Transformers: The Artists of Self-Creation.* New York: Bantam Books, 1992.

Those of us who would labor long and hard on behalf of viable utopian ideas are well-advised to also recreate long, often, and to our taste. While admittedly a hoary cliché, it remains true that all work and no recreation tends to dull one's creativity—and one's capacity to promote good ideas. The poetic account below of a magical enriching moment helps underline the importance of increasing the chances of such occurrences in one's own life.

17. Surprised on the Run!

Diane McManus

". . . the more of the outdoors I get, the more I want. That alone—that growing appetite for being out in the natural world—is a debt to running that I can never repay."
—John Jerome, *The Elements of Effort* (Breakaway Books, 1997; 89)

I head out for my hill workout thinking, "It's getting late, have to work, don't have time to do this today"—the voice of guilt. Yet, despite this, I know I need to be out there. I know because I will be running Mount Washington. I know because if I ever pass up a scheduled workout, the sense of deprivation makes me too distracted to work effectively. I know because running gives back in multiples what you give to it. And I know because an intuition keeps telling me that where I need to be is outside doing this hill workout.

So I head for my favorite park, a small township park only a few minutes from where I live, and use a trail that winds gradually uphill (the hill of choice was supposed to be gradual . . . this one is that)—nice easy surface, less pounding . . . and good for the soul as well as the soles. I suck wind—and with the wind, the scent of honeysuckle. After running the workout, I start my cooldown, trotting around a baseball field, then across a bridge, undergrowth twisting up around the railings near the bank of the stream, along another trail that leads to the edge of the water, then back, looking at the sunlit ripples and waves that splash over the rocks.

I think, "This is where I belong." I pick up bits of litter here and there and toss them into a trash can after I recross the bridge.

Further along, there is a children's playground, and I can't resist taking a few swings, feeling the contraction of my abs as I swing, feeling the body's rhythms. (As a child, while horseback riding, I used to put my hands on the horse's shoulders to feel their movement.)

Then it is time to let the swing dangle and stop and continue the cooldown. Turning, I see the bird, a long, thin, white curve—an egret. This park has been the home to unexpected wildlife, but until today, I never saw an egret here.

Surrounding this park are middle-class "burbs," row houses, grocery stores, fast food joints, pizza shops, and bars. Yet there, like an apparition from heaven, stood this beautiful bird. I stopped and could not move, perhaps I was as still as the bird, and we studied each other. The bird then waded away and swam calmly downstream.

A man came by in a tractor; he had been cutting the grass near the playground. I motioned to him and pointed to the bird. He nodded. He had to drive the tractor across a slightly submerged road to the other side of the stream— a little ways upstream but certainly within the bird's hearing distance. But he slowed the tractor so that it was barely moving, so that it would not raise a splash and frighten the bird.

Not a word was said between me and this tractor driver, but we both understood we were experiencing sacredness—two people meeting in the silence of a church who both sense at once the presence of God.

I knew then that this was the right time to be where I was—that I could not possibly be anywhere else that would make me richer than I was at that moment. The workout, the swing, the bird, the silent communication with the man driving the tractor—these were gifts to take with me through the day and remember when things get hectic or when I feel stressed . . . to remember that place of stillness and peace.

VI. Looking Homeward

Viable utopian ideas have always made a difference in our lives, though we have seldom been aware of this (save for the uneven attention we sometimes give to charismatic politicians, media pundits, professors, and pulpit spiritual guides). These ideas have generally been put to work behind the scenes—diplomatically, patiently, and persistently.

A fine example of this practice is explored in the revealing essay below, a mind-stretching consideration of the consequential relationship of utopian thinking and urban planning. Answers are offered to several intriguing questions: What are the ideologies that vie with utopian thought for the support of city planners? Just how utopian minded are the planners? Why? So what? How does utopian design differ from, or resemble, current urban planning processes? What should be the relationship?

If you have ever wondered what difference—at the end of the day—viable utopian musings can make in the real world, a type of wonderment common in our age of skepticism and ready disbelief, you may get a sounder appreciation for the practicality of utopian ideas from this essay.

18. Utopias and City Planning: Finding Strength in One Another

Thomas A. Reiner

What part can the idea of a utopia—and the long history of such ideas—play at present in the design of modern cities? Furthermore, what part should such ideas play?

To a large extent, market forces shape our environments—that and historical accident together with major and minor geographic elements (such as ocean ports, rivers, or floodplains). The presence of natural resources has a role: many cities are built around mines or close to agricultural products. And in a more complex way, so does how people have settled in the further out surroundings.

Our cities are also intentionally shaped by public policies, such as taxes; the placement of facilities, such as army bases, government headquarters, bridges, and so on; and the intentional design of the urban space, including the work of city planners, some of whom are inspired by utopian ideas.

Utopias are part of the planner's intellectual baggage when they strive to design better environments and as they work to implement programs to achieve these. Others are part of this process, of course, not the least as planners seek to intuit, or otherwise integrate into their mind-set and professional activities, what they understand to be the expectations and preferences of other partici-pants in city building, as well as the public at large: the people who are the planner's constituency. These, too, have been influenced by utopian thought—for example, as even today's political platforms incorporate, if indirectly, uto-pian precepts.

Utopias, however, are but one of many visionary constructs. Among others are ideologies such as notions of efficiency, social justice, particular aesthetics, and ecological sustainability. These, too, add to the underpinnings that affect discussions and negotiations and eventually result in our urban settings.

One interesting question we can ask is how these basic ideas and concerns relate to each other: Efficiency, for example, may be seen to be at variance with sustainability. Pursuit of social justice can fly in the face of aesthetic ideas. In this brief essay, I consider what some of these other ideologies have to do with utopias as urban plans are formed and put into effect.

Defining Our Terms: Utopias

In order to understand how utopias form an integral part of the city-planning process, we begin with a brief discussion of these two social inventions.

The essence of utopia—as presented in one way or another in each of the other essays in this book—is a vision of a social structure both good (in fact, a significant improvement over the existing one) and not yet encountered in human experience, except perhaps in some golden age in the past. A utopia looks at society as a whole; it is not particularistic with a sole focus, say, on the formation of community, or on production, or on the political decision-making system. It considers how the various components of the good society relate to each other, though one aspect may be given prominence.

A utopia ultimately is positioned in real space, and its elements are usually firmly rooted in the physical world. Homes, workshops, domains for leisure all have a given location. They require space, and there are interactions over distance. Thus, a utopian pattern may seek to minimize the gap between home and work—as do many policies in city plans. With just a little exaggeration, then, a utopia has the characteristics of a master plan.

Defining Our Terms: Planning

Planners, like the creators of utopias, see their mission as improving that part of the world over which they have responsibility. They seek a central role in the shaping of the physical environment. The visible piece may be the master plan, a mapping of intended, future, and desirable land uses throughout the city—the location of facilities, transport and utility nets, and so on. This master plan will also set forth the regulations and standards determining these uses. Such plans have been prepared for cities in most countries of the world.

In tandem with this effort, there will be a set of institutions: an organizational structure mainly in the public or government sphere, but also embracing the communal domain. Underlying all is a process: a sequence of choices by which appropriate actions are taken to shape the environment of the future. This process engages a wide range of agencies in the public sphere, but also major actors in the private domain. Finally, planning is an ideology: the conviction that one can indeed shape the physical setting and thus improve the human lot. For many planners, this means that where, and in which surroundings, people live, work, trade, and recreate will significantly affect their well-being.

Planning institutions include departments and commissions at the local and regional levels, part of municipal, county, and other levels of governance. These have a part to play in controlling where, how, and to some extent when the development of land can take place. The planner works in a dense net of organizations, agencies, and institutions, public and private, and may well be overwhelmed by those more powerful (for example, departments of transportation, banks, or real estate lobbies). In order for the planner to have control, there must be an analysis of existing conditions as well as a vision of the future. At the center (but by no means alone in its actions) will be a planning staff that engages in studies and is responsible for managing the implementation of the plan.

Getting the Job Done

The planning process is thus one that is both technical and political. It is among other things a sequence of choices which justifies the application of sanctions and rewards, for example, landowners seeking to develop land. Planners take part in the steps that first establish standards for density of housing in a particular area, and ultimately pass judgment on whether a particular proposal to build warrants acceptance in a specific site.

Planning also reflects an ideology—that the present state (often a pretty sorry one) is subject to amelioration. With this comes a belief that the human lot can be improved through social (political) intervention. Another aspect of the city planning worldview is a conviction that the urban setting constitutes a system of interacting parts—that one cannot affect one without also impacting others.

Note, then, how planners, with their concern with the interrelation between facets of urban life (for example, with the needs for transportation as intimately linked to the use of land in a particular area) resonate to the utopianist's holistic view of society. Planners and designers of utopias also share a concern with the idealized environment, or at least one that is significantly improved. More generally, therefore, both planners and utopianists are intimately engaged in the world of values.

On the Relationship

Utopias, thus, have significance in planning and for planning in three ways:

1. As a template for planners in the design of ideal communities
2. As a model for the real world in the integration of related facets of the urban setting
3. As an illustration of the notion that values permeate all social interactions and processes

(1) Planners have visions of preferred or ideal environments as they design and seek to achieve improvements over the present environment. Utopias offer a spectrum of relevant images; for example, a pastoral ideal, or an efficient machine-like production unit, or a commune. Consider such utopias as those that seek a return to nature (paradise) with humanity dwelling in a state of perfection, or the utopias which, byproducts of the Industrial Revolution, sought to offer a positive alternative to a destructive factory world. Many utopias have been designed in search of a harmonious, creative, productive, and life-enhancing community.

Such visions have their subsequent formalization in what may be called ideal communities, often created by architects, which emphasize the physical structure of the ideal place. One significant facet is the underlying belief that physical features serve to enhance social relation and human values. For example, close ties can be expected to follow on high-density living: proximity enhances community.

Some years ago, a novelist and architect team of brothers worked on city plans to test their ideals. Percival Goodman and Paul Goodman's wonderfully evocative *Communitas* was designed on alternate plans for a city based on such a sequence of visions of an ideal. One ideal was the notion of housing as a "machine for living." A second ideal gave prime attention to building up resources leading to community. The last, gave predominance to harnessing resources for production, while fostering the good life. The three ideals had distinct layouts, social structures, and lifestyles.

Utopias can be seen as the working out of an idea: What would happen if a certain concept (such as the ideal of seeking close human relations) were to be given recognition and full commitment? As such, the utopian approach can serve as a model for planners who also might wish to know the consequences of the pursuit of a particular objective. What, for example, would be the implications of curbing urban sprawl? Or for that matter, what would be the consequences in terms of sprawl of minimizing the administrative interventions in making locational choices, such as those which otherwise result in the sprawl of metropolitan regions?

(2) The planner's belief that the city constitutes a system has close parallels to the construction premises of utopias. Both emphasize that components are interrelated. The utopia may be premised on the links between moral virtue and productive system. Or may illustrate how living arrangements impact on lifelong learning. The planner, in turn, considers how the economic (or production) base affects the size and composition of the population in place, which, in turn, have consequences for the housing that is needed and service requirements. These translate into the way in which land would best be used. Once land use is introduced, transportation facilities must be given attention. Finally, the productive sphere is intimately linked to the economics of transport, coming full circle.

Failure to recognize such relationships results in high costs and inefficiencies and, quite possibly, social conflict. Much of the planner's work involves study of these links. So, too, utopians explore such interactions.

(3) The whole premise of the utopian endeavor is to design and construct a social environment that enhances the attainment of certain values. These values may be social justice, or rectitude, or communality—or some combination of these. The underlying quest of the city planner is to help shape the environment so as to bring about such an enhanced good life for the residents.

Tackling Fundamentals

Utopianists and planners must consider two questions. The first question concerns what makes up the good life. What are the values that define it? The second asks us to consider how, or whether, the environment, as well as adjustments or improvements to the environment, has consequences for the good life, as defined.

Planners and utopianists both work in the world of values. What then are the values in this context? Briefly, they are statements, such as goals, standards, preferences, likes, and dislikes. One way of viewing these are as propositions which stand in contrast to facts: the latter, unlike values, can be challenged, "disconfirmed," found to be true or false. Values (and facts) are further distinct from what have been called axiomatic statements, which hold by definition.

Consider the following propositions: *Value*: all workers' incomes should be equal. *Fact*: the lowest one-third of the nation's employees earn less than the top 1 percent. *Axiom*: income includes wages, rents, and dividends (but not transfers and subsidies).

These types of statements are highly related. We can make factual statements about values (how many people hold one value rather than another), and we can have values about facts (our reaction to measures of injustice, for example). Axiomatic propositions underlie each (as where we define what we mean by an inequitable income distribution). Moreover, we can have value positions on these—rejecting the exclusion of the worth of food stamps in the determination of income, for example.

We can study the values with some degree of scientific rigor: What is the effect of one on another? If we seek to promote equity, what is the impact on wealth or income of various strata of society? What are the costs of raising one or the other? Can two or more objectives be jointly sought without diminishing one or the other or both? Or, as an example of how doing well with respect to one objective affects commitment to another, does the quest to attain environmental objectives increase with rising income?

The writer or designer of a utopia has as a first task the specification of which value or values are to be promoted by the enterprise. Sir Thomas More, for example, created Utopia with a learned society in mind. The rationale of Edward Bellamy's *Looking Backward* was a search for the good life accommodating to the consequences of the Industrial Revolution (and taking advantage of the revolution).

The planner might well reflect on such a design strategy. He or she needs to think through what goals shape the design of the city and thus which measures are proposed. What, for example, are the ends that are to be served by a series of standards for the density of housing? What stands behind the rules that would exclude a facility for the mentally retarded from a residential area—a use that some might find noxious. Without such a way of strategizing, there is no justification for the choices made.

Impact of the Physical

One of the underlying questions, which both city planners and utopianists have to explore further, is whether an ideal environment and physical setting affect behavior, satisfactions, and ultimately the values of people who live in it. Is there a link between the setting and the quality of life? Can we enhance the good in people's existence by shaping the conditions in which they live?

This is an issue not only of interest to utopianists and planners. Geographers confronted this issue and, indeed, have gradually moved away from a belief in ecological determinism—that where people live defines how they live, as well as their economy, social structure, polity, and culture. Cultural anthropologists have similarly sought to establish the range of links possible between environment and social organization and institutions, linkages between individuals, groups, and culture. We now read of "possibilism"—that a given physical environment affords a range of behavior, interactions, and values.

Comparisons and Contrasts

Utopias, of course, are different in many ways from planning. First, few utopias give explicit guidance of planning as a process—how the good world comes to be is not generally part of the story. That is, little attention is given to the steps that must be taken all the way from conceptualizing the good life to implementing specific projects. Utopias lend themselves to a critique that implementing the vision determines the desired result: the "triumph of the will."

Second, while utopias have the virtue of dealing in an integrated manner with many (not all, to be sure) facets of the human condition, they tend to be closed. That is, they are seen to exist in a domain isolated from the rest of the world (at times even incorporating sanctions against interaction with the outside—perhaps with the intention to protect those who benefit from its goodness). The planner, by contrast, functions in an environment in which trade, migration, flows of capital, information transfer, and more general impacts from the rest of the world are of paramount significance and deeply affect all communities.

Third, utopias can be faulted when—by virtue of the good life promised—dissent is not admitted, or deviation made part of the scheme. Planning, to be sure, has also been afflicted by an authoritarian streak—a tradition going back to the redesign of Paris under Baron Haussman through the initiatives of Robert Moses in mid–twentieth-century New York. Even today megaprojects surface, some of which are regarded as oppressive.

In the last twenty-five years of the twentieth century, at least the public face of planning was one that acknowledged conflict; the diversity of participants, clienteles, and viewpoints about development; and an institutional commitment to allow and, indeed, facilitate interaction between those who differ. The good plan comes out of the dissension and discussion of many people.

Another difference between planning and utopia design has to do with what might be called a reality check. The utopian flies in the face of what is—and seeks to build a new world which is in stark contrast with the limited, immoral, unjust present environment. What the planner has to do, on the other hand, is to confront reality and build starting on this base. The planner must be aware of the constraints presented by reality. If the utopian approaches his or her task as a whole, the planner can be thought of as an "incrementalist." To be sure, the planner sees, as we have noted, an integrated, systemic, and interrelated city or community. But ultimately, the ideal is achieved step by step.

There are, of course, instances in which there is an opportunity to design on a clear slate. Postwar reconstruction (or postdisaster rebuilding) represents one such example. The building, in the United States and in other countries, of what are called "New Towns" is another. They may reflect a strategy in response to an objective as simple as reducing congestion, or providing the physical infrastructure (housing, shops, facilities, etc.) for a resource-based investment, such as a power station, mine, or military post. The New Town may also be built to provide a lifestyle that challenges features of mainstream society, for example, heavy dependence on the automobile.

Finally, there is a qualitative distinction between utopian and planning efforts. At first blush, it would seem utopias are essentially creative endeavors, while the work of contemporary planners is largely technical, scientific. This distinction, of course, is only partly true as a generalization and is not entirely valid. Ultimately, the values that govern a particular planning process, and which underlie a resulting planning document, have intuitive components. The planner's values do enter into making choices, particularly where information is incomplete, as it often is. On the other hand, utopias are not without their scientific calculations and determinations—demographic, engineering, and such.

Here, as in so many other ways we have noted, city planning and utopias show important similarities which go beyond their distinctions. Each has much to learn from the other . . . and each did over the previous century.

References

Catanese, Anthony J., and James C. Snyder. *Urban Planning*. New York: McGraw Hill, 1988.

Fishman, Robert. *The American Planning Tradition*. Baltimore: Johns Hopkins University Press, 2000.

Goodman, Percival, and Paul Goodman. *Communitas* (rev. ed). New York: Columbia University Press, 1990.

Horch, Charles, and Linda Dalton. *Practice of Local Government Planning*. Washington, DC: International City Managers Association, 2000.

Krueckerberg, Donald. *Introduction to Planning History*. New Brunswick, NJ: Center for Urban Policy Research, 1983.

Sies, Mary Corbin, and Christopher Silver. *Planning the 20th Century American City*. Baltimore: Johns Hopkins University Press, 1996.

Web Resource

Site for the organized planning domain in the United States: www. planning.org.

As explained by the author, "This essay proposes a novel approach in the attempt to find one or more versions of utopia: A distributed matrix of hundreds or thousands of cities that float on the oceans, holding physical life-support technologies and high standards of living constant across all cities, and making slight variations in the social fabric from city to city, based on local resident preference. This is not so much a blueprint for any one utopia, but rather, a plan for a testing laboratory to allow individual people and whole societies to find their own versions of utopia using the scientific method on a grand scale."

19. Distributed Floating Cities: A Laboratory for Exploring Social Utopias

Patrick Salsbury

Given the space constraints the editor put on all of the volume's essays it is impossible to demonstrate the possibility of building a floating city, nor outline the technical details of how this could be accomplished.[1] Please take my word that it is possible to build hundreds or thousands of floating cities and scatter them across the oceans of the planet.

Why bother? Because they put a buffer of several hundreds or thousands of miles of ocean between people with differing ideologies, so we can hopefully avoid the frictions brought about by close proximity. My general idea is to let people of a similar mind live near one another.

A major difference between floating cities and traditional landlocked cities is that once land cities become established and grow to their respective boundaries, they really are not going to expand. They reach maturity although they continue to age. Eventually, some areas become run down and go through various stages of urban renewal.

My floating city model, however, offers a radical departure. The design is based upon a simple biological model that has been in use for billions of years: cell division. As a sea-based city grows, it will draw energy and nutrient resources from the sun, wind, and sea. It will produce more physical area for its growing population, as well as more economic opportunities.

Unlike a landed city, a floating city can self-replicate, then split apart. It can go through a process of "budding" to produce smaller "seed colony" copies of itself, and these may split off and float away in a new direction, both physically and ideologically. Rather than letting a city grow beyond its social or physical carrying capacity, and suffering through waves of crime, unemployment, social dissension, or overcrowding, the people of a floating city can simply start a new colony at sea (or on land), according to their new definition of a utopian goal.

The implications of this are fairly profound: no more need for wars of independence, no more need to fight over occupied zones of control, no more fighting over so-called holy land since a floating city will be drifting around, no need for rebels fighting against the powers that be. With an amicable shaking of hands, a few thousand like-minded individuals can hop onto a seed colony and head out to sea to find out if they can make their idea of utopia work.

The general idea is to create a controlled laboratory environment, where most of the variables are held constant, and change just a few things. In this case, we attempt to hold life-support and living standards constant (and high) for all people. In a biology lab, it is common to see dozens or hundreds of Petri dishes with the same substrate of nutrients, while some other factor is manipulated in a controlled fashion. In this proposed planetwide sociology lab, the "Petri dishes" would be large-scale floating cities which are each home to somewhere between 5,000 and 150,000 people.

Once adequate life-support needs have been established at a high standard of living for all people, no one can blame continuing social failings on poverty, inequity, and so on. The ideas that knit together the individual societies may then be examined in a rigorous way, and we can begin to explore the ideologies that either make a society function well or fail to do so.

In this thought experiment, a high standard of living could not be defined as the way in which many Americans live today; that would spell ecological disaster when replicated across the globe with billions of people. Rather, in this case, we should strive for a standard of living that is higher than is common in America or in other industrialized nations.

We need to create environments in which everyone has enough personal space, food, water, sanitation, energy, shelter, education, health, and time to pursue their ideas of fulfillment and growth. This should be done without being wasteful, without polluting the environment, and while utilizing the latest advances in technology and knowledge to repair the damage done to the planet during the twentieth century. This sounds utopic, doesn't it?

Once the physical infrastructure of several of these self-supporting, eco-friendly floating cities is in place, slight variations can be made in social structure. And controversial issues, which have proven complicated in the uncontrolled, often very densely populated environments of current cities, states, and nations, can be explored.

Would you like to live in a certain type of political system, or with a specific religion, or no religion at all? What should be the status of guns, drugs, abortion, race, gender, or sexual orientation? Should a community be made up of a people with a similar disability—where most people are in wheelchairs, or are deaf? This city will differ significantly from one in which most people can

walk and hear. An all-gay city, a city of gun owners, a city of legal drug users
... suddenly, these people, who are used to being a marginalized minority,
find that they are the majority. How will that change their society? Will they
be able to achieve their vision of utopia without the oppressive yoke of whatever has kept them down for centuries? Or will they become oppressors themselves? (Hopefully not.)

A crucial thing to keep in mind during this thought experiment is that
participation in this proposed laboratory environment is completely voluntary.
This is not a proposal for concentration camps where minorities of whatever
sort are forced to go off and live with "their own kind." It is rather a haven
where they may flock by choice, to be with people of similar mind-sets. The
goal is to reduce friction as much as possible by letting each group pursue its
own idea of utopia, without the interference of detractors. Of course, anyone
who would rather live in our current societies and land-based cities may do
so. This is not a plan to replace the existing world, but to expand the options
and possibilities for those in the world.

Some people may question the idea of going off to live in a place where
everyone agrees with you, and insist that it is better to stay and fight for your
rights where you are. This choice will leave you unhappy, and it may make
other people unhappy. Two groups of unhappy people do not make a utopia.

Each society will have its own local constitution with the rules for that
group. To make sure that everyone in any given city is content with their
situation, there should probably be some sort of mandatory "happiness index"
check every year, if not more frequently. Perhaps a system in which each
citizen (which will probably vary with age based on different societies) is
required to sign and renew his or her adherence to the local constitution yearly.
In essence, they will be signing the "social contract" we often hear about but
rarely see in our current societies.

Times change, people change, and laws change. What sounded like a great
idea a few years ago might not actually be so good in practice. For example,
perhaps you have a family now, and all those guns everywhere in the free-
gun society are making you nervous. If you are not happy, then you are not
in your personal utopia. Under the provisions of the floating cities experiment,
you should be able to pursue your happiness elsewhere—perhaps another floating city or on the mainland. There should be some sort of "travel agency"
service to help you find just what you are looking for. If everything in your
current location is perfect, except for the guns, maybe you need a socially
identical city without guns.

Will letting people live their dream lead to social failure? Possibly. In fact,
in some cases, probably, which is a valuable thing to know. For example: A
city of 50,000 democratic, pro-drug, pro-choice, anti-gun people might thrive,
whereas a city of 50,000 communist, pro-drug, pro-choice, pro-gun people
might not. Holding other things steady, we have two variables. Was it the

communism or the guns that caused one city to fail? Or was it some combination of the two?

Even if some cities fail to succeed, this information will be useful for the rest of humanity, specifically in the next 50 to 100 years as we begin to move off the planet and out into space. This utopian testing lab will hopefully provide pointers into what sorts of social systems tend to produce extremely happy people, less happy people, or extremely disgruntled people. That information might mean the difference between life and death when a ship carrying 100,000 people or more heads off into the interstellar void.

It should also prove useful to people still living here on Earth.

Note

1. These are topics covered in more depth on the floating-cities mailing list and the Reality Sculptors Web site, http://reality.sculptors.com, where you can find archives of past discussions, or join in future ones. This essay will also be further expanded on the Web site.

––––––––––––

What might a life resemble if its possessor were a pioneer in formulating and advocating a viable utopian idea? What difference might it make if the idea were independently "invented" decades later by many others? The odyssey recounted below offers a bevy of instructive answers. The author has spent the last thirty years promoting a sparkling idea—the Resort Circle—which has since become a mainstream concept (see the Marien essay for additional possibilities). Details of the plan, along with valuable ideas of how to "sell" a viable utopian idea, help make this an especially empowering essay.

20. I Am a Utopian: Creating the "Resort Circle"

Ernest Vlahos

I am a utopian . . . a philosopher . . . a truth seeker . . . a do-gooder . . . an altruist . . . an idealist . . . a generalist. . . . I am a proselytizer.

In 1970 I quit my job teaching elementary school in Mississippi. Burnt out, poor, father of four, watching my wife die of cancer, I wanted to fulfill my life's ambition of contributing to making the world a better place. This occurred at the height of the commune movement—a counterculture sort of utopia.

I visited a Unitarian commune on the fringes of the Garden District in New Orleans, where I ran into an old acquaintance, Lenny, who was one of the leaders. When I noticed a member who seemed to be having a drug problem, as I had already read about the problems of the communes, I told Lenny that his commune was not viable, that it was not going to last.

Lenny then said two things. First, this was just an experience that they were enjoying at the time, just for its novelty. It was a fad of the moment among liberal freethinkers or free doers: drugs, free sex, anarchy, free living, and other bonding. Second, if I did not care for their little commune, I should go out and create a better one.

I continued to study ways in which to help people live better. I examined utopias, cooperatives, kibbutzes, and villages. I decided that the concept of the village was viable enough, since it has been around for hundreds, even thousands, of years. But I saw that in the future we will need a "village plus," one which incorporates more and more modern technology.

I read soon after in a magazine about a pineapple plantation in Hawaii which was being closed down and converted to a new destination resort. I realized that a leisure/resort lifestyle would be a large part of the future.

I began to collect brochures of different places to travel to. At a travel agency in Gulfport, Mississippi, I found a twenty-page brochure describing the *Acapulco Princess*, including beautiful pen-and-ink and watercolor drawings throughout, done by a gifted artist. It looked like a heaven on earth, a most perfect of perfect worlds. The people were fine of figure and elegant of dress. It was a futuristic Garden of Eden. Everything was provided for them. There was no work to be done—just super-refined living. Everything was here: beautiful people, beautiful surroundings, beautiful food . . . beauty incarnate. Everything was beautiful. To the eye it was beautiful; to the mind's eye it was beautiful.

Magazines and travel brochures taught me about other resorts with package plans that included everything at one price. I read about Club Med with its worldwide network of theme resorts in beautiful, exciting locations, with activities for the whole family.

The Resort Circle

My vision continued to come together in the 1970s, and eventually it developed into the idea of the Resort Circles, a nationwide (and worldwide) network of communities designed to bring together the best elements of an ecovillage, a small college, and a modern resort. It would enable people who are not wealthy to work only four hours a day, and live like millionaires, in a healthy, viable and sustainable lifestyle, without being wasteful of resources. I called this way of living a "live-better lifestyle."

A Resort Circle is a 1,000-acre leisure community located in the countryside, with modern resort accommodations for 1,000 families or single individuals. It goes far beyond the resort idea, however, in also including the facilities and activities of a trade school, college, spa, camp, art colony, summer stock, production plant, farm, and so on.

Only 5 percent, or fifty acres, of the 1,000 acres of land area will be built upon, including roadways. The other 95 percent will be left in a natural state. A certain amount may be used for farming and food production. Some of the land will be left with its natural trees and greenery, some will include a lake or ponds, and some will be set aside for recreational activities.

In the city a Resort Circle might be a middle-sized hotel near the downtown district or a fair-sized motel complex. It could be two, three, or four buildings adjoining one another, or it could be a city block, including all buildings, or it could be some other structural arrangement.

In high-cost ideal resort locations, such as the seashore, mountains, or lakeside, where land carries a high price because of its scarcity and ideal setting, a smaller parcel of land could be purchased and a high-rise built. Satellite facilities could be built, and their use commercialized, to be used by both members and the general public, who would pay.

At times, there might be ideal locations for Resort Circles, but enough land might not be available for various reasons. A Resort Circle could be built upon 300, 400, or 500 acres. Since this might not provide the full range of land necessary to meet most community needs, there could be satellite areas for food or goods production. These areas could include several hundred acres to accommodate a dairy farm, vegetable or truck farms, food-processing plants and storage facilities, or plant production facilities.

At times, it may be desirable and feasible for two or more Resort Circles to adjoin one another. They could have a central, common community, as well as their own Resort Circle community.

The Resort Circle enables one to live a dual lifestyle: two lifestyles in two different kinds of environments. In the lifestyle directed toward work, most of one's time and energy will be spent in a productive capacity. (It is better if residents put their own sweat into it, plus costs are greatly reduced.) The other lifestyle emphasizes the wise and enjoyable use of leisure time: self-discovery, self-improvement, self-enjoyment—maximizing the pursuit of happiness.

Resort Circles are designed to provide a live-better lifestyle: to conserve energy, to be ecological, to work well with the future, to make the future work even better, to reduce the causes and effects of social problems, to reduce the causes of city problems, to conserve resources, to provide a more natural lifestyle, to prevent boredom and its ill effects, and to make it easier for people to be successful.

Making Progress

In 1970, when I first began designing a Resort Circle, my thinking was clearly utopian. Now, in 2002, aspects of my early ideas are becoming mainstream.

The world is catching up to me. Thirty years ago, my utopian village concept of resort living was fresh, new, and ahead of its time. It is still a utopian ideal, but resorts are commonplace now, and there seems to be a resurgence of the village concept. Happily, my ideas appear closer to the mainstream and far more feasible than thirty years ago.

However, whenever you are talking about a utopian vision, it is never the same for everyone. Different cultures, different time periods, and different levels of sociocultural development produce different utopian visions.

For example, Iceland is a utopia along the lines of a Resort Circle. The people do not have to work because they receive sizable funds for the fishing rights around their island. They never worry about invaders. They have a lot of extra time to engage in leisure activities. Another modern utopian example is a well-known Japanese village that has changed little in 500 years. The villagers enjoy a healthy natural flow with the seasons and nature.

We also see on television variations on today's utopian concepts—enjoying the outdoors, going to a Club Med, vacationing in a destination resort, such as the Disney Institutes which promote lifelong learning along with resort living, or sailing on the luxury condominium cruise ship *The World*, where a condo costs at least $2,000,000.

I am encouraged by the fact that some of the experimental communities which began in the 1970s, such as Twin Oaks, in Virginia (a Walden Two prototype), and The Farm, in Tennessee (which began as a hippie commune in California), have survived, adapted, and changed. They now share their experiences and transferable lessons through modern websites.

Newer ventures of the 1980s and 1990s include cohousing in Europe and Washington state; "New Towns," like Columbia, Maryland, on the east coast, and in England; intentional villages, like Sea Side and Celebration in Florida; and futuristic company towns like New Oroville, India. These communities and hundreds of others join together to share information through global Internet networks such as GEN, the Global Ecovillage Network (www.gaia.org).

The Art of Promotion

Now, as a utopian, a truth seeker, a teacher, and a preacher of sorts, I have learned I also have to be a proselytizer. We have to motivate people. We must sell any utopian ideal that we put out there. People have to sign on the bottom line, and agree they bought what we sold them. And the more complex or difficult an idea is to understand, the more we have to sell it.

What am I trying to say? People must make a mighty leap, and they need all the motivating force they can gather to generate the leap . . . a leap of faith. As a visionary, I know that if they can see the vision, and if it is highly desirable, they will welcome it, embrace it, and build it.

Getting a good idea is one thing; getting people to listen to it is something else. It is not enough merely to build a better mousetrap; you have to promote it. Today there are too many new ideas that compete in the marketplace. If you create something new, you must shout it to the world.

The question as to how good a utopia is depends on the quality of your utopian vision. I have had a lifelong interest in what shapes people's lives . . . in what might encourage believers to choose the good road to the good society . . . to utopia . . . to Resort Circles . . . and beyond. I remain encouraged by the progress we are making in this matter.

Pulling It All Together

Over thirty years after I first started working on this Resort Circle idea, I still have lots of notes and written thoughts which have not yet seen the light of day. I am sure that will be corrected soon. Today we can use computers to research topics which once took months and years to explore. A blend of the old and new is easily available. Today the Internet offers a way to reach millions of people worldwide, even on a poor man's budget. Like-minded individuals can learn and share and link together through giant networks on the World Wide Web.

Hell, I am seventy-one years young, and I still have enough fever/fervor/manic/gentle fanaticism to never end promoting this cause. I believe utopian means "making it better," and I'll never stop trying.

Note

If you would like to learn how the Resort Circle concept can be used as a tool for creating all kinds of utopias, I am looking for kindred souls. Dialogue and correspondence are welcome. E-mail: justernest@cableone.net; address: Ernest Vlahos, The Resort Circle, 2603 Catalpa Avenue, Pascagoula, MS 39567; phone: 228-762-4980.

References

Campbell, Carlos C. *New Towns: Another Way to Live*. Reston, VA: Reston Publishing, 1976.
Cohousing, The Cohousing Network: http://www.cohousing.org/.
Critchfield, Richard. *Villages*. New York: Anchor Books, Doubleday, 1981.
DeSoto, Hernando. *The Mystery of Capital: Why Capitalism Triumphs in the West and Fails Everywhere Else*. New York: Basic Books, 2000.
Erasmus, Charles J. *In Search of the Common Good: Utopian Experiments Past and Future*. New York: Free Press, 1977.
Etzioni, Amitai. *Next: The Road to the Good Society*. New York: Basic Books, 2001.
Fairfield, Richard. *Communes USA: A Personal Tour*. Baltimore, MD: Penguin Books, 1971.
The Farm, Summertime, Tennessee: http://www.thefarm.org.
Frantz, Douglas, and Catherine Collins. *Celebration USA: Living in Disney's Brave New Town*. New York: Henry Holt, 1999.

Global Ecovillage Network (GEN): http://www.gaia.org.
New Oroville, India: Catalytic's Company Resort Community: http://www.catalytic software.com.
Nordhoff, Charles. *The Communistic Societies of the United States.* New York: Schocken Books, 1875, 1965.
Reich, Robert B. *The Future of Success.* New York: Alfred A. Knopf, 2001.
Ross, Andrew. *The Celebration Chronicles: Life, Liberty, and the Pursuit of Property Value in Disney's New Town.* New York: Ballantine Books, 1999.
The Seaside Institute Seaside, Florida: http://www.theseasideinstitute.com/.
Silverman, Justin. "Welcome to the Cubicle Dome." *Wired* 9, no. 7 (July 2001): 42.
Skinner, B.F. *Walden Two.* New York: Macmillan, 1948.
Spiro, Melford. *The Kibbutz: A Venture in Utopia.* Cambridge, MA: Harvard University Press, 1956.
Twin Oaks Intentional Community, Louisa, Virginia: http://www.twinoaks.org.
Weinberger, Eliot. "Paradice." *The Nation,* February 10, 1997, p. 36. (Reprinted as "Heaven on Ice," *Utne Reader,* May–June 1997, 29–30).

While we commonly associate utopian ideas with the big picture—as with institutional reform (schooling, wellness) or with the really big scene (the nation, the globe)—it is vital that we pay comparable attention to matters much closer at hand, as close, for example, as our own homes.

Guided by the engaging essay below, we are drawn to ask how our home contributes to or detracts from our well-being? What is its psychological value? In what ways does a home constitute a personal utopia? And, looking ahead, what are the gains and hazards posed by "Gee whiz!" technological gadgets and services? Especially valuable are pragmatic reforms suggested to help us stay on top of the hazards that threaten us—each such reform, in its own way, a viable utopian idea.

21. Personal Utopia: Technology's Effect on the Meaning of Home

James Mitchell

In Mali, West Africa, the Natomos family of eleven shares two mud houses, which would provide a moderate efficiency apartment for an adult couple in the urban United States. Their total possessions, aside from the clothes they wear in their family portrait in *Material World* (1995, Sierra Club Books), number forty, including a "ritual cane."

Bill Gates, billed as the world's richest private individual, a few years ago moved into his 40,000-square-foot "ecology house" sliding down a west-facing hill to the edge of a Seattle lake. His family of four (not counting the nanny and multiple unidentified support staff) consume more than 10,000 square feet per person. At the standards of the Natomos, an extended family of about 450 people could live in Gates's house.

Social sermons about inequality are not the point of this comparison. What it raises are questions of what constitutes a house, and how it contributes to the well-being of those who live in it. The Natomos represent the majority of humans throughout history. For them the house is a place to shelter from the weather, to sleep, cook, procreate, argue, study, sing, sicken, age, and finally die. They have no running water, no electricity (though they do have a battery-operated radio), two rough chairs, no table, no beds, and no decorations. A bicycle is their only form of transportation. Undoubtedly one of the first things they would add would be a television if reception became possible and they could afford it.

We do not have pictures of the Gates family relaxing in their mansion, but one can assume that Bill and Melinda Gates are reasonably happy in it. Aside from space enough to win perpetually at hide-and-seek, they have every amenity imaginable, all of it polished to the highest level of craftsmanship. They are not, for instance, bothered by the ugliness of electrical outlets—these are hidden, though the many appliances are certainly present. Music to suit the individual taste can follow them throughout the house (does Bill win when he and Melinda enter the same room?). The images on the wall change to suit individual whim. If Bill Gates pushes the proper button in his car, the bath will be waiting at the exact temperature.

It seems fair to say that Bill Gates enters a personal utopia when he passes the last security guard. The world he enters is the one he and his wife imagined—with the help of many talented professionals. Without leaving his grounds he can work, exercise, sleep, dream, communicate, play, escape, and entertain. If he wanted to be like Howard Hughes he could disappear from sight and have a complete existence within his home. He has everything.

The Natomos, despite a house and possessions that probably would not fill one of Bill Gates's walk-in closets, smile apparently happily to the camera. Because they are connected via their radio, they undoubtedly know that many in the world own far more than they do. Would they change places with the Gates family? Certainly they would far more readily than the Gates family would move to Mali. The evidence of rural-to-urban migration throughout the world testifies that the amenities and opportunities of city life are a continual draw.

Yet the Gates and Natomos families share much once they cross the boundary to their property—a boundary that can even be movable as it is with nomads around the world. The worst of weather is excluded from the family space. At mealtimes the family can gather to share food and talk with only those they choose to invite. At night each person has a sheltered place to rest. When they leave during the day their possessions remain behind awaiting their return. For the children, home is the place where they are fed, loved, guided, and eventually released to form their own families. For the adults, it is where love and the sharing of the goods and information gained in the outside community support and bind the family.

As it serves these physical functions, the home acquires a psychological value for each inhabitant, one that is both unique to each individual and shared within the family. Only the family knows the physical space and the possessions so intimately that they form a shared mental space that can be discussed and occupied even when not in it. Many of life's most emotion-filled moments have occurred in that space, from lovemaking to birth to death. Each view, each room and nook carries memories for the family, creating another vocabulary shared only by those family members. So too with the objects that fill the spaces.

For the Natomos, the ritual cane, for instance, almost certainly binds them to the husband's or wife's parents, and perhaps to many generations beyond. The cooking pots are places of sharing between mothers and daughters where first menses, or hopes for a new dress, have sunk into the fired clay. Even the radio is endowed with memories of a drought extended or the coming of tax relief.

For each member of the family, there is more than the shared physical and mental space. There are also personal triumphs, miseries, and quiet pleasures that can be savored anew in memory. The ability to pin a futbol star's photo to the wall, or recreate the moment the red sun was first seen streaking through the crack in the door, extend one's self through time and anchor memories to place. The future, too, is greatly shaped by the thoughts, plans, and fantasies that develop buried in night hours or amidst the afternoon lull of family bustle.

Home, then, molds creation of personal and family history and plans, as well as permits the activities that define family life. While it is never perfect, it provides a personal utopia in each member's organization of memory and vision of the future. For the Natomos and the Gates families, the function is the same.

Of course, the Gates family has many more objects, rooms, and views, but their lives are still bound within the same number of hours, and the activities of family life must follow the same general pattern (albeit with many more variations). For our purpose what differentiates them from the Natomos family most dramatically are the changes brought to their personal utopias by technology.

We see the beginnings of that change in the Natomos family's radio. That single object, the extreme leaf on a vine that covers the world, has brought new memories, new knowledge, and new dreams to their lives. Through its news, music, and story functions it will create new worlds in the children's heads, ones that will likely lead many of them to leave the family home and depart for the urban center where the stem of the vine is stouter.

For the Natomos family, the radio is a single object which is probably played only occasionally—if only because the batteries are expensive. Its impact on the family member's vision is real, but limited. For the Gates family, and those of us who will follow his technology lead as declining electronics prices make his extravagances commonplace, the probable impact is enormous.

Leaving aside what biotechnology is likely to provide in the way of sensory manipulation, the house of a few years hence is almost certain to affect us even more than telephone, radio, and television already have. Bill Gates's house tracks each individual and modifies the pictures on the wall and the sound in the air, creating the first steps to a physical utopia as well as a mental one. Robotic technologies promise that in the future entire walls will reform and move. Display trends make it likely that those same walls will take any vista—current, historical, or imagined—that we choose. Electronic fabrics will change the appearance of the furniture in the space—and it too can be readily moved. Internet communication will soon allow three-dimensional presence in another place, as well as interaction with another person.

The most likely effects will be similar to the proliferation of the special-interest magazines of the past quarter century. From a few read-by-everybody magazines, which barely filled a few display shelves in a drugstore, we've fragmented and specialized to the point that bookstores now present a dozen tightly packed racks displaying titles touting single-flower gardening to mercenary training.

In a similar way, it seems probable that the ability of the house to tailor the environment to each individual within its space is likely to fragment the family even more than today's frenzied, pop-tart dispersal through suburbia. The Natomos's grandchild could live in a house in which what he sees is endless futbol replays in virtual stadiums. Or she might wander amidst the romance world of Mali's golden age with perfect warriors always inviting her to join them in delight. The sons may coast on spacecraft and peer around them at the Martian surface, while the daughters may live amidst tribes of Disney characters, always finding the rainbow.

We see these tendencies already. With multiple telephones, radios, television sets, and computers in each home, the family seldom gathers for a common experience—even the shared meal is on the wane. The coming technology will take the devices that currently sit isolated and make them nearly the entire environment. One will not be locked to a chair to experience one's fantasies; the fantasies will follow from room to room.

For each individual family member this enhancement will apparently create a more perfect utopia. I will never need to see my sister's stupid teddy bear characters or the old man's retread sports. I can see what I want, when I want it, and quite literally not see or hear what the rest of them cherish.

The family's utopia of shared experience and space, however, will be vastly diminished. No longer can there be the assumption that we have all lived in the same set of spaces. Even though the outer walls may remain fixed, the inner ones will have moved to suit individual whim, and what those walls appear to represent will not be shared. Procreation, birth, work, illness, and death will not disappear, but even they are moving more and more out of the home to other locations that are not shared within the family.

If one is disturbed by these possibilities there appear to be two possible reactions. The first, which has seldom been effective, is to limit the new technologies—the houses that restrict television use today are rare indeed, though the benefits are clear. The appeal of the digital dream is too great for most families. Second, conceptually tougher, but more rewarding in terms of our social heritage, is to develop links between the electronic world and the physical one which have permanent psychic meaning. We need to replace the traditional bonds of shared place with ones that can utilize the new technology.

The first steps in this direction are the online shared genealogies and the Web-based family photo albums which are already prospering commercially. If shared events can be frozen in digital space and then linked, perhaps they can create a new sense of family unity. If the coming house, for instance, incorporates cameras and recording devices that monitor every space (already in existence at the Aware House at Georgia Tech), then it may be programmed to save critical events for future sharing with family members (far more radical uses, good and bad, are easily imagined).

Perhaps there may develop family games similar to the multiplayer computer games currently expanding on the Web. These could use the enhanced environment and the physical proximity of people to explore issues relevant to family growth, thus providing learning. At the very least they could provide shared experiences that would be similar in nature to those traditionally bonding families.

It may well be possible that the geographically dispersed family can be reunited through electronics-based experiences—an expansion of the role of today's telephone, e-mail, and instant messenger services.

At a community level there are many possible ways of using the new tools to replace the direct contact of the traditional neighborhood. We see first steps in that direction with eBay's and other commercial service's "trust" ratings which create and incorporate validated history into individual interactions.

The family and individual home, however, are likely to remain the basis for social life. What happens within the family's walls, however malleable, will still be the foundation of each new member's vision and his or her creation of a personal utopia. It will undoubtedly expand and morph, but it will always start at home.

VII. Schooling Possibilities

*Not all viable utopian ideas have to be obvious blockbusters. Some can pro-
mote what at first may seem to be small changes but—on closer examination
and with further reflection—may actually contain far-reaching implications. A
fine example is found in a low-keyed essay below advocating intriguing
changes in K-12 education. Offered by an experienced teacher with an obvious
love for her craft and her wards alike, the essay shares pragmatic and seemingly affordable reform ideas; for example, schooling might go outside of the
school building, peers might help as educators, neighborhood resources might
get finer-than-ever educational utilization. These and other sound notions add
up to a heady mix of viable utopian ideas . . . well worth rapid implementation.*

22. A Future Vision for Public Education

Marilyn Vlahos

Consider this scenario for the utopian public school of tomorrow one morning
in the next twenty years. It could take place tomorrow in the United States or
even in a Third World country. It could still be viable 50 to 100 years from
now. It is a worthy dream to work toward.

A Primary Vision: Learning Is Fun

The children enter laughing and talking about what has happened since we last
met. They put away their personal belongings from home or daycare and ease
comfortably into their school-day experiences. Some work by themselves,

some together, some with me, some with our assistant. Other adults or older children may linger with us for awhile to exchange information or just to visit.

This week our assistant is a parent of one of the students. Next week it may be a high school student, a college student, a teacher trainee, a student nurse, or a volunteer. Or we may have a paid assistant who comes every day. Some children may arrive with an individual assistant. Special professionals may come one or more days a week to work with children individually or in small groups.

We have books, school supplies, several computers, laptops, games, cameras, video cameras, televisions with VCRs and DVDs, radios, and CD players. We have chairs and tables, couches, stove, refrigerator, washer, dryer, and other appliances, as well as inside and outside work and play areas. We have toys, tools, art materials, software, hardware, plants, animals, and more. We have bicycles, skates, and a small van.

Depending on our local population size and density, my class may consist of preschoolers, lower elementary or upper elementary students, or a combination. We have boys and girls, children of all races and economic conditions, with and without handicapping conditions. Our class has from four to eight students and two or more adults. We do not have a school building. We meet in my home several days a week.

The children learn to talk, read, write, calculate, problem solve, experiment, and use technology. Our four hours together pass quickly. We may cook together some days or go on a field trip. We share what we have learned. We teach each other. My job is to teach and facilitate learning of basic literacy, language, and social skills. We practice individualized mastery learning. We apply what we have learned in natural settings.

When the children leave my class for the day, they go with their parents, siblings, or caretakers to their next activity. Several groups may join together at the community gym, sports complex, pool, library, counseling center, dance studio, or music, video, or art studio. There they will continue to work in small groups led by specially trained teachers with paid and volunteer assistants. Then they will go home or to small group day care or night care. We have school year-round, with two or three week vacations between terms.

This is not a university model program, a special pilot program, a private school, or a homeschool program. It is the worldwide primary school of the future, and I am a public school teacher of the future.

I love my work. Every day I see happy children, who are learning and growing in a safe, stimulating environment and who will grow into productive and peaceful world citizens. Our society has finally realized the value of small groups, constant positive interaction with adults and other children, healthy activities that develop demonstrable skills, natural settings, useful technology, and active learning.

A Secondary Vision: Moving into the World

Our older children move through a basic four-by-four-block day throughout the community. They meet two hours at a time in different settings. Sometimes they meet in individual teacher houses. Sometimes they meet in community specialty buildings. Sometimes they meet at a community college or a work site.

Their day consists of literature/social classes, math/science classes, arts/languages classes, and sports/leisure activity classes. Group sizes remain small with from eight to twelve students and two or more adults. Adult accompaniment outside class time gradually decreases according to student age and individual needs. Technology and introduction to work experiences are included within each block.

Year-round schools help provide for continuity in learning and improved use of time, including the development of lifelong recreational skills and a wiser use of leisure time. Small group trips to other communities, cities, states, and countries are planned on a regular basis to introduce students to each other and to other cultures at a young age. Exchange student activities are encouraged to promote tolerance for diversity and cultural differences.

As students reach what we have traditionally considered the high school years, an additional block of formal work or volunteer work experience is added to the school day. Students transition to formal college or apprentice programs, as they are ready individually. They may choose to complete a secondary diploma either by examination (in parts or all at once) or by attendance for a specified time period.

A Viable Utopian Vision for Education

The two preceding scenarios may sound like a teacher's dream. They are, but they also provide a simple outline for a process that solves and prevents many of society's current and future problems. Some similar small primary school groups already exist in our country and in other civilized countries worldwide. Secondary programs in some countries have already moved closer to our secondary vision.

We like the neighborhood concept for working with groups of human beings. Small communities need to have, and frequently do have, a variety of public and private special-interest activity centers where small groups can participate in a variety of activities. Larger towns and cities comprise many small communities and smaller neighborhoods. Children of all ages can learn to get around and become good citizens in a neighborhood.

We do not need to continue to build large school buildings nationwide and worldwide to house large groups of children who are heavily regimented, and are expected to conform to increasingly strict standards of behavior and achievement arbitrarily imposed to meet the needs of large-group management.

Many of the growing ills of society are furthered by continuing to attempt to educate students in groups too large to be learning effective, primarily under the guise of being more cost effective. To be truly cost effective, we need to invest our money in the personnel and technology necessary to make our children socially and academically successful from birth. We can then stop wasting so much of our money on dinosaur school buildings, prisons, rehabilitation centers, and all the related content and personnel costs of these ever-growing bureaucracies.

More and more individuals who do not fit into a certain mold are being pushed out and excluded from school life, under the excuse that their removal from regular programs is needed so that the larger group will benefit. This exclusion is taking place at a younger and younger age. We need to reverse this trend and begin to "take in" more and more children now. We need to work diligently to help them be successful members of our small groups and neighborhoods at a young age, so that they can continue to be successful and participating members of society as adults.

Our primary vision of the neighborhood-enriched teacher home can be implemented in any society. It has strong possibilities for improving educational opportunities in emerging and Third World countries. It would be a good use of both public education monies and donations from private foundations.

Our secondary vision involves expanding the full-time use of community public and private facilities. Both students and adults can participate in building and enjoying special activity areas in the community. A practice of healthy participation in and enjoyment of community activities can be taught at a young age, and enjoyed for a lifetime.

Recommended Web Sites

Autism Society of America (ASA). The Autism Society of America Homepage: The Voice of the Autism Community. "Nationwide support group that promotes lifelong access and opportunities for persons within the autism spectrum." This is a model support site that is very interested in research and future planning: http://www.autism-society.org/.

National Education Association (NEA). Welcome to the National Education Association: "America's oldest and largest organization committed to the cause of advancing the cause of public education": http://www.nea.org/.

Phi Delta Kappa (PDK). Phi Delta Kappa International Home Page. "Phi Delta Kappa is an international association of professional educators. Our mission is to promote quality education, with particular emphasis on publicly supported education, as essential to the development and maintenance of a democratic way of life": http://www.pdkintl.org/.

Only as we succeed in drawing everyone into the dialogue can we hope to bring along viable utopian ideas likely of success. To date, to judge cautiously from the formal literature in utopian studies, the vast majority of authors have been white males, commonly of the grey-hair variety. (This volume, despite my best efforts, has no representation from Asian Americans, Hispanic Americans, new immigrants, or others we would like to have heard from.) We cannot do enough fast enough to remedy this imbalance. To achieve far broader representation is to take pragmatic actions like that one explained below and to do so soon.

23. Blue Sky for Black America: Utopia and African America's Future

Jesse Rhines

First as a graduate student, and now as a professor of African American studies, I have written about approaches to African American development for over twenty years. While my work on African American development has been future oriented, I now include study of the future itself in my teaching curriculum through the device of utopian imaginings, as a means toward achieving that development. My goal here is first to weaken student acceptance of the status quo, and to then provide them agency sufficient to challenge and change that status quo more to their own individual liking.

This is where the concept of utopia comes in, for it provides the vessel for possible futures that students can consider in designing that new status quo. After reading a few utopias and acknowledging that they are fictions, the fact of African Americans' real situations seem much less a necessary product of history than a conditional product of human choice and actions.

After reading Terry Bisson's *Fire on the Mountain* (1990, Morrow, William, & Co.) for example, students expressed genuine surprise at the impact a single event—in this case, a successful Harper's Ferry raid by John Brown in 1859—might have had on the course of African American history and development. As a result of this discovery, the student's own individual human agency becomes a central feature in the shaping of African America's destiny.

Since the early sixteenth century, Europeans have united space and time orientation with sociopolitical aspirations within the concept of utopia. Utopias stretch time orientation and can both invigorate and broaden one's conceptual approach to one's own future. Blacks, however, have largely ignored utopia as a venue and have abrogated possible real-world benefits of a long-range purview. African American protest against the absence of black characters in the futuristic 1977 film *Star Wars*, however, demonstrates that blacks do consider their representation in works imagining the future to be important.

In big business, utopian reasoning girds the blue-sky concept. Blue-sky projection of a company's hopes for the next 100 years is not fantasy. It asks, if there were no clouds on the horizon, what would be the company's best situation at a given time? In *Reason Enough to Hope* (1998), MIT physicists Philip Morrison and Kosta Tsipis describe blue sky as "what is possible within the broad objective constraints that delimit our options: the laws of physics, energy, and food availability, population, global wealth, geography, weather."[1]

As an IBM systems engineer trainee I was frequently asked to "blue-sky." Instructors told us to contemplate IBM 100 years hence. What would technology and customers be like? Would the company expand or contract? Blue sky gave trainees a hopeful image to shoot for something no matter how fanciful. It was inspiring. It generated an esprit de corps. My idea is that blue sky, in the form of utopian imagining, has a role to play in combating hopelessness and encouraging development in the African America community.

In their article "Imagining a Future in America: A Racial Perspective," William Nichols and Charles P. Henry declare that nonwhite authors, African Americans specifically, have produced very few utopian works.[2] More recently, however, Maria Giulia Fabi has analyzed newly discovered African American literary utopias of the late 1800s: *Iola Leroy* by Francis Harper and *Imperium in Imperio* by Sutton Griggs.[3] George Schuyler's *Black Empire*,[4] which appeared as a serial in the *Pittsburgh Courier* between 1936 and 1938, was a utopia that envisaged a Black International—composed of highly skilled Africans, African Americans, Caribbeans, and others under the dictatorial command of Dr. Henry Belsidus—all committed to the destruction of global white supremacy.

In the 1990s, Toni Morrison's *Paradise* and Octavia Butler's *Parables* series were said to have significant utopian elements. *Dark Matter* (2000), edited by Sheree R. Thomas, a collection of science fiction produced by African Americans from the nineteenth through the twentieth centuries, includes three utopias created since 1990. One of these, "Space Traders," was written by Derrick Bell who quit his job as a professor at Harvard Law School in protest against university's hiring practices. Bell also wrote a short story, "Afrolantica," perhaps the only hint at an African American Eutopia ever written. It is eutopias, imaginings of good societies, that blacks should be encouraged to write. Virtually all the utopias thus far written by blacks are dystopias, imaginings of bad societies.

In "High-School Utopian Writing Project—A Viable Utopian Idea!," in *The Declining Significance of Race*, sociologist William Julius Wilson called "hopelessness" a major impediment to African American development. According to Wilson, antisocial values and concentrated criminal activity, resulting from poverty and isolation precipitated by extreme job loss since the 1970s, have clouded underclass residents'—particularly the young's—view of the future.[5]

Hopelessness is revealed through concatenated and myopic imaginings of the future which seem to bear little strategic dimension or long-term time orientation. Time orientation is important because it is the canvas upon which individuals and groups conceive of the range of sociopolitical possibilities available to them. A short time orientation imposes severe limitations on the range of possibility perceived.

In addition to college classes like the one described above, I propose, in this regard, that blacks undertake a national project in which African American high school students read utopian literature, then compete in the writing of utopias depicting alternative ways for blacks to live in a multicultural world. The reason for the contest is to take the shock of the new from the future by allowing students to map out the future. By orienting students toward the future, and their own place in it, we will stimulate in them hopefulness and feelings of agency.

I specify utopian literature as the basis for this project because, unlike other fictive works, utopias, by their very nature, contemplate complete and integrated sociopolitical systems. Utopias force readers to take stock of the specifics of contemporary reality. They always compare that reality with an imagined alternative which highlights unfortunate aspects of the real world and suggests ways of improvement.

Utopia is not only the tool of the creative writer, but of both the social worker and the social scientists as well. Writing utopias will provide students with a base for normative reasoning. The writing of utopias is also an automatic rebuke of the negative racial images that still exist in America and around the world, because the writer can explore the rationale for those images and immediately confront them by creating viable utopian remedies.

Notes

1. Philip Morrison and Kosta Tsipis. *Reason Enough to Hope* (Cambridge: MIT Press, 1998), p. x.
2. William Nichols and Charles P. Henry. "Imagining a Future in America: A Racial Perspective." *Utopian Studies* (Spring 1978): 39–50.
3. Maria Giulia Fabi. " 'Race Travel': Towards a Taxonomy of Turn-of-the-Century African American Utopian Fiction." In *Viaggi in Utopia*, ed. Raffaella Baccolini, Vita Fortunati, and Nadia Minerva (Italy: Longo Editore Ravenna, 1996).
4. This refers to the 1991 joint publication of "The Black Internationale" and *Black Empire*. George S. Schuyler, *Black Empire* [Pittsburgh *Courier*, 1936–1938] (Boston: Northeastern University Press, 1991).
5. William Julius Wilson. "High-School Utopian Writing Project—A Viable Utopian Idea." In *The Declining Significance of Race* (Chicago, IL: University of Chicago Press, 1980).

Viable utopian ideas often turn things on their head. For example, Bill Du Bois makes a convincing case in the essay below for affordable delinquency prevention and rehabilitation programs which youngsters actually embrace. He offers an appealing blueprint for a new type of Youth Center, one likely to help delinquents help themselves as no other has or currently does. Delinquency prevention and rehabilitation can be turned to utopian-building advantage—and a pragmatic plan below suggests how. What are we waiting for?

24. Inventing Utopian Delinquency Reforms: Being There in Ways That Work

William Du Bois

We need to create programs kids run to rather than from. Even when we barely glimpse them, our theories about the possibilities and perfectability, as well as our underdeveloped notions about a more utopian life, shape how we spend public money on social reforms, determine what types of programs we develop, and how we evaluate their worth.

As an applied sociologist interested in helping young delinquents, I think it is time we applied sociological theories in imaginative new ways. Theories and research findings, which have been sitting there for years, will lead us in practical, utopian directions (Shostak 2001: 123–143).

Envisioning a Better Youth Center

Most young delinquents fall through our net, and they surface only when a crisis becomes extreme or when authorities force them into treatment. At such times, delinquents may or may not be willing to listen. They may define treatment as punitive. By the time they get to their counseling appointment, the crisis may have subsided. A Youth Center guided by fresh assumptions about possibilities and perfectability would offer so much more.

Counselors must be available at the crisis time. People with problem-solving skills—helpers familiar, accessible, and perceived as friendly assets—must be immediately available and accessible to people with problems. How? Consider this actual neo-utopian achievement: In the 1960s, a Wisconsin training program for psychiatrists interested in alcoholism had the interns tend bar. The approach was simple: Bartenders have traditionally given a layman's type of "psychiatric" advice. If you are interested in alcoholism, you go to where the alcoholics are.

Similarly, a Youth Center guided by utopian theory might have staff counselors who actually work other functions, such as cooking and waiting tables. They would then become familiar, available, and approachable when problems arise. Young people might actually consider such a "counselor" a genuine friend—someone on their side. Bonding is crucial. We need an opportunity to talk over our lives and develop significant insights at critical junctures with someone we trust, someone who cares about us. College students majoring in sociology might be perfect for this role.

Resources for prevention should actually be enjoyable, not programs from drab and shabby social service agencies. A miniature golf course might be designed with a clubhouse which serves as a teen center. The local mall could have a youth hangout with video machines, ice cream, dance floor, and counselors working the floor. The local parking lot could be equipped with carnival type booths where counselors could sell soft drinks and other items. Dating classes could be taught by attractive females who were two years older than the boys, and by attractive males who were ten years older than the girls. Here, a conversation about social skills, conflict resolution, and power skills would draw an eager audience.

A car rental agency stocked with sports cars or luxury cars which youths could rent with tokens earned from attending conflict-resolution classes may seem far fetched, even utopian, but is it? Even this seemingly absurd suggestion makes economic sense. The money we spend on prevention may well be worth it. We are willing at present to spend $100 a day or more to treat youths when they are convicted and confined as delinquents. The average adult prisoner costs taxpayers $25,000 a year: a $1 million investment over a lifetime.

The question is where do we want to spend our money: at the front door where it is inexpensive as prevention or at the back door where it is expensive and problematic? The car idea above illustrates the boldness and the trust in utopian possibilities with which we must approach new solutions.

Community, Meaning, and Opportunities

Creating community is a significant preventive factor in reducing delinquency. People who make their way out of delinquent environments have significant others to support them and perceive their opportunities, even if initially only as dreams that are supported by someone. For example, kids who overcome bad environments often have a mother who believed there was something special about them, who saw possibilities and sought to cultivate them, rather than mold their children in an authoritarian way (Currie 1985).

Community is also crucial for rehabilitation. Despite the myths of what we say we are doing, most people actually get out of the criminal justice system by becoming interested in someone or something. Close bonds, the sense of community, and being interested in someone or something are all crucial factors.

We know a great deal about creating neo-utopian communities. We can design neighborhoods and community centers to facilitate position interaction. We can provide the resources that increase the probability of friendship formation. We can commission product champions when youths have good ideas, and thus get people involved in and committed to their communities. We can provide meaningful roles which promote a sense of doing something worthwhile (Du Bois 2001a; Du Bois 2001b).

If opportunity theory is correct, much of youth delinquency occurs because of perceived blocked opportunities. A resources model would create healthy environments in which community, opportunities, and meaning can flourish. Specifically, our approach should be to provide the participatory resources people can utilize to create their own meaning.

This does not mean simply pumping money into the delinquent areas. The familiar proverb of providing a fish versus teaching a person how to fish is appropriate here. To extend this utopian-promoting metaphor, it means providing access to poles, hooks, fishing maps, trips with old fishermen, fishing books, and upbeat opportunities to learn fishing.

This means more than getting an after-school job. The research is muddled at best concerning the benefits of a job on decreasing delinquency. There is not much meaning in, "Do you want fries with that, ma'am?" It makes more sense for the delinquent youth to put on their gang colors and strut down the street. There, at least, it is possible to be a hero, and heroism is crucial for youth.

Instead, we must invent healthy opportunities for heroism. At-risk youth need meaningful roles, something beyond hamburger flipping. Midnight basketball, for example, never looked like crime prevention to many, but it provides an example of how positive youth recreation and after-school programs can provide positive activities and reduce delinquency (Mendel 1995).

Crime prevention should take nontraditional turns. Does falling in love, for example, decrease one's likelihood of engaging in youthful delinquent acts? I know of no research here, but I would suspect as much of this neo-utopian state of grace.

Research, after all, shows those in relationships become more conservative in attitudes, stay home more, and get more involved in positive directions and goals. Research on commitment and family membership from Durkheim (1951) on suggests that creating solidarity decreases delinquency and anomie. Research on gender roles shows relationships take the roughest edge off of masculinity, making men gentler and helping them get more in touch with their feelings (Rubin 1983).

Perhaps we should design neo-utopian structures which facilitate youths in forming loving relationships. We might create a network where young singles can meet and match. We may need more matchmakers and fewer counselors.

Matchmakers could learn to match not only lovers, but also mentors, friends, and even opportunities for new schooling or better employment.

Youths can be involved in solving problems. Teen court programs empower people (Godwin 1998). With the crack of a gravel, kids go from being part of the problem to being part of the solution. Restorative justice programs, including victim-offender mediation, family conferencing, and circles, provide new ways to empower community members and to help solve delinquency problems (Zehr 1990; Umbreit 1994; Galaway and Hudson 1997; Van Ness and Strong 1997).

Peer mentoring and peer tutoring programs may or may not be more effective than traditional programs for the mentored and the tutored. However, they are worth their weight in gold for the student mentor and the student tutor. They provide an opportunity to be a hero, a star.

Reaching Out to Parents

Parental involvement in their kids' education is one of the greatest factors related to low delinquency. However, how do we get parents involved in their child's education if they don't care? They may have negative memories of school from their own experience. Any attempt to force them to get involved will only increase their bitterness. Somehow, we must invite them into the school for their own purposes and help them decide to change their attitudes toward school.

The first step is to turn the neighborhood school into a free community center. It should provide relevant programs (a day-care center, a tool lending library), recreation (a midnight basketball league), and social functions (a singles group). Periodically there could be a flea market, club meetings, income tax help, and a food stamp booth. There may be a garage sale or a concert or an auto repair clinic or assistance in turning a hobby into a small business. They may even take classes, or use a potter's kiln, or work in the workshop, or play on the computers.

There could also be games and activities which combine youths and adults. We can introduce positive roles for students, paying jobs in the center for youths and adults, and make it a gathering place for all types of people. We can create a stage people can use for their own positive purposes.

Parents who participate will meet their neighbors and form community. They will legitimize the importance of school. When they talk about it at home, the idea will now be associated with something positive, something rewarding. All of this should reinforce the utopian-building notion that school is important. Such public relations can help change parental attitudes toward school and possibly influence the attitudes and performance of their children in all the best ways.

The key is inviting participation and providing resources for people. This involves parents in their kids' education in a roundabout way which could not be accomplished in a straightforward fashion with the at-risk families we want to serve. It is a pull, rather than a push. Programs should be designed synergistically so that there is something in them for everyone.

Power skills, problem solving, and conflict resolution classes might be introduced, although there would have to be tangible, meaningful rewards for attendance. More important, these skills need to be programmed into the organizational culture of the center. Counselors should be doing something— ideally something for their own purposes—working in the wood shop, or having their car fixed, or tending bar in the restaurant area. Perhaps the local psychologist would love to teach billiards, or play the piano, or fire pottery in the kiln. The local domestic-violence counselor could hang out the first and third Monday nights each month. A child-abuse counselor might become involved in games and projects thereby becoming known and familiar to youth (Crawford and Bodine 1996).

Summary

All of these neo-utopian ideas are relatively inexpensive: They require a talented and inspired coordinator, an office which can be housed almost anywhere, and adequate meeting space. None will get going, however, until we have an informed public that funds imaginative solutions. We need to appreciate and applaud way-out possibilities for reform and set our sights on the sort of perfectibility at the heart of this delinquency reform vision. When it comes to delinquency programs, we are implicatively involved in deciding what kind of people and what kind of world we want to make.

References

Crawford, Donna, and Richard Bodine. *Conflict Resolution Education: A Guide to Implementing Programs in Schools, Youth-Serving Organizations, and Community and Juvenile Justice Setting.* Washington, DC: Office of Juvenile Justice and Delinquency Prevention, 1996.

Currie, Elliott. *Confronting Crime: An American Challenge: Why There Is So Much Crime in America and What We Can Do about It.* New York: Panthon Books, 1985.

———. *Crime and Punishment in America.* New York: Metropolitan Books, 1990.

———. "The Prevention Game: Thinking Creatively about Reducing Crime." In *Utopian Thinking in Sociology: Creating the Good Society,* edited by Arthur B. Shostak, 123–43. Washington, DC: American Sociological Association, 2001.

———. *Reckoning: Drugs, Cities, and the American Future.* New York: Hill and Wang, 1993.

Currie, Elliot, and Bruce Berg. "Crime in Society: Sociological Understandings and Societal Implications." In *Using Sociology: An Introduction from the Clinical and*

Applied Perspectives (3d ed.), edited by Roger Straus. New York: Rowman and Littlefield, 2001.

Du Bois, William. "Design and Human Behavior" in *Applying Sociology: Making a Better World*, edited by William Du Bois and R. Dean Wright. Boston: Allyn and Bacon, 2001a.

Du Bois, William. "Transforming Community Attitudes and Morale." In *Applying Sociology: Making a Better World*, edited by William Du Bois and R. Dean Wright. Boston: Allyn and Bacon, 2001b.

Du Bois, William, and R. Dean Wright. "The Sociologist as Artist." In *Applying Sociology: Making a Better World*, edited by William Du Bois and R. Dean Wright. Boston: Allyn and Bacon, 2001.

Durkheim, Emile. *Suicide, A Study in Sociology*, translated by John A. Spaulding and George Simpson, edited with an introduction by George Simpson. Glencoe, IL: Free Press, 1951.

Galaway, Burt, and Joe Hudson. *Restorative Justice: International Perspectives*. Monsey, NY: Criminal Justice Press, 1997.

Godwin, Tracy. Peer Justice and Youth Empowerment: An Implementation Guide for Teen Court Programs. Washington, D.C.: American Probation and Parole Association, 1998.

McGillis, Daniel. *Beacons of Hope: New York City's School-Based Community Centers*. Washington, DC: National Institute of Justice, 1995.

Mendel, Richard. *Prevention or Pork: A Hard Headed Look at Youth Oriented Crime Programs*. Washington, DC: American Youth Policy Forum, 1995.

Rubin, L. *Intimate Strangers: Men and Women Together*. New York: Harper & Row, 1983.

Shostak, A., ed., *Utopian Thinking in Sociology: Creating the Good Society*. Washington, D.C.: The American Sociological Association, 2001.

Umbreit, Mark. *Victim Meets Offender: The Impact of Restorative Justice and Mediation*. Monsey, NY: Criminal Justice Press, 1994.

Van Ness, Daniel, and Karen Heetderks Strong. *Restoring Justice*. Cincinnati, OH: Anderson, 1997.

Zehr, Howard. *Changing Lenses: A New Focus for Crime and Justice*. Scottsdale, PA: Heralds, 1990.

VIII. High-Schoolers on Utopia

Since today's teenagers were born after the advent of the digital revolution, many are now members of what is known as the "N-Gen," the first cohort to take the Web for granted. They are arguably in a position to know more than any previous generation did at their age, thanks to the many hours spent Web surfing and learning through e-mail dialogues, competitive gaming, and search-engine explorations.

What if one were to ask such teens to design a utopia? What sort of viable utopian ideas might they suggest? To judge very cautiously from the essay below, high-schoolers may be increasingly open to the challenge—open in ways that raise fresh hope that these young Americans may soon formulate a politics and public policy agenda more aligned with, than different from, ideas shared elsewhere in this book. While one sparrow does not a summer make, and one field report begs for further extensive validation, it is encouraging to find below hints of more imaginative and caring views than often associated with teenagers.

25. Posterity in Their Hands: High School Students and Their Hopes for Utopia

William McKenna

How do high-schoolers envision utopia? In the winter of 2002 I asked this of a Cheltenham, Pennsylvania, high school class taking a course in futuristics. Answers from juniors and seniors stirred both hope and doubts, as might be expected from their thoughtful and nuanced approach.

My small sample (about 25 students) comprised students of varying academic abilities from a diverse economic, racial, religious, and ethnic pool.[1] I make no grandiose claim of representativeness, but I do think my students speak for many in their generation.

What follows is organized thematically, as I asked the class to design a utopian society which incorporated five basic and interdependent institutions: economy, religion, the family and society, education, and government. They were to address the components and exclusions inherent in a utopia, as defined by Rosabeth Moss Kanter in her essay "A Refuge and a Hope and the Limits of Utopia."[2] They drew as well from essays in the "Historical Antecedents" and "Problems with Utopian Societies" sections outlined in my curriculum. While I asked them to be pragmatic, they were also asked not to be afraid to explore possibilities and take risks.

Government

Apropos matters of governance, my high school students offered these thoughts:

> Each country became a state under the United Nations *[and]* each state in the United Nations had an equal role and say in the government and economy. The leaders of each state would represent their state in government policies. No senator had more say than the next. Since each state is under the U.N. there is no need for a military. They would handle *[conflict]* with debates.

> Third World countries don't exist because in the beginning of our utopia they were given equal technology and resources. Cities were rebuilt and education and medical facilities were important priorities.

> The government provides all services. This will avoid competition. A checks and balances system will be *[included]*. All of the citizens will vote.

> Government and companies work together to create fair pricing that correlate with supply and demand. Exploitation is reduced by setting a *[limit]* that each company may take as profit before further earnings are given to the community or charity of choice.

> Environmental laws are strictly enforced. Every product is made with recyclable material. Equal health care is provided for everyone.

Car taxes will be extremely high to encourage public transportation and
to cut down pollution problems.

Local towns and not corporations own farms. Recycling, water conservation, pollution, and packaging are all controlled by the local police.
Helping the environment is a major responsibility for each citizen wants
to live in a clean world.

With the course now completed, I ask myself if the concerns expressed here—a
truly representative government—are viable utopian ideas? I also wonder if
the remedies proposed by my high-schoolers—altruism, charity, and government regulation of industry for the good of the people—express false objectives? On reflection, I would now say *no* to the former and *possibly* to the
latter.

Somewhere between high school and adulthood, the passion for humanity
and justice revealed by idealistic teens seems to become blunted by life. I say
possibly to the second question because if schools can instill an awareness that
we are the fortunate ones, the 20 percent of the world's population who absorb
89 percent of its global income (Brown, 1994, 5), it *will* make a difference.
Students can then be confident that their opinions do and can continue to
matter.

Economy

Where economics is concerned, my high school students offered the following
thoughts:

Capitalism was eliminated so that not one person or state has an advantage.

There are no social classes.

Everyone is paid equally for their jobs, there are no class differences.

Since some jobs take longer schooling there may be a difference in pay,
but not enough to create a rich and poor class.

No longer do citizens live in poverty. They don't have to live with the
fear of war. They can enjoy the clean outdoors, get a good education,
and live comfortably. All states are equal in power and in wealth.

The radical ideals expressed in this section are utopian. I know it, and the
students have no false hopes about their realization in the near future. We

discussed at length the difficulty of fulfilling all humankind's wants and needs at the expense of competition, coercion, conflict, and exploitation in a capitalist society. This is, no doubt, why the solutions presented here appeared socialistic to many in our class.

Materialism and greed are part of our socialization from birth, and many of us transfer our selfish tendencies to our children. They have more pocket money per year than the poorest people alive. According to the World Bank, about 60 percent of the world's six billion people live on less than $2 a day (Thompson 2001). We are also provided ample opportunity for anticipatory socialization through ubiquitous corporate logo bombardment. Brand loyalty, driven by media-promoted societal icons, stimulates our materialism. These tendencies to "Buy! Buy! Buy!" will be difficult to change, and my daily observations of my high school students reinforce this troubling view of mine.

Education

In the matter of schooling and formal learning, my high school students offered these thoughts:

> Excess money that the government makes goes to school funding, better technology, and smaller classes so students get more attention. There are no private schools so that everyone has an equal opportunity.

> A teacher's job is the most important of all. Government must have strict regulations and standards. Every student must get an education.

> Schooling *[censors]* sex and violence for the young, *[and]* teachers teach a truthful and unbiased education.

> Education teaches "crucial" tolerance towards races, gender, religion, sexual preferences, and the mentally and physically handicapped.

Education historically has been viewed as the great equalizer, yet it is perhaps the most dystopian institution in America. The need for greater equality of educational resources and caliber is strongly stated in virtually all of my student papers—irrespective of the student's race, religion, ethnicity, or gender. Perhaps they know, better than do many adults, what works, and where education is failing contemporary America.

We struggled over questions of class size, access to higher learning, tolerance, truthfulness, staff competence, student learning styles, academic ability, and district funding. While a utopian education system was difficult to conceive of, my students especially wondered where the contemporary trend for allowing profit-seeking companies to run privatized, formerly public, schools fits into a utopian model of education.

Religion

My high school students offered these thoughts in regard to religion and religious beliefs:

> *[My utopian society includes]* the right of religious freedom, excluding any religion that incorporates persecutions or is not open-minded to other people practicing a different religion.

> All religions are tolerated. Citizens have the freedom to pick what religion they want as long as they tolerate all others.

> Religion in our utopia is open. Every child attends Sunday school to learn about the aspects of every religion. Parents are not allowed to force a religion on their child, and the child can decide to choose whichever religion *[to follow]*. There would be no religious persecution because of the complete understanding of every religion.

Thomas Paine said that every religion is good that teaches man to be good; and I know of none that instructs man to be bad. Why, then, is religion a difficult topic to explore with adults and students? It is the only topic that causes me apprehension prior to any class discussion across my instructional curricula, including courses in American history, sociology, the future, and contemporary issues. It is an area so personal and inflammatory that some students react more from passion than from rationality.

Is this reaction socialized? What do we teach our children here? What behavior do our world leaders model? Historically and at present, their leadership lacks in rationality, and it is certainly contrary to many utopian models. My utopia-designing students explored religious issues with a welcomed objectivity lacking in other high school classes of mine.

The Family and Society

In the matter of family life, my high school students offered these thoughts:

> Contraception courses are taken by every student and contraceptives are widely available; this helps population control. There may be accidental pregnancies, but not often because everyone is educated and understands the need to keep population levels low.

Overpopulation is not a problem. My utopia has reached the third stage of the demographic transition, meaning that death and birth rates are equal. Everyone is taught about sex and contraceptives. Contraceptives are widely available for anyone to use.

Equal housing helps eliminate the poor class. There is only a small crime rate as a result of providing everyone in the community with common necessities, and eliminating the need to commit crime. *[Where crime does exist]* therapy and recovery programs are put into play.

Cars are used less because of widespread public transportation. The few cars that are used run on renewable energy, like solar power.

Every race is seen as equal along with equal rights given to both genders.

Homosexual couples could also get married. If a homosexual couple wants to have a child they could adopt.

The family and society component of this assignment was designed to afford an opportunity to explore a less abstract matter—what the students and their own (distant) children might someday do with their personal lives—a topic with which they could draw on direct personal experience.

In sum, I believe we adults underestimate the depth, reach, and creativity of certain high-schoolers. My students had an opportunity to slide into selfish or frivolous "stuff." They chose instead to grapple with far tougher, deeper, and even loftier matters. They helped me get a better understanding of what is really on their minds, and I find inspiration in their hopes for the future they dream of helping to make . . . their hopes are fantastic.[3]

Notes

1. Cheltenham Township is a suburban community of approximately 35,000 located on the northern border of the city of Philadelphia. Although comparatively small (only nine square miles), Cheltenham Township is rich in its diversity, as is also the school district. Its 5,200 students in the 2000–2001 school year included 35 percent African American; 9 percent, Asian; and 54 percent, Caucasian. (See http://cheltenham.org/Information/InfoDefault.htm)

2. This essay appears in the anthology, *Scanning the Future, 20 Eminent Thinkers on the World of Tomorrow*. Edited by Yoric Blumenfeld. London: Thames & Hudson, Ltd., 1999; pp. 256–275.

3. Student contributors from the Cheltenham High School Future Class of 2001–2002: Kyle Bady, Leah Birek, Reuben Burrows, Bariq Fluellen, Dan Krause, Dennis McCloskey, Bill Michel, Ben Novack, Zabrina Noyes, Stephanie Paaske, Jordan Seltzer, Kevin Seidman, and Erica Quint.

References

Blumenfeld, Yorick, ed. *Scanning the Future: 20 Eminent Thinkers on the World of Tomorrow*. London: Thames and Hudson, 1999.

Brown, Lester, ed. *State of the World 1994*. New York: W.W.Norton, 1994.

Paine, Thomas. *The Rights of Man*. Part 2, Chapter 5. (Encarta bookshelf 2000).

Thompson, Morris. "How Most of the World Lives on Under $2 a Day." *Philadelphia Inquirer*, May 25, 2001, p. A25–26.

Imagine a utopian design so appealing that Americans en masse vote it into law. What might it resemble? As envisioned by a creative high-schooler in the essay below it includes a wide array of viable utopian ideas, ranging from federal government dictation of local school curricula to rule by a religious panel of local "judges." However you come out on the controversial particulars, please do recognize this sort of expansive reflection is a healthy starting point for a lifetime advocacy of viable utopian ideas. The sooner more teens are invited in high school to take up this sort of design challenge, the better.

26. Conception for Perfection: A Practical Utopia

Kyle Bady

My utopia exists in the near future of our current nation. It is in the United States in the year 2006. The shift to my utopia has been totally accepted voluntarily, not through violent coercion, propaganda, or any other evil methods, but because a few enlightened individuals shopped a concept in the year 2001. Federal, state, and local employees shared the concept with other people, and so forth and so on. It became so widely spread that the nation as a whole voted for and adopted my utopia.

Education in my utopia is strictly and equally government funded. All school districts, facilities, and services are centralized. There is one large district that includes the entire nation. No one is excluded or turned away from seeking education. To eliminate parents' concern with the quality of education a particular school is giving their child, all curricula will be the same. Standards for academic performance will be raised considerably.

This will work because the teacher to student ratio will be 1:3. A concept known as "a friend for life" will be the driving force. There will be one teacher for every three children born. Three newborn babies will all have one teacher for the rest of their lives from grades K to 12 and through any graduate or undergraduate college courses. Students will reach high standards because the relationship between student and teacher is improved significantly by the personal attention being paid to academic problems. Students will not be apprehensive in the classroom, and they will feel comfortable with experimenting and learning.

Occupations and the economy will be handled in the same fashion as capitalism in the United States. As a result of the child prodigies that will have spawned in my utopia (as a result of the amazing education system), every occupational salary will be paid according to a theory I like to call "natural necessity."

If your job is essential to the survival, safety, care, or development of my utopia, you will be paid higher wages than if the jobs are not essential. High-paying jobs include such jobs as doctor, firefighter, police officer, carpenter, trash collector, social worker, and teacher. If your job is a needless luxury, you will be paid the least. Jobs like professional athlete, actor, or entertainer fall in this second category. For instance, a police officer will be paid a $100,000 salary; a professional basketball player will be paid between $50,000 and $70,000. If society were faced with a catastrophe and times were crucial, we would need law enforcement rather than sports . . . someone hitting a three-pointer from thirty feet away!

Money will rapidly flow into my economy because there are more people occupying essential jobs than nonessential jobs. In our society nonessential jobs are held by a privileged few; the majority of people hold essential jobs. This will put money in the hands of the essential job holders, since they are the majority. Consumerism comes in, they buy, and this feeds my economy and makes it healthy.

Religion, Religion, Religion. My utopia will be 100 percent tolerant of every practice, expression, or belief of any religion. If an aspect of my society conflicts with a particular religious pillar, you do not have to bend or yield to federal, state, or local law. The issue will be settled by a panel of five varied local judges from the person's particular religious sect. In every community, no matter how big or small, there will be "The Judges" from a person's specific religious sect. This religious judicial system will be separate from government control or influence. It will totally be organized by the corresponding religious sect, and the government will honor every verdict handed down by The Judges.

For example, imagine you are Muslim and you wear a Sunni (a beard worn by men of the Sunni Muslim sect) as a symbol of your religious pride. Your workplace, however, requires you to be clean shaven. You will bring the issue to your local panel of The Judges for area Muslims. They will decipher the issue and decide to judge in your favor or not, based on the pillars of your religion. If they decide you have the right to wear the Sunni, then The Judges will inform the employer of their decision, and the employer will yield. If The Judges decide otherwise, then the man will be quickly prompted to cut off his beard, and the conflict will be resolved. If you refuse to cut off your Sunni, you will face prison time or fines. Religious freedom will be a staple in my society.

Government will be structured like the capitalists in the United States do so well. There are, however, a few major differences. What is the main problem common people have with government officials and politicians? It is that they make decisions, policies, and laws from a detached perspective or from only one angle. The government is basically out of touch.

In my utopia the face of government will change often. In contemporary times the government is largely 40 to 60 percent white males raised in suburbia. This is because the largely white members of government know the right people, and have favors owed, and connections that help them. As a young black man, I personally have asked myself the question—Why is government bleached one color? I know the answer. The white majority runs the country.

However, in my utopia, every race will be in government. People well known in any race can occupy a government position. There will be a black female president, and even a Chinese male vice president. Government positions will alternate by race once every four years. This varied perspective will improve government significantly in decision and lawmaking. The more information one has about a situation, the more one can change one's approach to it. My government is an exemplary model because it will see problems and issues from every possible angle and be able to make the best decisions.

Family will also be a capital pillar. From personal experience, I know that when parents abandon or leave children to be raised by just the one parent, or by a relative, it develops deep internal problems. In my utopia it will be a life sentence for any parent who does not support financially and emotionally. The only exceptions are death or a mental or physical handicap. As for divorce, this will continue. A parent does not have to live with the other one, but he or she must be there for the child. Leisure time will consist of the same activities that we partake in today: movies, clubs, restaurants, games, watching professional sports, and the like.

There are some ripple-effect type weaknesses in my utopia. The first concerns holes in my education system. Centralized schools may lack attention to kids who may be above or below normal intelligence. People might look at this as an attempt at conformity and rebel because the individual cannot excel by being in an honors class or a mentally gifted program. Another hole in education concerns the student/teacher relationship. The personal relationship that is developed by this system might forge a bond that is too comfortable: Certain children might take school lightly because it is like having a friend teach them, rather than a teacher.

Another type of weakness concerns gaps in my religious system. People might feel their freedom compromised by the fact I am giving power to five randomly selected members of their own sect and giving them the right to judge. Finally, a hole in my government system is that I bias positions because of race. I would give a federal job to a Puerto Rican just to add variety to the color palette, while ignoring a better qualified applicant.

Science fiction is a remarkably strong aid in conceptualizing, conveying, and employing viable utopian ideas. Fans like myself learn much from such masters as Isaac Asimov, Ben Bova, Octavia Butler, Arthur C. Clarke, Philip K. Dick, William Gibson, Ursula LaGuin, Walter Mosely, Neil Stephenson, Bruce Sterling, Jules Verne, H. G. Wells, and scores of others. All the more pleasing, therefore, is the example below of a new imaginary utopia, crafted by a talented high-schooler, a world strong in viable utopian ideas well worth pondering in the here and now.

27. Settling the High Frontier: Castles in the Sky

Benjamin Novack

The Free Worlds' League consists of fifty-four member habitations. Twenty-five of these are positioned at the Earth-Luna LaGrange points; six are bubble habitats on Mars; five orbit Mars, twelve are nomadic within the asteroid belt, five are currently in the vicinity of Neptune and intend to travel to the Alpha Centauri system, and one—New Arcadia itself—travels in a wide loop around Earth, Luna, Mars, and the asteroid belt.

The first orbital habitats—New Jefferson, New Arcadia, Nomad City, and Athens Reborn chief among them—were settled by former residents of so-called First World countries, who were discontent with the hypocritical and self-destructive attitudes of their old homes. These habitats, ten-kilometer-long cylinders, with circumferences of more than six kilometers, spin fast enough to simulate gravity. Their populations rarely exceed ten million.

The general tone of the ideologies espoused by these first settlers was enough to discourage others from coming to the habitats, and so politics and opinions were largely homogenous within each habitat; this trend is still true. Differing opinions do arise. However, people with drastically different views from those of their fellow habitants usually depart for another world, one more suited to their tastes.

In the early days, the orbital habitats were nearly all the same—distrustful of religion, practicing direct democracy whenever possible, and embracing new technology. However, as more were built, and more people left Earth, the range of opinions grew. Free-worlders generally hold that technology is the key to humanity's definition—a view hard to avoid when one's home exists only because of scientific advances. (Those who desire a more pastoral life tend the massive food-producing colonies. These worlds have surface areas three or four times those of the usual space-borne city, filled with crops except for the few human habitations).

The unified government of the artificial settlements is the Free Worlds' League (FWL). Its formation was the result of the life work of Lucas MacAllistar, one-time U.S. Senator. Its Constitution, based on many of the ideals espoused in his former country's Declaration of Independence, officially protects the rights of the pursuit of happiness and liberty. In some ways, the FWL resembles the United States shortly after its formation; member states are left to form their own laws on most issues.

However, it does provide for a strong federal government, the League Senate, and an executive, the League President. The League Senate's primary role is coordinating the material transfers between the many habitats, while the president's main purpose is overseeing the justice system, which is standardized throughout the worlds.

In addition, the policing forces of the FWL have been charged with ensuring that the basic rights enshrined in the Constitution are not violated by member states; although that is a possibility, it has never occurred. Free-worlders believe strongly that, as their Constitution's preamble states, "The role of Government is to safeguard the liberties of the people whom it represents. This is its most basic and essential task—indeed, all other tasks it engages in are in support of that goal."

Local governments range from direct democracy in Athens Reborn, to New Arcadia, where an elected executive alone wields as much power as many Earth-bound governments do. All of the member settlements, however, are fiercely democratic.

The habitats themselves—aside from the Martian bubble-cities, which are involved in terraforming and farming the red planet—are generally of similar design. The basic cylindrical shape has not been improved upon since humankind first set up homes off the Earth, but newer cities, such as Amaurot and Thoreau's Nightmare, are nearly three times as large as the first ones. They receive their electricity from massive arrays of solar cells, converting the light and heat from the Sun entirely into usable power. Everything, from public transportation to the massive lighting systems (powerful enough to simulate daylight) to the local computer nets, is run using this virtually unlimited font of energy.

The physical materials needed to make things—metal, plastic, wood, and the like—are produced either on the agricultural worlds (in the case of wood) or by mining the asteroid belt. Twelve cities in the belt process the great rocks to obtain raw materials, including iron, gold, and silicon, which are sent to the other habitats in return for finished products, including the silicon-derived pseudoplastic which finally eliminated the need for fossil fuels.

Among the habitats, there is no specific medium of exchange. Inspired by Sir Thomas More's Utopia, all colonies send to each other whatever is needed and use the rest for their own desires or to construct daughter-worlds. This has led to little discontent; even the mining worlds harvest far more material than they could use themselves, and sending automated cargo ships over long distances with high-power lasers and light-sails is easy. Currency exists for everyday transactions, but most of the usual expenditures are provided for the public at large: transportation, medical care, housing, and basic nourishment. Individuals repay their fellow citizens for this largess by working for the general good.

Free-worlder society, morality, and employment are often difficult to separate. While religion varies from habitat to habitat, most of the basic philosophy behind it is the same. All Free-worlders believe in the importance of the individual as a distinct part of a unified community, in the preeminence of enhancing the human condition, and in the importance of action.

Free-worlders do what they are good at—those who are talented create entertainment; those who are charismatic serve as diplomats and political leaders; those who are scientifically skilled develop technological improvements for their worlds. Most menial tasks—trash collection and the like—are automated; those individuals who can best find satisfaction in physical work usually move to a food-producing habitat or join in the Martian terraforming effort.

The individual worlds are small enough that everyone's contribution can be recognized and appreciated as playing a part in keeping the world running smoothly, if nothing else. Those who fulfill particularly demanding roles—doctors and judges, for example—receive larger salaries than others, but these credits can be used only for the most luxurious items. Nearly everything is so easy to make and power with the resources available to the habitats that money is quickly becoming an anachronism.

With the enormous amount of automation and technological aids available, however, most Free-worlders who want leisure time have plenty of it. They indulge in reading, writing, debating, singing, and nearly every other pastime imaginable. Chemical enjoyments of any type are legal, but are strongly frowned upon, especially when they interfere with the fulfillment of one's job. To a Free-worlder, every task is being done for the common good; there are no frivolous professions.

Education is truly a lifelong endeavor. Most citizens attend school full-time until their late teens, at which point they begin to practice a profession. The great universities are open to all who want to learn, and it is customary to become educated in an entirely new field every ten birthdays—thirtieth, fortieth, and so on.

Religions in the habitats are relatively uncommon; most citizens prefer a morality devoid of a supernatural element. Some religions, however, have survived and even thrived; faiths that promote social action have found followers.

Religious beliefs that conflict with the general morality are simply not present. Adherents to religions that violently disagree with Free-worlder morality never emigrated from Earth.

Crime is rare, with poverty nonexistent and a social environment available for nearly every frame of mind. Criminal acts tend to be the result of mental illnesses, which are treated by dedicated professionals. There is some unavoidable stigma associated with formerly violent individuals, but the fact that a person was once violently unstable is usually unknown to anyone but the patient and those he or she chooses to tell.

Family structure in the habitats varies more widely than anything else, and preference for a family type is the most common reason for departing one's home world for another. At one end of the spectrum is New Jefferson, with its strict monogamous customs. At the other end is Athens Reborn, where the world "marriage" is nearly a foreign word, and everyone is an aunt or uncle to every child. Most worlds' policies lie somewhere in the middle, with most people preferring a two-person marriage, but group arrangements are far from uncommon.

Children are born by a number of methods. Most are conceived by traditional biological methods, but a sizable minority are conceived in artificial wombs. If a genetic mix of something other than one man and one woman is desired, genetic engineers alter eggs and sperm to match the DNA of one of the participants who lacks that cell type. Multiple individuals' DNA can be combined in this way as well to share parentage among group members.

The founders of the Free Worlds designed them to be paradise for all of their inhabitants, but nothing human is perfect. People who want to live a truly low-tech lifestyle are without options—the habitats are universally technophilic, and the artificiality of the feed worlds is oppressive as well to many neo-Luddites. Mars will not be human habitable for centuries to come, and Earth's overpopulation has become a sick joke. Billions upon billions are straining the resources of the thousands of square miles of hydroponics facilities built into the megalopoli of America and Asia, sited next to desalinization and water-purification plants the size of twentieth-century towns.

As much as they like to think so, the Free Worlds' League is not a utopia for everyone; there are just six hundred million Free-worlders, compared to the nearly uncountable swarm of humanity on Earth. Their number is so large that many in the habitats have declared the situation helpless, and they are content in their knowledge that the Free Worlds will survive without difficulty, even if the Earth suddenly were to become totally lifeless and worthless.

For those who take most strongly the traditional Free-worlder philosophy of improving humanity, this grim outlook is intolerable, but the Terran problem, as it is known, has yet no solution. The only thing keeping the situation from exploding is the Terran governments' prohibition on emigration to the habitats. Some Free-worlders despise this violation of the right to choose one's home; others are quietly thankful that their small homes have not been overrun by desperate Earth-siders.

Personal Note: The biases of this "utopian" vision are obvious. Because I believe technology is a force directed for good or evil, my utopia is driven by technology harnessed for good. The nontechnophilic have no real place here. Because I believe the role of government is to protect liberties and freedoms, my utopia does this. A product of a middle-class environment, I do not see hard work for its own sake as a virtue or relaxation as a sin, so my "perfect" world embraces hedonism and learning for their own sakes, which some would see as just as pointless. I personally find religion in general antagonistic to my own secular humanistic morality, so I exclude it from my utopia, knowing full well that real human beings very often desire a link with something greater than themselves. This vision bears many marks of being the product of a mind raised in an environment that separates religion and morality, where technology is perceived as morally neutral if not outright good, and where unproductive leisure is regarded as a valid way to spend time. Largely because of the morality instilled into me by my society and my parents, I consider any family structure that provides a stable environment for its participants and any children as valid, a view that is certainly not universal.

IX. Choices: Very Personal

Abortion is arguably one of the most contentious subjects in modern life, here and elsewhere around the globe. Thanks to the unusual approach taken in the imaginative and caring essay below, we have fresh clues to ponder, fresh leads to a way out of this mean-spirited situation. A persuasive case is made for daring to get beyond a focus on reform, and daring instead to think of transformative possibilities . . . of ways by which this sorest of subjects might yet prove to be available for viable utopian reformulation.

28. "How Do You Want Your Abortion?"

Margaret R. Johnston and Claire Keyes

We are abortion providers, each with over twenty years in the field. We are constantly looking for ways to change the experience of abortion in a field that has remained nearly unchanged since its legalization in 1973. From our perspective, the abortion issue has been stigmatized, polarized, and essentially frozen in time, with disastrous effects on real people.

In real time, women—and men—make thoughtful choices that are sometimes painful and sometimes empowering, but they have nowhere to go with their feelings, thoughts, and experiences. Will the future hold promise for breaking the deadlock around the abortion issue? If so, what do we really want?

As longtime abortion providers who talk to women every day, we recognize that many women do not know how to even begin, what questions to ask, or what to ask for. Because of the silence surrounding the abortion experience, this is uncharted territory for the women and men who come to us. So we peopled our model world below with "guides" and a menu of options. A trustworthy guide is always a good thing, whether you are facing a death in the family or learning about Australian wines.

In the abortion world, you hope to be lucky enough to find a guide who will listen to your story, who will pass on the wisdom of others who have traveled this same path, someone who will tell you what to expect and how to get through the bumps and twists along the way. Most of all, you hope to find someone who can notice the good things—the gifts—that this unexpected—and unwanted—journey can surprise you with.

We hope, and expect, that in the future the popular culture will include complete information and perspectives on a multitude of abortion experiences. Women will be able to talk freely about their decision with trusted friends or family, get accurate information in health books as well as on television and in movies, easily find a counselor, get abortion services readily, and enjoy seamless, ongoing care. They will be able to buy self-help books and DVDs or attend workshops on postabortion feelings. Taken together, women may find that they can piece together, on their own, the parts they need to create their own ideal experience, including the appropriate emotional and physical recovery afterward.

Interestingly, all of the options and the complete menu of packages we present below could happen today, not in the distant future. The future may yet bring us further options, new technology, and hopefully better birth control. The recent advent of abortion with a medication (now known as RU486, or Mifeprex™) has already introduced the idea of different methods for accomplishing an abortion. Breakthroughs in genetic research, cloning needed body parts, and gene therapy will alter how we regard life on a cellular level and, perhaps by extension, the issue of abortion.

What the future promises most is the open consideration of all aspects of pregnancy, without judgment and with compassion. Choice will finally mean choices. Some day, perhaps not too long from now, someone may ask you, "How do you want your abortion today?" Hopefully you will meet Jane: "Hi, my name is Jane and I'm going to help you decide what kind of abortion is right for you. First of all, let me say that I'm sorry you are in this situation, but it may help to learn what's available and then decide what's right for you. We have a number of packages available, or you can customize an experience that fits with your situation and needs. Let me describe our most frequently requested packages to you.

1. *Economy*—Our most popular package, this has been offered since 1973 and used by several million women in the United States. You can expect to be in an abortion facility about four hours. Several other clients will join you as you learn about the basics of pregnancy termination, birth control, and

aftercare. Outpatient surgery is simple, quick, and safe. A personal review of your medical history and emotional "check-in" are available; beverages and snacks will be served, and a choice of pain relievers is yours, all for a reasonable fee of $350.

2. *The Lunch Hour Special*—This option is designed for the busy woman for whom time is more valuable than money. You can make your appointment on line and submit your personal medical information for review in advance of your appointment. Lab work can be performed at your convenience ahead of time. The physician is kind, quick, and gentle. Some sedatives may not be available in this time frame, but we guarantee service in one hour for $600.

3. *The Family Package*—Since this is an important decision in your life, you may want your loved ones around you. You can be accompanied through every phase of this process by the person you choose. Counseling is available for all family members, and it includes training and suggestions for them to participate in your care. Flowers, breakfast in bed, babysitting; just tell us what you want and we'll pass it along. We stress support and coping skills before, during, and after your abortion. Choice of abortion pill (additional $100) or surgical abortion for $650.

4. *DIY (Do-It-Yourself)*—Are you the kind of person who does a lot of research? Someone who knows what you want? Do you want to avoid the bustle—and waiting time—of a busy clinic? Would you like to perform your abortion in the comfort of your own home? Take a pill today and choose when you bleed anytime in the next three days, safely, completely, in your own home. Full instructions and educational video are included, and our 24-hour advice line is open to you. This option is available only in early pregnancy, and some restrictions apply. You can have this experience on your own terms for $550.

5. *Deluxe Spa Treatment*—Get the luxury and personal attention you deserve!! Check into our special suite at the Jetson Hotel where you will meet with our experienced guide, who will be available to you for your abortion experience. After extensive orientation for you and your partner or family, enjoy a relaxing massage and jacuzzi. Full emotional support is available to you and those close to you, tailored to your needs. A full range of sedatives and pain relievers to choose from make for a pain-free procedure by our experienced and friendly physician. Recover in your suite and choose from three relaxing options: a foot massage, a mud-pack facial, or a rebalancing of your shakras by our expert Reiki master. Then, enjoy room service from a four-star restaurant. Our guide will be available to review aftercare and discuss any emotional issues. Full cable and choice of video entertainment are available. Enjoy our feather pillow beds for a good night's sleep. $3,000 is the price for the total package.

6. *Spiritual Journey*—Ending a pregnancy is not just a physical act, but also a spiritual process. Meet with our spirit healer and guide a week in ad-

vance to plan the ritual journey that will meet your spiritual needs. Native American (Taino clan tradition), Eastern philosophy, nature-inspired (pagan), or custom-designed ceremonies are available to you and to the support people who will accompany you on your spirit quest. Or, design your own rituals with the help of our experienced guides. Check in to our mountain retreat Friday night for a ritual cleansing and spiritual preparation. Have the surgical procedure when you are ready for a separation of paths with the spirit child within you. Miscarriage with medicines and herbs is also available early in pregnancy. A follow-up ritual a year and a day later is included in this package for $5,000.

7. *Full Emotional Support*—Deciding to end a pregnancy may well be the most difficult emotional crisis a woman or couple may face. Our experienced counselor will spend two hours with you and a support person of your choice, and your appointment will be scheduled for between two and seven days later. The counselor will explore relationship and identity issues, personal goals, religious and spiritual concerns, and will offer interactive skill building to you and your significant other. A choice of three self-help books is included, with additional suggestions for grief work and emotional aftercare. The procedure will be performed by an experienced, kindly physician in privacy with your choice of pain relievers and sedatives. You may also choose to miscarry with medicine taken at home ($100 extra). Two follow-up visits with our licensed and experienced counselors are available one week and one month after the procedure. Consultation by phone with the clergy or spiritual leader from your belief system is included, if desired, for $1,000.

8. *Discount Package*—A basic no-frills package is available for women who need no ambiance or additional support. No additional sedation is available without additional cost. Licensed physicians perform the safe surgery in less than five minutes. Expect delays and waiting time. No support people are allowed in the counseling or medical areas. If you want to spend the money on something else, this package may work for you, but we encourage you to consult our website for a complete overview of the abortion experience. This option costs $250, cash only.

9. *Abortions Anonymous*—For the woman who wants to tell no one, keep it secret, and have no record of having been there, we offer an anonymous service with private hours. Counseling is offered to explore any feelings and potential emotional side effects. No names are taken. This option costs $950, cash only.

Note: All materials for emotional healing, aftercare, and information on women's wellness is available on our website, www.pregnancyoptions. info.

Disclaimer: Matters of pregnancy, including abortion, are profound and complex, and they should be attended to in accordance with your personal needs and preferences. The medical process, though not usually complicated, still needs your complete cooperation and disclosure of information. Our first concern is your safety and health, and medical concerns supersede all other plans, agreements, and considerations. Thank you for your understanding.

Do you have any questions?"

In most utopian scenarios, price tags are not offered because we assume money will be replaced by a better system of valuation. However, we have included these imaginary prices, in 2002 dollars, as a way to think about what an experience is worth to us.

It may seem strange to think about market forces at work in abortion services, but, actually, the stigma long associated with abortion has kept the principles of market economics from working for the consumer of abortion care. Abortion fees have been historically low in relation to medical inflation, and consumers have few choices.

Abortion services, by and large, have not changed much in the last thirty years. If people were given real choices of how they wanted their abortion experience to be the market would reflect a range of price tags as well as desires. When the stigma of abortion dissipates, women will actually have more choices and more recognition of the range of their feelings, circumstances, and needs in facing an unintended pregnancy.

As providers, we are impressed most by the women's stories. Each story is different, complex, and nuanced, depending on her history, her stage of life, the support she has, how she reacts to this turn of events, and many many other factors. It is difficult to represent this variety of stories in the rich detail each one deserves.

Indeed, we are painfully aware that we are sometimes the only ones who hear these stories, since society is largely deaf to the real experience of abortion. An abortion provider we know said, "A woman can have a profound experience while she is in the clinic, but when she leaves, what is on the other side of the door? Frequently, silence."

The future of abortion must recognize these separate and different realities of the millions of women who have had and will have an abortion. We live in a multicultural society which sometimes feels like a culture-less society. American culture does not offer much helpful advice about pregnancy loss. Sometimes we say to our patients who choose abortion, but also feel a sense of loss, "There is no Hallmark card for what you are feeling. No one will drop by with a casserole. You have to figure out your own grieving." In a future and ideal world, the culture will find many ways of offering solace to women in dealing with the social and emotional aspects of an unintended pregnancy.

Of course, in our ideal world, birth control works, sex goes beyond trading fluids to a trading of souls, and society is understanding of the emotional and spiritual issues in the rare situations in which pregnancies happen and are not desirable. Of course, we also realize that even in the future, enlightened or not, people will take risks with sex, love will still be blind, and, abortion will still be needed.

However, in our vision of the future, abortion is a non-issue; pregnancy is regarded as a profound and life-altering event, and everything about it is treated as sacred—even, or perhaps especially, its ending. Children are miraculous and welcomed, miscarriages are mourned, and abortions are considered carefully and carried out lovingly, with the support and comfort of the woman's community. Men may be involved in all aspects, and grandparents, aunts, uncles, siblings, and friends rally around to support the woman in her chosen path.

At the same time, a couple's decision not to have children is equally honored. The pregnant woman recognizes that she is the gatekeeper of life, and she creates a special place for herself to consider this question: "Is this the right time for new life to come into the world through my body?"

In this question, at least, there is no difference between the future and the present. Every day thousands of women, and men, answer some variation of this question. It may be surprising to anyone outside the abortion field that the query "Do I want an abortion?" is not the question at all, but one answer (and usually the last resort) to the real question about what we want from life and what we can offer to life. Most people we talk to say, "I never thought I would be here" or "I always thought I was against abortion." The denial around the possibility of being faced with an unintended pregnancy is nearly universal, yet 43 percent of all women will have an abortion before they are forty-five years old.

When the question becomes a real one for you, it is like a bright light shines on your life. Frequently, the light seems harsh and all the flaws show up, but sometimes you can see the perfect parts, too. One of our patients said, "Since I've been making this decision, I have been appreciating my three daughters. They are such a blessing to me."

Here is a partial list of women's concerns:

"Where am I going?"

"How will a child affect my other children? My career? My education?"

"Who is with me on this journey? What do they think about me and my life?"

"What are my beliefs about life, death, and doing the right thing?"

"How is my health? Who is depending on me to care for them?"

"How strong is my relationship with my partner, my family, my friends?"

"What can I handle financially, emotionally, physically?"

In this internal quest for the right decision, a woman soon notices that she is part of a web of relationships where what happens to each person affects others. Obviously, the woman is the nexus for many threads, and her own desires, needs, and strengths get the most consideration. The threads connecting her to partner, children, and family must be fully considered. It is important to realize that the decisions each woman makes affect the entire web, from the earth we stand on to the spirituality and culture of a society.

When we thought about the future of abortion, we knew it had to include many different perspectives and experiences. We also knew that the interesting questions were not about legal rights or access, but about the quality of the abortion experience. We realized that the question about abortion for the twenty-first century had to be, "How do you want your abortion?"

The answer to the future of abortion is to be found in many people standing in the future and answering the above question. This "Stand in the Future" technique has enabled us to think about a world in which we would like to live. The technique is also valuable in understanding how to map a course from the present to that vision of the future.

It is tempting for those of us in the abortion field to say, "If we could just get rid of restrictive laws" or "Let's get rid of the stigma around abortion." What is more useful in shifting our perspective is imagining a utopian world in which each of us constructs how we would like abortion—indeed, all pregnancy experiences—to be. We are not looking for reform as much as transformation. When we focus on how we want an experience to be, often we discover that meaningful change is within our own power right now, in the present time.

Difficult to introduce without "spilling the beans," the essay below ventures boldly where pro-utopian activists must go, however reluctantly, namely, the indelicate problems (challenges) that keep males and females unnecessarily and painfully apart. Written in an engaging style, it helps us explore "heavy" matters with a light touch. It surfaces costly errors in a forgiving way. It clarifies what a New Manhood and Womanhood might resemble. And it closes on a welcome note of hope . . . for us all.

29. Read 'Em and Weep, Boys

John E. Glass

Disclaimer: Please note that the following essay contains an embedded sociological intervention. By reading it, you will be exposing yourself to the possibility of change. Maybe even the possibility of profound transformation. Heck, maybe even the initial inspiration for creating a utopia. So . . . read it at your own risk.

For Males Only

Male privilege has been, and remains, a considerable hindrance to the emergence of utopia. In fact, this "thing" has inhibited the emergence of utopia for millennia. And you and I have it.

So, I want to help us discover something about ourselves that some of us have previously been totally unaware of.

Okay, now, are you ready? Do you want to help create a utopia? Well, if you do, then there are certain moves that need to be taken. I am not sure about all of it, but I can tell you I am pretty convinced that the following twelve steps need to be taken, and need to be taken by all men if we want to have any shot at everyone's soon being able to make more utopian lives for themselves.[1]

So, get ready to first "read 'em and weep, boys," and then resolve to do it all a hellova lot better.

1. We admit we are drunk with male privilege, and that our treatment of women and other oppressed groups is abhorrent.
2. We agree we are ignorant of the extent to which our privilege has infected our lives, and we now commit to shutting up and listening to others about how much it has and still does.
3. We make a decision to turn our lives over to the principles of responsibility, accountability, critical self-examination, equality, and allegiance to women and other oppressed groups. And we work hard to end male privilege and entitlement.
4. We make a searching and fearless inventory of ourselves, identifying all of the ways in which we have and currently do maintain our privilege, and ways in which we may have caused harm to women and other oppressed groups in the past through the invoking of our privilege.
5. We admit to a woman (preferably a woman well-versed in feminism) all that we learned in step 4 above.
6. We become entirely ready to be challenged by others (and ourselves) on all aspects of our privilege.
7. We boldly ask others to confront us about our privilege, and we humbly listen without any comment, taking in every word and considering for at least three days what we heard (this step may also include writing down what others say, so we can reflect on it for

those three days) before even thinking about what to say in response. (You will know when you have mastered this step when you have absolutely nothing to say in response, except "Thank you.")

8. We make a list of the ways in which we have (and still do) inflicted ourselves on others by the invocation of our privilege (especially women and other oppressed groups) and specific individuals/groups if applicable.

9. Instead of making direct amends to those we may have harmed by our privilege (we chose not to do this because in all likelihood we would end up exerting our privilege and convincing the others that it was actually *them* that harmed *us*), we share this list with either the same person in step 4 above or someone else (preferably the same person in step 4 to ensure our accountability).

10. We continue to be ever vigilant of our privilege and the ways we use it, and when we are aware that we have used it, we promptly admit it and plan how not to do it again, followed up by a commitment to enact that same plan.

11. We seek through humble and respectful interaction with women (and members of other groups that are oppressed) ways in which to increase our awareness of our privilege and subsequently reduce it, along with ways to further live out egalitarian principles.

12. Having gotten an inkling of the extent to which our lives are dominated by our privilege as a result of working all of these previous steps, we commit to ending male privilege in all its forms and practicing these principles in all of our affairs.

For Men Only

People who do not have male privilege (basically women) will read these steps and say, "Wow, somebody got it right!" They are not angered by them. They are not angered by them because they do not have them. Those of us who are identified as "male" in our society (and I am not sure what society is not included in this) do have them, and do get angered by someone saying that they have them. It is as simple as that.

Now, there are other forms of privilege, and chances are you have those, too. I know I do. I will let you find out what those others are on your own, though I am still recovering from going through *these* twelve steps. (A hint, they have to do with ethnicity, social class, education, access to power, and so on).

There is not enough space here for me to write more about male privilege. Believe it or not, the best people to educate us about it (actually about privilege in *any* form) are those that do not have it. So, since I do have it, I am probably not the best person to teach you about it. I still cannot see it all the time in myself.

It is enough for a start for you to know that you have it, and that somehow it contributes to the inhibition of utopia making (hey, you just worked Step 1!). I cite some references below to assist us in finding out more about it.

For Men Only (Conclusion)

You did well to face the twelve-step challenge and resolve to do something healthy about it. You are in a better position to help create that utopia you deserve, but first you must let go of the privilege. Trust me, privilege in *any* form serves no one. It causes only harm. So, do no harm to anyone, ever. Take care, and take responsibility for yourself, and go and help create that damn utopia.

For Women Only (Conclusion)

I can only speak for myself, but if I could speak for all of my gender, this is what I would say: Thank you for being who you are. Thank you. There is no way we can ever repay you. We are especially grateful that you treat us far better than we have ever treated you. Thanks for caring for our children, for putting up with our immaturity, for not doing away with us entirely. Hang in there, there's hope for the male gender yet.

For Everyone (Conclusion)

I pray the utopia we deserve—men and women alike—we soon craft together. If what I have written contributes in some small way, I will be forever grateful.

Note

1. Although the ubiquitous twelve steps is the primary vehicle for the delivery of the intervention, it is used solely for heuristic purposes. In no way am I advocating the emergence of one more twelve-step program. In some ways, this would be anathema to the intent of this intervention.

Further Reading

Clarke, D.A. "Male Privilege," 1981. http://www.tufffemme.com/femmers/121599 femmers.html.
Daly, Mary. *Gyn-Ecology*. Boston: Beacon, 1990.
Hobgood, Mary E. *Dismantling Privilege*. Cleveland: Pilgrim, 2000.
Jensen, Derrick. *The Culture of Make Believe*. New York: Context, 2002.
Kivel, Paul. *Men's Work*. Center City, MN: Hazeldon, 1992.

Schacht, Steven. "Teaching about Being an Oppressor," 2002; http://www.nostatusquo
.com/Schacht/teaching.html.

Reference

Ellis, C., and A. Bochner, eds. *Composing Ethnography: Alternative Forms of Qualitative Writing*. London: AltaMira, 1996.

---

*Finding our way, an extraordinary lifelong challenge, has a special component
in the choosing (and re-choosing) of a job and a career . . . perhaps a dozen
job changes and half as many career changes over the course of a work life.
Help with this sort of decision-making is available from a conceptual tool
popular with serious futurists. It identifies three major types of future, and
thereby facilitates better-than-ever thinking (and feeling) about vocational options. As gracefully explained below, the tool makes more likely securing relevant utopian notions—and thereby contributing "to the good things of life."*

30. Choosing Your Future

Wendell Bell

During more than four decades of teaching, I have often served as a sounding
board for students who were deciding what to do with their lives. I learned
that I could be helpful by listening carefully to them and asking questions to
find out what they really wanted to do. Usually that did not take long. Then,
I urged them to state their goals clearly and to examine them both in the light
of alternatives and their own values. I asked them to imagine, if they pursued
these goals, how their future lives would be ten, twenty, and more years ahead.
After that, if they still thought that was what they wanted to do, I advised
them to go for it.

Not all cases, though, were as simple as that. I remember one young man,
let's call him Bill, whose dilemma was that his father was pressuring him to
become a lawyer, while his grandfather was urging him to become a doctor.
Whichever he decided to do would please one but displease the other, a double
bind. After an hour or more of conversation, during which, among other things,
he rejected the possibility of becoming both a doctor *and* a lawyer and focusing
on legal cases dealing with medicine, I was still puzzled about what he himself
wanted. Finally, exasperated, he said, "Okay, what I really want to be is a
stand-up comedian."

I was surprised, but not totally thrown. (After all, Yale graduate Garry
Trudeau's *Doonesbury* comic strip appears in newspapers daily. Careers such

as that are not inconceivable.) I asked him to tell me more. As he talked, it became clear that he was serious and had done a lot of thinking about it. We explored his image of his future self as a comedian.

We looked at the uncertainties and obstacles, the chanciness of it, the potential lack of stability and security, what it might mean to his future wife and children, and how he knew that he had enough talent to succeed. We also talked about the creative challenge, fun, satisfaction, and, possibly, even the financial success that he thought it would give him. Clearly, in Bill's mind, being a stand-up comedian was a viable utopian idea.

In the end, he was determined, so I suggested that he talk to his father and grandfather, explaining his hopes to them and saying that he wanted to try being a comedian for a year or so. If it did not work out, he would go either to law or medical school, satisfied that he had given his dream a chance.

Some weeks later I received a call from Bill's father who wanted to know what kind of an idiot I was to advise his son to do a dumb thing like becoming a stand-up comedian. Given his father's anger, I could understand why Bill shifted the "blame" onto me.

My talk with Bill was years ago. Since then, I've learned more about how people can make good choices and take the right actions to create desirable futures, not only for themselves, but also for the people around them and even, sometimes, for the communities and societies in which they live. In a nutshell, my advice is simple: Consider what is possible, what is probable, and what is preferable. When you have done that and have made a decision, pursue your goal with tenacity.

The Possible

First of all, one must consider what is possible. Most people most of the time fail to do this adequately. They do not take into account anything close to the full range of alternatives for their future. Rather, they usually consider only a few of the real possibilities. As a result, many people trudge through life ignorant of most of the things that they could have been, some of which they might have liked better than what they become.

To explore all the possibilities, look at the present situation and the opportunities in the world around you, your own talents and values, and the resources available to you. Also, break out of the straitjacket of conventional thinking. Include, but go beyond, the expectations of your family, friends, and socio-cultural setting. Stretch your imagination, asking not only what is, but also what could be.

Remember that present possibilities for the future are real. They exist, even if they are only potential. Some things, for example, are breakable, but may never be broken; achievable, but may never be achieved; or buildable, but may never be built. Just as some people are teachable, but will never be taught;

curable, but will never be cured; and funny, but will never be stand-up comedians. Thus, we ought to search the present for clues as to what is possible.

Moreover, all decision making is future oriented. We all live within a constantly moving stream of time. Although we make decisions to act in particular
ways now in the present, the consequences of our acts always occur in the
future. Thus, we ought to scan the emerging future. To make informed and
intelligent decisions we must think ahead, charting the trends of social change
as well as forecasting the consequences of our own actions.

Although Bill did somewhat better than some people, because at least he
looked beyond the conventional careers urged on him by his family, he did
not do a satisfactory job of searching the horizon for a variety of other
possibilities.

For example, ask yourself how the world is changing. How will technological revolutions in energy, information, materials, and genetics affect your future? What new occupations are coming in renewable energy resources, in the
Internet and other high-tech means of communication, in the development of
new building materials, and in a coming age where everything from food to
human beings can be genetically altered?

Ask yourself, too, what new expertise will be needed as globalization continues and peoples of different countries increasingly interact and come to
depend more and more on each other. If Asian countries become the driving
economic forces of the future, what opportunities will they offer for new
careers?

What new possibilities will occur if nanotechnology becomes widespread,
for example in medical therapies? Should you become a specialist in the design
of personal robots because such robots are one of the waves of the future?
What new services will be needed for an increasingly aged population? What
new job opportunities will come with the exploration and colonization of
space? Will housing and transportation be different in the future than now? If
so, what new occupations will they require? What about education? Will it be
increasingly carried on at all ages? Will there be new Internet universities?
How will new information and communication technologies alter conventional
colleges and universities? In these developments, what are the possibilities for
new professions?

Of course, not everything and anything you might imagine is possible, but
there are two kinds of errors that we can make when thinking about what is
possible. We can err by believing things to be impossible when, in fact, they
are possible, or we can err by believing things to be possible when they are
not. Although both types of errors can lead to bad decisions, try not to dismiss
what seems impossible too quickly, if it is something that you want. The reason
is that when you try the impossible and fail, the world as it really is impinges
on your consciousness and invites you to change your beliefs. You learn. (And
if you have taken a course in which the professor has told you that "the world

as it really is" does not exist, then politely ask that professor if he or she would like to jump in front of a speeding truck. Splat! End of argument.)

To the contrary, when you do not even try to do something because you falsely believe it is impossible, you do not learn. Such untested false beliefs become the walls of a prison you construct for yourself, walls that confine you as much as if they were made of some of those plastic wrappings around packages that no normal human can open without a crowbar. Thus, when you are making decisions about your future, consider all the alternative possibilities relevant to your hopes and desires that really exist in the present. Free your powers of observation, imagination, and creativity.

The Probable

Second, ask yourself, what is probable? There are a lot of things that may be possible, but they are not equally likely. For example, under certain conditions, nearly all the people on the earth might learn to speak Chinese in the next twenty years, but it does not seem very likely given present trends. Once you have surveyed the alternative possibilities relevant to your interests and hopes, consider how likely they are. Do not base important life decisions on forecasts that have low probabilities of actually occurring, unless you want something enough to take a large risk of failure.

Here the methods of futures studies can be of help. Futurists do not look into crystal balls or watch their navels and meditate in order to discern the future. Rather, they deduce probabilities for alternative futures from a variety of data. They use existing knowledge about causes and effects; they chart long-term trends and project them into the future.

Futurists use the results of survey research into how people intend to behave in the future—for example, when and what they plan to buy or for whom they intend to vote. They study the opinions of experts in particular fields about future advances in their fields. They do computer simulation and modeling based on a variety of assumptions as, for example, in studying the future of the life-sustaining capacities of the earth and population growth. They engage in gaming, looking at the interaction of players in the game for clues to the outcome of real-life situations as they do at the War Gaming Department of the Naval War College. They scan and monitor activities and social indicators, including the world's newspapers, in order to detect changes. They use other methods, too.

With knowledge of your present social setting and accurate forecasts of the future, you can increase the wisdom of your decisions and the effectiveness of your actions. If you had been around in the early part of the twentieth century, for example, you would not have wanted to go into any business dependent on the horse and buggy unless you were collecting relics for a museum, since the automobile was then beginning to replace them.

In addition to social trends, you ought to consider your choices and the consequences of your own actions in any given situation. Ask yourself, for example, what is my most probable future if I keep doing what I have been doing? (Perhaps that has been serving burgers at McDonald's, which, of course, is a lot more respectable than loafing at home freeloading off your parents.)

Ask yourself, to take the choices that Bill faced, what is my most probable future if I go to law school, or medical school, or become a stand-up comedian? These are alternative and contingent scenarios for the future. What different scenarios can you think of for your own future? What probabilities can you assign to them, if you did choose this one or that one and worked to achieve it?

In sum, you should consider social trends and their probable future trajectories as they may affect your future life. In addition, you ought to assess your own possible actions, and those of other people who may influence events of concern to you, for their probable consequences for your future.

The Preferable

Third, ask yourself, what is preferable? What kind of a future do you really want for yourself? Even though you have discovered what is possible and what is probable, you cannot intelligently choose what to do until you also know which of your alternative possible futures are the most desirable to you.

Some of the goals that people use to make such personal judgments include having good health, a happy marriage and family life with children, and having close friends. Also, they usually take into account doing something that will give them a sufficient income to have a comfortable life, although many people are not interested simply in making enormous amounts of money and becoming extremely wealthy. In making their life's decisions, people often give considerable weight to being good at what they do, having a sense of teamwork in their work or community activities, and being appreciated and respected by others.

At a more profound level, people hope to lead meaningful lives and to feel at peace and harmony with themselves about their relations with others. Moreover, they wish to have some control over their lives, some sense of freedom. In addition, most people strive to find some moral purpose to their lives.

Put another way, most of the world's people want a certain amount of freedom and personal well-being. They want good health, a job, a decent level of living, decent housing, a happy home life, education, and opportunities for their children. They also want to fulfill their obligations to other people, and they balance their desires for freedom with being responsible and loving members of families, communities, and societies.

For most people, these things taken together are not always easily achieved.

They take hard work, effective decision making, and, perhaps most of all, tenacity. No doubt you will face disappointments, obstacles, and setbacks. When you do, reassess your methods and even your goals as necessary because things seldom work out exactly as planned, and because we constantly get new information and feedback. But do not give up easily. Although you may have to change your strategies, be persistent. Paying proper attention to the preferable, to your basic values, and to a balance among them can keep you from becoming one of those people who hate their jobs but have twenty-five more years until retirement.

Once you know what is possible, probable, and preferable for you, stop and consider one more thing: How can the life that you choose help to create the kind of world in which you—and your children and grandchildren—would like to live?

Creating a World in Which You Want to Live

The values that you use to judge your preferable future, of course, are not yours alone. Many of them are widely shared by other people as well, not only by others in your own country but by people nearly everywhere on earth. Such values often express the wisdom of millennia of human development. They are not arbitrary; rather, they are part of an evolving system of human morality which gives meaning to our lives and more or less guides us in our actions.

Such values derive in part from the type of bio-psychological being we are. For example, we cannot survive without air, water, food, sleep, and personal security. As human beings, we have other needs for comfort and flourishing, such as needs for clothing, shelter, companionship, affection, and sex. Thus, the human community has learned to value such things.

Still other human values derive from the nature of group living. In addition to our bio-psychological needs, we have social needs. For example, our needs for love, approval, emotional support, and communication can be satisfied adequately only by interaction with other humans. Moreover, social life itself has shaped human values. Morality importantly functions to make social life possible. It encourages people to live and work together and to learn from one another. Through the trust, cooperation, honesty, and mutual regulation that it provides, morality promotes the multiple payoffs of organized human effort that allow individuals and societies to thrive far beyond what would be possible if each individual tried to work alone, in isolation from or in conflict with others.

Today, there is an emerging global ethic. It is partially described in many documents, including the United Nations Universal Declaration of Human Rights and the Parliament of World's Religions' *Towards a Global Ethic*. All persons, both religious and secular, can affirm the ethical convictions contained in these documents.

Values in the global ethic include individual responsibility; treating others as we wish them to treat us; respect for life; treating all other people with dignity, patience, understanding and acceptance of one another; forgiveness; solidarity and relatedness with other peoples of the world; kindliness and generosity; caring for others; compassion; love for one another; equality between men and women; nonviolence; economic and social justice; peace and global order; nature-friendly ways of life; respect for human rights; constancy and trustworthiness, truthfulness and honesty; moderation and modesty; loyalty; safety and security; freedom as long as no harm is done to others; tolerance; and sexuality that expresses and reinforces a loving relationship lived by equal partners.

Do we now live in such a world? Well, yes and no. Although there are many violations of such moral rules, many people, perhaps most of the time, live up to them within their families and neighborhoods, even in their casual social contacts. Some people certainly do not—those, for example, who are locked in deadly conflict with others, who are living in poverty without jobs or hope, or who are dominated by greed and narrow conceptions of self-interest. The question is—Would you like to live in such a moral world?

Or would you rather live in a world whose life-sustaining capacities were constantly under threat by air, water, and land pollution, in a world dominated by prejudice, hatred, theft, greed, arrogance, mistrust, hostility, violence, envy, jealousy, resentment, terror, oppression, torture, mutilation, killing, ruthlessness and brutality, lies and deceit, swindling and hypocrisy, demagoguery, fanaticism and intolerance, opportunism, domination, and the degradation of people?

Most of us, obviously, would prefer to live in a good society, characterized by peace and human decency, dignity, well-being, and freedom. Wouldn't you? If so, then, when you are choosing what you want to do with your life, think about how your life might contribute to creating a good society.

Does this mean that you have to give up caring for your own needs and hopes? Definitely not. Your first moral obligation is to yourself, to take care of yourself and not to be an unnecessary burden on others. You are being morally responsible when you seek your own survival, comfort, and self-fulfillment. Beyond that, it is also your moral obligation to do no harm to others and to help others when you are able, without impoverishing yourself.

Remember that you are choosing not only a career, but also a life and the kind of person that you will become. No matter what career path you choose, think of yourself as the world—even if only some small part of it—for those people with whom you share your life. Like most of us, you may not be able to control the actions of nations and multinational corporations, or the momentous events of history, but you can learn to control yourself in the way that you treat other people.

Thus, it is within your power to create a world of self-restraint, empathy, understanding, and generosity for each person with whom you interact. Within that part of the lives of others that you constitute, you can—as each of us can—create the good society that you hope will become the future. Such behavior on your part is not mere selfless altruism, because what goes around comes around. As you act, you create the world, not only for others but also for yourself.

Conclusion

Looking back, I wonder if Bill ever tried to be a stand-up comedian or if he became a lawyer or a doctor. I wonder, too, if he even remembers his college dream. Whatever he is doing, I hope, of course, that he is happy and leading a useful and self-fulfilling life. Knowing what I now know, though, I wish that I had had a chance to tell him the following:

"When all is said and done, Bill, it is your life. Thus, after you have examined what is possible, what is probable, and what is preferable for your own future, and after you have listened to what your family members (including your irate Dad) have to say, and you have respectfully explained your views to them, if—all things considered—you still want to be a comedian, then do it.

"You may face some pain. But be what you want to be. For nearly everyone, it takes some pain—hard work, self-discipline, sacrifice, and risk—to lead a satisfying life. The only right answers are perspicacity, patience, perspiration, and persistence."

Then, I would add, "But Bill, think not only of your career. Think also of the mark that you are leaving on the world and the kind of person that you want to be. Yes, of course, try to be successful at whatever you do, but also remember that you are more than your job, your wealth, your fame, or your power.

"Try to be a decent, understanding, generous, and caring person. As you live your life, be concerned not only about yourself, but also about the freedom and well-being of the other people who share this planet with you. Show concern, too, for the as yet nonexistent future generations who will follow you, so that their future will be better than the past and present. Do so because it is the right thing to do. Do so, too, for your own self-respect.

"Finally, Bill, remember that there are many ways to contribute to the good things of life. Lawyers can do so by bringing order and justice. Doctors can do so by bringing good health and longer life. Comedians, too, can do so by bringing a genuine smile to a face and laughter to the world."

References

Barbieri, Eleonora Masini. *Why Futures Studies?* London: Grey Seal, 1993.
Bell, Wendell. "A Community of Futurists and the State of the Futures Field." *Futures* 34, nos. 3–4 (April/May 2002): 235–47.

———. *Foundations of Futures Studies.* 2 vols. New Brunswick, NJ: Transaction, 1997.
———. "Making People Responsible: The Possible, the Probable, and the Preferable." *American Behavioral Scientist* 42, no. 3 (November/December 1998): 323–39.
———. "New Futures and the Eternal Struggle between Good and Evil." *Journal of Futures Studies* 5, no. 2 (November 2000): 1–20.
Coates, Joseph F., John B. Mahaffie, and Andy Hines. *2025: Scenarios of US and Global Society Reshaped by Science and Technology.* Akron, OH: Oakhill, 1996.
Dator, James A., ed. *Advancing Futures: Futures Studies in Higher Education.* Westport, CT: Greenwood Press, 2002.
The Futurist 35, no. 6 (November-December 2001).
Hicks, David. *Lessons for the Future: The Missing Dimension in Education.* London: RoutledgeFalmer, 2002.
Küng, Hans. *Global Responsibility: In Search of a New World Ethic.* New York: Crossroad, 1991.
Parliament of the World's Religions. "Towards a Global Ethic: An Initial Declaration." Chicago, IL (August 28-September 5), 1993.
Shostak, Arthur B., ed. *Utopian Thinking in Sociology: Creating the Good Society.* Washington, DC: American Sociological Association, 2001.
Slaughter, Richard A., ed. *The Knowledge Base of Futures Studies.* 3 vols. Hawthorn, Victoria, Australia: DDM Media Group, 1996.

X. Choices: Societal

In your utopian society, what would organizations, in general, and businesses, in particular, resemble? What do they owe society? In turn, what do we owe them? How should we assess businesses, especially their actual worth? How likely is reform of a business when necessary, and how likely is backsliding thereafter? What part does an organization's communication climate play in all of this? What viable utopian ideas might business be well advised to honor anew?

31. The Journey Counts Most: Building Deserving Organizations

Douglas Bedell

"Your trusted guide on your financial journey," proclaimed billboards announcing a bank merger. It may be a great idea, but there is a problem with claiming trustworthiness as a corporate journey begins. Trust is earned during a journey, and it has continually to be renewed. It cannot be self-conferred at the start.

There is nothing wrong with aspiring to be an institution that builds and maintains trusting relationships. That is a form of utopianism in progress, and it is to be encouraged.

Unfortunately, organizational leaders do not always give trusting relationships a particularly high priority. If they do, they may lack awareness of all that it takes to nurture and sustain them. Bold, energetic managers may be handicapped from the start. Removing blind spots that block the development of deserving organizations is a key need in our economic system, a truly viable utopian objective.

We have passed through an industrial revolution into an information economy, and we still do not know how to value organizations, how to assess their actual worth. The arbiters of corporate value have it largely wrong, and people with money invested in the stock market increasingly are catching on.[1] Wall Street decrees that quarterly earnings are the appropriate indicators of value and, in its streaming depiction of the economy, CNBC-TV hypes the earnings reports. But how many analysts know, close up, what is really happening in organizations to merit trust and confidence? How much bearing do longer-term or deeper-down factors have as the television tape flashes by?

As Enron demonstrated, a booming organization can go bust before its actual nature becomes known. "In fact, earnings have no predictive value whatsoever," Harris Collingwood, a former senior editor of the *Harvard Business Review*, wrote in the *New York Times Magazine*. "Rapidly growing profits," he observed, "are as likely to be produced by accounting tricks as leadership skill."[2]

Organizations need somehow to be valued by the quality and acumen of the relationships taking place within them. That is a utopian ideal worth pursuing. To what degree are commitment and creativity, along with respect and regard for individual capacity and potential, driving a business? Although these factors are not easy to assess, they are the truly critical ones.

Case Study: The 1979 Accident at the Three Mile Island (TMI) Unit 2

Afflicted with hubris and overconfidence, the nuclear plant's designers and managers thought they had anticipated everything that could go seriously wrong in a reactor. They were confident that backup systems would always keep the fuel core covered by heat-removing water. A loss-of-coolant accident would never happen.

Thus, when a puzzling sequence of events began at Unit 2, the possibility that it could lead to the core's becoming uncovered was not considered. The control room operators had not been equipped to defend against something that would never happen. Mistakenly, the emergency cooling pumps were turned off, and the superheated core *did* lose some of its coolant for a while.

The accident's salutary result was a major reversal in the approach to nuclear plant emergencies. *Recognize* that the worst may happen, and deal with it up front. When alarms go off, ensure that the core is covered before you worry about what broke. With this change in the mind-set, that is relatively easy to do. Nuclear plant operators are now trained to confirm that reactors retain cooling before turning to anything else.

Even so, there is more to responsible management than hindsight in the training department. Building a safety culture at a nuclear plant—one worthy of the public's trust—requires that the roles and capacities of everyone working at the plant be respected and reinforced. Mistakes do not matter as much as the response they get. If someone makes a mistake, but owns up to it—reports it and learns from it—there should be no penalty. If a mistake is covered up, there should be no tolerance.

Going from Good to Bad

General Public Utilities (GPU), TMI's owner at the time of the Unit 2 accident, formed the GPU Nuclear Corporation (GPUN) to operate its two nuclear plants afterward. GPUN sought to institutionalize safety by instilling core values across the company. Its defining values became integrity and trust, respect for nuclear technology, accountability, teamwork, and cost effectiveness.

GPUN's employees themselves were asked (in a series of meetings and feedback sessions) to identify behaviors in support of the values, and they did. The system was not touted outside the company, and it might not have been credited anyway. Nevertheless, it became deeply rooted in the plants, and it was accompanied by open and constructive relationships with the communities around them.

With the commitment of its employees effectively mustered, GPUN restarted the undamaged TMI Unit 1, got high operational grades, and began setting world records for uninterrupted runs at Unit 1. GPU's fortunes overall rebounded, until its directors made the unfortunate decision, as deregulation took hold, to sell all of its generating stations and become a wires-only utility.

Sadly, TMI's new owners, the Chicago-based Exelon Corporation and British Energy have not seemed as attuned to relational values in the workplace or the community. As the plant's operator, Exelon has taken a more draconian approach to plant operations, and it virtually shut down TMI's community relations program. The Harrisburg, Pennsylvania, *Patriot-News* reported in spring 2002 that human resource directors at Exelon's TMI, Limerick, and Peach Bottom plants had resigned and that the human resources manager at Oyster Creek was seeking a severance package after less than a year on the job. "We recognize that there are problems," an Exelon spokesman said. "We've admitted it internally. We're trying to resolve it."[3] We can hope they will, but the indications are that an overly controlling management took a wrong turn. [As this volume went to press, Exelon announced it was considering selling its share of TMI and Oyster Creek.]

On Taking a Viable Utopian Stance

Why do wrong turns keep happening at this point in our economic development? Shouldn't we be a bit closer to the utopian ideals of responsiveness and trustworthiness after more than a century of experience at industrial management?

It is true that, for nuclear plants, the newly heightened threat of terrorism makes relational issues more complex. It may not be a good idea to give plant tours as readily as did GPU Nuclear. But a technology that continues to require public understanding and support can ill afford to turn away from the public, or slight the capacities of its employees.

Over and over, we find the hierarchial style of management still has too tight a hold on the way we do business, the way we run organizations. Top-down direction still unduly limits initiative and responsiveness. There is too much emphasis on short-term profit over longer-term prospects. We do not yet know how to correct for the subtleties of management style in valuing organizations, despite all the cheering that has been done in recent decades for empowerment, employee involvement, teamwork, and shareholder value.

To be trustworthy, a business has to function in the public interest with, as W. Edwards Deming, one of our management prophets, put it, "constancy of purpose."[4] In a knowledge economy, the dispersal of authority and accountability among the people who do the work is critical. Management sets the aim and enables people using their hearts and minds to fulfill it. Leadership is shared, objectives are widely understood, standards are maintained, sound procedures are followed, and personal needs are respected. These appear to be more distant utopian principles at this point in our "post-industrial society" than they ought to be.

Organizational climate really matters. In 1960 Douglas McGregor wrote in *The Human Side of Enterprise*, "More important than the existence of particular policies or the formal statements concerning them are evidences of how they are administered."[5] The overall communication climate in an organization is more important than anything else.

Good communication does not just happen. It takes a patient, highly intentional approach, starting with the CEO, to make a true learning organization. Clear, consistent values, training in teamwork and leadership, the banishment of defensiveness, close connections with customers, receptivity to ideas and insights wherever they might be voiced, and the continual digestion and circulation of what is being learned (in the form of corporate stories) are all vital.

These are worthy goals to pursue. Confidence in our economic system requires they be increasingly honored, not tomorrow, but at this very time in our journey.

Notes

1. Kurt Eichenwald, "Audacious Climb to Success Ended in a Dizzying Plunge," *New York Times*, January 13, 2002, p. 1.
2. Harris Collingwood, "The Earnings Cult," *New York Times Magazine*, June 9, 2002, p. 68.
3. Brett Lieberman, "Bonuses Reduce Discord at TMI," *Patriot-News* (Harrisburg, PA), April 29, 2002, p. 1.
4. W. Edwards Deming, *Out of the Crisis* (Cambridge, MA: MIT Press, 1982), p. 23.
5. Douglas McGregor, *The Human Side of Enterprise* (New York: McGraw-Hill, 1960), p. 133.

Recommended Web Sites

The Quality Movement: http://www.insidequality.com/.

The Association for Quality and Participation, a great workplace participation organization: http://www.aqp.org/.

The W. Edwards Deming Institute, the great prophet of quality: http:///www.deming.org/.

Lots of quality resources from John Hunter: http://deming.eng.clemson.edu/onlineq.html.

American Society for Quality's Community Quality newsletters: http://www.asq.org/net/divisions/cqcc/.

Great teamwork development firm and newsletter: http://www.qci-intl.com/home.htm.

Communities of Practice: http://www.tcm.com/trdev/cops.htm.

The Wharton School's Center for Leadership and Change Management: http://leadership.wharton.upenn.edu/welcome/index.shtml.

Training and materials in communications skills: http://www.innovations-training.com/.

Organization Development Network: http://www.odnetwork.org/index.html.

Organization Development Survey site: http://odsurvey.cjb.net/.

Materials on Appreciative Inquiry, an organizational development technique: http://www.mapnp.org/library/commskls/appr_inq/appr_inq.htm.

The American Communication Journal: http://acjournal.org/.

The Center for Management Creativity: http://www.cmcsite.com/.

Darwin, a good business information age magazine: http://www.darwinmag.com/.

Fast Company, another good business magazine, aimed at up and coming people: http://www.fastcompany.com/homepage/.

Emerald, another online business magazine: http://www.emeraldinsight.com/reviews/coolsites/index.htm.

Insights into differences in learning styles: http://www.allkindsofminds.org/.

Almanac of Policy Issues: http://www.policyalmanac.org/.

Workforce Trends: http://www.workforce.com/.

Electronic Journal of Social Work: http://www.ejsw.net/.

The New Social Worker Online: http://www.socialworker.com/.

International Association of Facilitators: http://iaf-world.org/index.htm.

Social Capital, sources on same: http://www.worldbank.org/poverty/scapital/.

A wealth of stuff on creativity: http://www.mindtools.com/page 17.html.

Fun on creativity: http://enchantedmind.com/.

The Society for Organizational Learning: http://www.SoLonline.org/.

––––––––––––

More than 16 million Americans are members of labor unions and thereby part of the nation's largest social movement. Older than the nation itself, its ranks include actors, ballplayers, cooks, doctors, electricians, engineers, lumberjacks, musicians, nurses, pilots, waitresses, and zoo keepers, including nearly every imaginable job title in between. It impacts every aspect of American life, and it has Internet-boosted ties with comparable labor bodies in nearly every other country in the world.

Visionary at its core, the American labor movement helps put utopian ideas on the radar screen of working men and women. It boasts time-honored alliances with major activist organizations fighting for reforms on 101 fronts. Were it ever to achieve the influence which it aspires to earn in current events, it would likely promote scores of viable utopian ideas, many of which are cited in the far ranging and informative essay below.

32. The Society Unions Can Build: Toward a Utopian Social Democratic America

David Reynolds

Today, fewer than one of every six American workers, or only 14 percent, are union members. According to the latest polls, however, 50 percent of the 110 million Americans who work in nonunion workplaces would form a union if given a chance.[1] Were these 55 million people to join the ranks of the existing 16 million union members, the labor movement would encompass nearly two-thirds of working Americans. How might this transform America? In what ways might this be regarded as a viable utopian achievement?

In the workplace the answers become obvious simply by observing any unionized firm. Union workers average $146 more per week than nonunion workers. They enjoy better access to health, pension, vacation, and other benefits. Their workplaces are cleaner, healthier, and safer. Most important, people form unions to win basic respect. Without a union, the boss can fire you anytime. That is a fundamental imbalance of power. If you are mistreated, there is no binding grievance procedure. Experience, loyalty, and years of service may not mean much if a company's unilateral cost-cutting leads to replacing you with a cheaper worker.

Unions allow workers to sit across the bargaining table and negotiate what occurs in their workplace. They can win seniority systems, grievance procedures, and basic job protections. They also gain far greater access to opportunities to better themselves through training, higher education, and leadership experiences. The result is a more committed, more motivated workforce. One recent study discovered that union workplaces were 16 percent more productive than nonunion workplaces.

What about outside the workplace? Since their beginning, labor unions have always been agents of broader social change. Indeed, at times in the history of the labor movement, building a more just and democratic society had a greater focus than collective bargaining in the workplace. Reforms that at the time seemed like starry-eyed, utopian dreams are taken for granted today, including the eight-hour workday and the two-day weekend. By looking at the kinds of social changes unions have fought for in the past and fight for today, we can imagine what our society would look like if all who wanted to join or form unions got their wish.

Higher Public Standards

While workers can gain much at the bargaining table, so long as other employers in the same industry and the larger economy do not play by the same rules, business competition always threatens union gains. This why the unions have fought for broad public standards which all businesses must follow.

A unionized America would have far stronger laws to promote the union principle of a fair day's wage for a fair day's work. For one, the current $5.15 an hour federal minimum wage would increase to reflect the half-century increases in the cost of living. At least $9.00 an hour reflects a minimal wage above poverty by 2002 standards.[2] Second, there would be a maximum wage cap on executive compensation. In the 1950s through 1970s, CEO pay at *Fortune* 500 companies averaged forty times what an average worker made. Today, the ratio has skyrocketed to nearly 500 to one.[3]

Third, workers in female-dominated occupations would have tough new regulations to ensure that they receive wages fully equal to those in comparable male-dominated professions. Fourth, similar laws would require employers to provide part-time, temporary, and other contingent workers—many of whom are younger workers—the same wages and pro-rated benefits as their full-time employees. Today, with nearly one-third of Americans working under contingent arrangements, many companies use such work to undercut basic wage, benefit, and employment standards.

As unions were the main lobbying force behind the establishment of the federal Occupational Safety and Health Administration in the 1970s, they would strengthen the existing system to reduce the grim reality that every year 10,000 workers are killed on the job, and 100,000 die prematurely as a result of work-related health problems. Legal penalties would increase to eliminate the practice whereby management weighs the costs of health and safety improvements against possible weak fines for breaking the law.

Although employer cries of "job losses" occasionally get individual unions to oppose specific environmental regulations, overall, the labor movement has fought for environmental protections. More people in unions would mean far higher pollution standards, better land use regulations, higher fuel economy standards, and so on. Unions would be key players in helping our communities and nation develop more comprehensive plans for environmental recovery.

One of the biggest battles animating union organizing in the nineteenth century was control over work hours. Labor's great victory in winning the eight-hour workday and two-day weekend came after decades of struggle to first win twelve- and then ten-hour days. The forty-hour workweek is now seventy years old. Worker productivity has more than doubled and tripled over this time; however, companies have used such gains to shed workers and to persuade people to buy more stuff.[4] Rethinking the workweek down to thirty-five or thirty-two hours is long overdue. With a union majority, all workers would enjoy legally mandated paid vacations of at least four or five weeks each year, and workers would enjoy far more options for negotiating with their employer over work time flexibility.

A strong labor movement would also establish completely new public standards. All workers would enjoy protection from job loss because the boss would have to document valid reasons for firing an individual. Furthermore, companies could not simply close and leave a community. They would have to give notice and explain the economic rationale for their proposed decision before a public body. Such an authority would block the decision if the company's action would undermine public standards.

Greater Public Wealth for All

Unionized workers bargain for health care, pensions, education, and other benefits, but such standards are often undercut by nonunion companies. Furthermore, when the quality of your health, retirement, and other opportunities depend upon your job, then your life has fewer options. How many people stay in a job they hate simply because they need family health care? By contrast, in a more unionized society, a rich array of public resources would open up to everyone.

The first obvious change would be some form of national health-care system. The only industrial country without such a system, the United States has the single most expensive health-care industry in the world. At least 40 million Americans have no health coverage. In our private-run health-care system, an estimated one out of every six dollars is consumed in insurance paperwork. With prescriptions averaging $65 a shot, the pharmaceutical industry is the most profitable in the nation. With insurance rates exploding, many unions see demands for health-care concessions as the number one item on management's bargaining agenda.

Under a fully public health-care system, anyone could walk into a medical facility and have their needs met at little or no cost to themselves. Public policy could then address our nation's shortage of primary-care family doctors and registered nurses by redirecting resources toward these needs. The single public system, which would cover prescriptions, would have the power to bargain down the inflated costs of drugs. It would also place far greater resources into less drug-driven, more holistic health practice.

Union political action would push a wide range of universal social programs. Just like high school, higher education would be free, with the government providing stipends for room and board. Each person would have a wide range of opportunities for lifelong learning. A fully comprehensive public training system, overseen by government authorities, and run in close cooperation with businesses and unions, would offer ongoing education outside of college. People would also gain time off from work to pursue learning. Indeed, in Organized labor's social democratic America, people would routinely meet in small study circles after work to discuss issues of common interest and public concern.

Greater public wealth would transform family life. Instead of the current law's twelve weeks of unpaid leave, parents would have the right to a year or more of paid leave from work to care for a newborn infant or an elderly parent. All parents would receive a per-child money allowance from the government to help offset the cost of raising that child—poorer parents would receive an additional amount. All local child-care centers would be subsidized; by law, fees would be based upon the parent's ability to pay. Parents would have the legal right to stay home from work to care for a sick child. They would also have the right to take a certain amount of time to participate in their child's schooling.

Routine family expenses, such as rent, mortgage, and car insurance, would be far less expensive from publicly run, nonprofit programs. Unemployment compensation would pick up most of a person's former salary until they get a job—not the current twenty-six weeks at a fraction of pay. Indeed, a constitutional amendment would guarantee all adults the right to a job—thus committing the government to providing whatever resources a person needs to train for and find work.

Social Security would not only continue to provide a retirement income and disability insurance, but the system would be expanded so that the public pension would provide most of a generous retirement living. The unpaid work spent on education and child rearing would count toward a pension.

In short, from cradle to grave, a person would have the freedom of knowing that their basic needs will be met, irrespective of who they work for or even if they work for pay. The funds for such public wealth would come out of a fair tax system based upon an individual's and company's ability to pay. Historically, unions fought for and won the graduated income tax as a fairer system than many flat taxes that hit rich and poor equally. Unfortunately, over the past fifty years, the corporate portion of federal taxes has fallen by half, while the burden on individual income tax has grown by more than 50 percent. Meanwhile the tax rate on the richest individuals has fallen from a peak of 80 percent to only 39.5 percent—and these top rates continue to fall (Collins and Yeskel 2000). A more unionized America would reverse this pattern.[5]

Democracy Everywhere

People organize unions under the belief that they should be able to participate in the economic decisions that effect them. This democratic value has broad application. For example, corporations are governed by the representatives of those who own shares in the company. Workers who make a huge personal investment of their time and energy have no say. Yet, since corporations exist only as a creation of the law, government could require that at least half a company's board of directors be elected by the employees. These worker "stake holders" would be voices for long-term planning. Under the current system, shareholder representatives all too often push short-term, ninety-day returns. Studies have shown that in the most productive workplaces, employees, not just management, are involved in making daily decisions.

Just as the law today requires that employers formally recognize the existence of labor organizations once they have won an official government-monitored election, the law could also mandate that management consult with their employees on a range of daily issues. Under a codetermination system, management would have to secure the formal approval of workers (through an elected Works Council) for policy changes concerning health and safety, transfers, hiring, overtime, layoffs, training, and shift scheduling. While such mandatory power sharing would complicate the decision-making process, it would foster well-thought-out decisions and quick implementation.

In large part thanks to unions, Americans own a good share of the financial wealth of the country through more than $4 trillion in pension assets. Laws could allow workers to set criteria for how their funds are invested. Wealth would not go to the companies that pursue strategies that are anti-union, environmentally destructive, killers of small businesses, and creators of weapons. Pension wealth could support such alternative strategies as cooperative management, environmentally friendly products, worker ownership, and commitment to the community. Unions have also been a voice for employee buyouts and ownership. In a more unionized America, government policy would actively support worker-owned firms—providing financial resources, technical support, and regulations supporting democratic management.

In a more unionized America, government at all levels would play a more extensive, more democratic role in planning the economy. Through new Regional Development Boards people could create long-term visions for their area. Regional rules on land use, business investment, and public expenditures would replace the current fragmented anarchy of uncoordinated city and suburban practices. Communities would no longer compete with each other for who will offer a footloose company the most lucrative public gifts.

To provide a greater public role in steering economic decisions, many of our nation's major banks and financial institutions would become publicly owned. A significant portion of the basic infrastructure, such as electricity, oil, phone, cable, trains, and airlines, would also become publicly owned companies, driven by democratically set needs rather than profits maximization. The public broadcasting system, which today relies upon corporate contributions, would become more extensive and would be paid for entirely by public funds.

A more unionized America would change the way in which government functions. Today various groups, with corporations the most powerful, lobby behind the scenes to influence lawmaking. A more formalized and balanced practice of social partnership would be far more democratic. By law, government bodies would be required to include representatives from various citizen groups and movements (unions, business, environmentalist, women's groups, civil rights organizations, etc.) formally in the decision-making process. Major policy decisions would also make much greater use of public referenda. The public could be asked, for example, whether it wants to continue to have half of all federal discretionary spending go to the military.[6]

Strong unions would transform our nation's political parties. Historically, political parties began as elite clubs. Indeed, initially only people who possessed a certain level of property were allowed to vote. Such restrictions fell away, and elections became more of a mass affair (at least among white men) because the early labor movement organized local labor parties and political clubs. A stronger labor movement would either produce a new political party or completely transform the Democratic Party.

In either case, electoral politics would focus on issues, rather than on candidates. People would get together in neighborhood meetings to develop an agenda for their local, state, and national party platforms. Unlike today, these platforms would act as actual guides for government policy. Grassroots party members would have the power to recall elected candidates who did not uphold their promise. In short, more unions mean a more animated democracy, as people in their workplaces, neighborhoods, and public press debate the crucial issues of the day.

It Is Already Happening

The above utopian vision is not merely an abstraction. Most of the public standards I have cited have been commonplace in Europe for years. Europeans, for example, enjoy from four to six weeks of minimal paid vacation. France today has a thirty-five hour workweek. Denmark's minimum wage was $14 an hour in 1994. The ratio of CEO pay to workers is more like 50 times rather than 500 times. Today, government policy in the Netherlands is guided by a comprehensive twenty-five-year plan for environmental recovery and restoration. Under German law, companies must give up to six months' notice and seek approval from a public labor board before making mass layoffs or closures.[7]

Public wealth is also far greater in Europe and Canada than it is in the United States. All of the examples mentioned above are taken for granted in the Scandinavian countries of Sweden, Denmark, and Norway. Recent cutbacks of unemployment, sick pay, and parental leave in Sweden reduced the rates from 90 to 80 percent of original pay—an amount still staggeringly above our nation's unemployment system, our nonexistent paid illness, and our parental leave. In the 1990s, Denmark and Norway extended the idea of sabbatical leave—common among college faculty—to grant every citizen the right, once in his or her life, to take a year of paid leave from work to do whatever he or she wanted to do.

While overall tax rates are high in Scandinavia, the tax rates for low- and middle-income families compare well with our country. Indeed, even traffic tickets are based on a sliding scale; speeders have to pay a certain percentage of their income. Free health care and higher education, family allowances, subsidized child care, and so on are taken for granted throughout Europe.

Worker elections for a company's supervisory board and works councils have been part of the German system of codetermination laws since the 1950s. Publicly owned companies, especially utilities and banks, have been features in Europe for over half a century. Until the 1990s, two-thirds of Austria's fifty largest companies were publicly owned, nationalized firms. Europeans routinely speak of "social partnership" in which labor and management participate in major social and economic policies. Austrian law requires that representatives from mandated "chambers" of business, labor, and agriculture that have a formal role in developing government policy. Worker study circles are a common way in which people in Scandinavia learn about and discuss the important issues of the day.

The strength of unions is a big part of the difference between the United States and Europe. In Scandinavia, at least 80 percent of adults are union members. Managers have their own unions. Clergy collectively bargain with their congregations. Prisoners have labor organizations to bargain over the job-training funds for life after prison. German rates reveal that 40 percent of German workers are in unions, and 75 percent are covered by union contracts. In Italy, union density is over 60 percent. In Britain and Canada, it is over 33 percent. Furthermore, in all but Canada, the labor movement has created the nation's largest or second largest political party.

This is not to say that Europe is problem free. Over the past twenty years, social and economic strains have caused sharp debates. Some voices call for becoming more like the United States. Others seek to build on the union/social democratic legacy by increasing public controls over corporate actions and establishing European-wide public standards and public wealth. A strong Green movement has highlighted many weaknesses and limitations in the old labor/ social democratic agenda. What is clear, however, is that for the past fifty years, Western Europe has been able to combine a far greater degree of public standards, public wealth, and democratic values with comparable (or even superior) long-term economic success and a measurably higher standard of living.

Organizing at Home Today

The lesson for America is not to copy Europe, but to realize that today's reform efforts have great potential. Indeed, the above vision can also be seen in the grassroots reawakening developing today.[8]

For example, several states have raised the minimum wage above federal standards, thanks to such efforts as the Vermont Livable Wage Campaign and labor-community coalitions in Washington, Massachusetts, California, and Oregon. In over 150 communities across the country, grassroots living wage campaigns have won, or are organizing for laws requiring companies that receive public contracts or financial assistance to pay wages above the poverty level. Reforms in states such as Minnesota and Maine lead a growing corporate accountability movement that requires firms to live up to binding community standards when they receive public money.

The National Alliance for Fair Employment provides a clearinghouse for labor-community efforts across the country trying to bring fairness to contingent employment. The AFL-CIO-affiliated Working for America Institute similarly aids grassroots partnerships among unions, the community, and management, to promote "high road" business practices in worker training, product quality, worker empowerment, and environmental responsibility.

Coalitions are also being formed between unions and environmentalists. The National Alliance for Sustainability and the Environment grew out of battles over timber cutting in the Pacific Northwest. Labor has begun to join the Smart Growth Movement. Across the country, citizen groups, environmentalists, government officials, and forward-looking developers are organizing to reorient our nation's development practices away from community- and environment-destroying sprawl and toward the kinds of integrated, compact communities that were once the norm. Reformers visit places such as Portland, Oregon, and

Chattanooga, Tennessee, to see how communities have combined environmental recovery with community redevelopment and economic health.

Unions and community groups across the country have fought to keep the anti-worker, small-business-destroying WalMart and other "big box" chains out of their communities. Unions have also been central players in establishing new nonprofits organizations like the Los Angeles Alliance for a New Economy and Working Partnerships USA (Silicon Valley), and Sustainable Milwaukee. These institutions help bring diverse groups together around building and implementing grassroots agendas for economic change.

A backdrop to all this activity is the rethinking the labor movement began in the mid-1990s. In 1995 the new leadership of the AFL-CIO—the national umbrella organization to which most American unions belong—looked at a future of potential death. Over the past half century, the labor movement had declined from representing one-third to less than one out of six workers. Employers had clearly become increasingly aggressive in opposing unions. Meanwhile, government protections of the right to organize had become so weak as to be meaningless.

The AFL-CIO concluded much of the decline was also self-inflicted. Having fought the organizing battles in the 1930s to the 1950s, many unions transferred their energies into bargaining and enforcing ever-better contracts, not organizing new workers. Today, with huge nonunion sectors even in traditional union strongholds, the American labor movement can ill afford not to make organizing a top priority.

The AFL-CIO has called on unions to place as much as 30 percent of their resources into organizing. It has promoted new ways to use collective bargaining, political action, and member volunteers to support organizing. Institutional change, however, is never easy. The labor movement is only at the beginning of a very long and bumpy road.

What has already emerged are labor leaders who see the need to organize and realize that the unions cannot go it alone. When unions have grown they have always done so in coalition with the community. Union organizing has always been not just a matter of economic justice, but also an issue of utopian matters—of moral standards, civil rights, community health, and basic democracy. As labor rebuilds itself, it cannot help but be part of the next great social movement to transform America.

Notes

1. Poll commissioned by the AFL-CIO.

2. $9.03 is the hourly wage needed for full-time work to produce an annual income at the 2002 Federal poverty guideline for a family of four. Many researchers criticize today's Federal guidelines for underestimating the minimal financial needs to support a family.

3. *Common Sense Economics* presentation from the AFL-CIO. See also Chuck Col-

lins and Felice Yeskel, *Economic Apartheid in America* (New York: The New Press, 2000); chapter two.

4. Juliet Schor, *The Overworked American* (New York: Basic Books, 1991).

5. Tax information comes from the newsletters of Citizens for Tax Justice. See http://www.ctj.org for more information.

6. This pattern is clear from the multi-decade yearly budget summaries found in the official publication of the 2003 Federal Budget. Once Social Security and Medicare—which are legally separate from the general budget—are removed and all the military related expenditures added together, the military becomes half of all discretionary spending.

7. For information on the standards, public wealth, and democracy found in Europe, see Part one of David Reynolds, *Taking the High Road Communities Organize for Economic Change* (Armonk, NY: M. E. Sharpe, 2002).

8. For more on these examples see David Reynolds, *Taking the High Road Communities Organize for Economic Change* (Armonk, NY: M. E. Sharpe, 2002); part two.

Further Reading

Reynolds, David. *Taking the High Road Communities Organize for Economic Change.* Armonk, NY: M.E. Sharpe, 2002. This is the source for all of the statistics in my essay above.
Collins, Chuck, and Felice Yeskel. *Economic Apartheid in America.* New York: The New Press, 2000.

Web Sites

The national umbrella labor federation: www.aflcio.org.

Corporate accountability and unions and sprawl: www.goodjobsfirst.org.

Union-business partnerships: www.workingforamerica.org.

Contingent work: www.fairjobs.org.

Living wage campaigns: www.acorn.org.

Union-sponsored site battling WalMart: www.walmartwatch.com

The Alliance for Sustainable Jobs and the Environment: home.pacifier.com/~asje/.

Model labor-community action in Silicon Valley: www.atwork.org.

Model labor-community action in Los Angeles:www.laane.org.

Art Shostak's ongoing dialogue about unions and computer power: www.cyberunions.net.

We think too seldom and with a too limited knowledge of the utopian-building gains possible via the third sector—our friends in community and voluntary organizations. Theirs is a record of long and vital contribution, much of it linked on these shores with this or that utopian effort in American history. The essay below helps fill in gaps in our knowledge and encourages fresh recognition of the part played, being played, and yet to be played here by viable utopian ideas.

33. Utopian Conceptions of Society's Third Sector

Jon Van Til

Utopians, as social theorists, typically present a four-sector conception of society. They describe ways in which the polity (government), the economy (businesses and corporations), the voluntary sector (community groups, nonprofit organizations, churches, foundations), and the informal sector (families, kin, neighborhoods) are organized, and explain how their interactions play out within an imagined and ideal society.

My special interest is in the "third sector," a colorful composite of the community or voluntary organizations which try to better our lives and those of others. We Americans pride ourselves on being a nation of joiners, and over half of us actively participate, in any given week, as volunteers in some sort of community activity. In addition, most of us also donate financially to community or nonprofit organizations, giving on an average nearly 2 percent of our income (Independent Sector 2002).

The broad range of our voluntary organizations includes neighborhood associations, which seek to restrain crime or encourage the cleaning of streets; faith-based organizations, which include churches, mosques, synagogues, and the like; and civic organizations, which often try to improve a city's economic climate. Other groups of volunteers attempt to reduce family abuse by direct service and legislative advocacy.

Contemporary estimates identify well over a million nonprofit organizations in the United States, many of which support paid staff as well as volunteer employees and board members. Surveys also find that 9 percent of all meaningful employment (and 7 percent of all salaries) emerge from the third sector (Van Til 1988, 2000).

Such organizations are voluntary in a dual sense: Much of their human resources are contributed by members as volunteers; and they are nongovernmental, nonprofit, and nonprimary. Thus, voluntary organizations may be seen as the key components of society's third sector.

Theoretical Foundations

Voluntary organizations are central to a number of important theoretical perspectives in social science (Van Til 1988). Writing at the turn of the nineteenth century, for example, Emile Durkheim, following in the footsteps of his countryman Alexis de Tocqueville, gave a major role to associations in his studies of social solidarity. The observations of Max Weber laid the basis for later neo-coroporatist thought, and the studies of Robert Michels illuminated aspects of elitism and populism within voluntary organizations.

Karl Marx, while never a voluntarist, nevertheless relied upon the power of a voluntary social movement to accomplish revolutionary tasks. More recently, in the late twentieth century, social theorist Talcott Parsons envisaged voluntary organizations playing a major role in the "integration" of societal institutions, a task extended by the contemporary communitarian and neo-utopian theories of Amitai Etzioni and Roger Lohmann.

Philanthropy, in turn, figures prominently in the work of classical utopians. Gerard Winstanley and James Harrington, for example, echoed Thomas More's judgment that righting the unequal distribution of wealth, income, and power was the basic problem a utopia could correct. The imposition of governmental policies could serve to distribute resources and benefits more equally . . . a notion that became a tradition of utopian socialism. It led to the communal constructions of Robert Owen and also to the revolutionary ideas of Karl Marx. Typically ignored in democratic utopianism's focus on public control of the economy were the utopians' own reliance on third-sector organizations to bring about structural changes.

To Marx, of course, philanthropy provided an instrument by which the ruling class maintained control of the workers it both employed and dominated. Like its cousin institution, religion, philanthropy served as an "opiate of the people," deflecting attention from the evils of class domination. Philanthropy, Marx asserted, masked greed and control in the veils of its purported beneficence. It created a submissive crowd of supplicants and recipients unlikely to give either voice or support to calls for redistribution and revolution. In the commonplace expression of contemporary philanthropy, the only problem seen as attached to "tainted money" is that there "tain't enough" of it.

Two leading Socialist utopians, Edward Bellamy (1888) and William Morris (1890), were particularly observant regarding the hegemonic uses of philanthropy. For example, in Bellamy's classic *Looking Backward*, Dr. Leete, the utopian host to the narrator (Mr. West, who had gone to sleep in the year 1888 and awakened in the year 2000), explained that even the physically challenged had come to play an important role in Utopia.

For Mr. West, as for so many contemporary Americans, caring for the needy was a duty to be rather soberly discharged, one that had to be carefully engineered by charitable organizations to ensure that those in need are not neglected. But in Bellamy's Utopia, as Dr. Leete explained, the division between the truly needy and the self-sufficient melted before the recognition that all persons are dependent upon each other, enmeshed as they are in one great social network of mutual support (see Bourdieu 1990).

Widening the Net

The tension between individual and collective provision of social support is one of a wide range of issues raised clearly and provocatively by the utopian tradition. Other issues pertaining to philanthropy and the third sector in that literature include the following:

- Population size and control (generally viewed favorably)
- Crime and punishment (with a particular concern for capital punishment, ranging from its abolition by More to its democratization by the Marquis de Sade)
- Voluntary suicide (advocated by More)
- National Service (widely viewed as an important part of civic education)
- Religious tolerance and pluralism (also widely approved)
- Educational pedagogy (developed in considerable detail by utopians like Rousseau)
- Communal social care (a favorite cause of utopians since More)
- Open sexual relationships (a pet topic of a few utopians)
- Guild organization (favored by evolutionary socialists)
- Residential patterning into a variety of ordered communal structures (of which Fourier's phalansteries are perhaps the most complex; see also Lang 2000).

Similar issues have been considered in the "dystopian" literature, which creates images of frightening or dysfunctional futures. These "negative utopias" have become highly popular in current mass culture, particularly in film and the novels of Aldous Huxley, Ursula LeGuin, George Orwell, and Ray Bradbury.

Two Case Studies

Perhaps the most intriguing construction in the utopian literature based on voluntary association is that of Charles Fourier. Building a communal society on the basis of "passional attraction," the eccentric Fourier imagined the erection of a series of "phalansteries," each consisting of a carefully selected population of between 1,500 and 1,600 residents joined in voluntary association. Located on a pleasant site within reach of the city, it would attract persons of various levels of wealth and income to a life of ever-changing leisure. (Sociologist Joan Roelofs suggests Fourier's complex vision would become viable only after a system of "computer dating" was introduced to better match enrollees; Roelofs 1985).

Industrialist Robert Owen, a more conventional philanthropist than Fourier, actually built two notable utopian communities to house workers he employed at below-market wages (but with generous medical, educational, and recreational benefits). New Lanark (Scotland), begun in 1799, featured a reduction in working hours from twelve to ten hours per day and a prohibition of child labor. Home to 1,400 workers, New Lanark was succeeded by the New Harmony community in Indiana, established in 1824.

Summary

The role of utopia, in short, has always been to expand the envelope, to extend the vision of what may be achieved "if only" we had the vision, the good luck, and the commitment to build a better society.

As Robert Nozick suggested, perhaps the best utopias emerge where process, rather than framework, is given primary attention. His conception of utopia is based in the third sector, resting as it does on our ability to choose between and among voluntary associations. Such a conception, he asserts, "treats us as inviolate individuals, who may not be used in certain ways by others as means or tools or instruments or resources" (Nozick 1974, 332).

Utopia, Nozick concludes,

> allows us, individually or with whom we choose, to choose our life and to realize our ends and our conception of ourselves, insofar as we can, aided by the voluntary cooperation of other individuals possessing the same dignity. How dare any state or group of individuals do more. Or less. (1974, 334)

Nozick is not the only theorist to note the primacy of voluntary and philanthropic action in society. The third sector has often been seen as "first" in its ability to innovate, the home of poets and dreamers as well as of managers and service providers (Young 1983). Accordingly, I believe all who would advance viable utopian ideas would do well to recognize the unique potential of voluntary action.

References

Bellamy, Edward. *Looking Backward.* New York: NAL, 1888, 2000.

Bourdieu, Pierre. *The Logic of Practice.* Stanford, CA: Stanford University Press, 1990.

Callenbach, Ernest. *Ecotopia.* Berkeley, CA: Banyan Tree Books, 1975.

Dauncey, Guy. *Earthfuture.* Gabriola Island, British Columbia, Canada: New Society, 1990.

Fourier, Charles. *The Utopian Vision of Charles Fourier,* edited by Jonathan Beecher and Richard Bienvenu. Boston: Beacon, 1971.

Harrington, James. *The Commonwealth of Oceana.* Cambridge: Cambridge University Press, 1992.

Independent Sector. *Giving and Volunteering in the United States 2001.* Washington, DC: Independent Sector, 2002.

Lang, Michael H. *Designing Utopia: John Ruskin's Urban Vision for Britain and America*. Tonawanda, NY: Black Rose Books, 2000.

Lang, Michael H., and Jon Van Til. "Utopia: Course Syllabus" (2002). http://crab.rutgers.edu/~vantil/courses/utopia.html, as of June 5, 2002.

More, Sir Thomas. *Utopia*. Mineola, NY: Dover, 1516, 1997.

Morris, William. *News from Nowhere*. London: Penguin, 1890, 1993.

New York Public Library. "Utopia." (www.nypl.org/utopia) (accessed June 5, 2002).

Nozick, Robert. *Anarchy, State, and Utopia*. New York: Basic Books, 1974.

Robbins, Kevin. Presentation to Seminar on Philanthropy. Presentation at Indiana University, Indianapolis, June 2001.

Roelofs, Joan. "Fourier and Computer Dating. *Telos* 65 (Fall 1985).

Royle, Edward. *Robert Owen and the Commencement of the Millennium: The Harmony Community at Queenwood Farm, Hampshire 1839–1945*. London: St. Martin's Press, 1988.

Van Til, Jon. *Growing Civil Society*. Bloomington: Indiana University Press, 2000.

———. *Mapping the Third Sector*. New York: Foundation Center, 1988.

Winstanley, Gerrard. *Law of Freedom and Other Writings*. Cambridge: Cambridge University Press, 1983.

Young, Dennis R. *If Not for Profit, for What?* New York: Free Press, 1983.

XI. Nation-Building Aids

Around the globe a wide array of grassroots movements are stirring the dust. What many lack in funds they commonly make up for in local popularity. What they may lack in discipline they make up for in adaptability ("undecidibility"). And what they sometimes lack in highbrow ideological sophistication they make up for in earnest and ceaseless reflection ("dissensus"). Colorful and courageous, grassroots movements adapt viable utopian ideas with enthusiasm and raise fresh hopes for their near-future realization. Valuable light is shed below on the subject's nuances, a vital front in the "war" against an untenable status quo.

34. Utopianism and Grassroots Alternatives

Valerie Fournier

Whilst it has become common to proclaim neoliberalism as "the only viable economic alternative," my aim here is to argue that many have sought—and are even now seeking—to escape from its shackles. After all, as H. Lefebvre put it, "People do not revolt to change governments . . . but to change their lives" (1971, 36). Out of necessity or hope, some have dared to believe that there are alternatives, to make a wager that there must be alternatives (Young 1996). It is to refer to this cultivation of possibilities by grassroots movements, this daring to imagine alternatives, that I use the term "utopianism."

Utopianism and Movement

I use the term "utopianism" rather than "utopia" to emphasize movement over static visions of a better order. Thus I follow several writers in defining utopianism in terms of its critical, transgressive, and transformative functions, rather than in terms of its form or content (Harvey 2000; Levitas 1990; Sargisson 1996). From this perspective, utopianism is not a blueprint for a "perfect society"—it may be better conceptualized as a movement of hope. It undermines dominant understanding of what is possible, and it opens up new conceptual spaces for imaging and practicing possible futures.

Utopianism is about movement and processes rather than "better states"; about journeys, rather than destinations. It is about opening up visions of alternatives, rather than closing down a vision of a better society. It is about what moves us to hope for, and to cultivate, alternative possibilities. And it is about establishing the conditions for the development of alternatives.

This "moving" nature of utopianism is well captured by the ambivalence inherent in Thomas More's (1516) discussion of utopia as a "good place" and a "no place." This ambivalence opens up a space for a continuous process of deferral, for perpetual movement. Or as L. Marin (1984) suggests, it creates "tension zones" which prevent movement from ever reaching an end.

Thus utopianism cannot end with a critique of the present, nor even with the construction of a better future; it cannot end at all. It has to resist the temptation of closure around another "best" alternative (Sargisson 1996). It lives off tension-zone disruption mechanisms which will stop it from settling.

Grassroots Movements

How are grassroots movements utopian? They are born out of and embody a wide range of concerns. Some may start as women's movements, simply because women often happen to be at the points where the material and environmental effects of global capitalism are most urgently felt (Agarwal 1992; Bennholdt-Thomsen and Mies 1999; Rocheleau, Thomas-Slayter, and Wangari 1996). Others may be about small farmers or landless people reclaiming the right to use common land to meet their subsistence needs, as in, for example, the Zapatista movement in Mexico (Holloway and Pelaez, 1998). Local people may be reclaiming their rights over traditional knowledge of life forms from corporate biopiracy (Shiva 1997).

These movements are not moved by a common vision or political agenda, but by a common enemy (Starr 2000): the "force" of neoliberalism. True, this common enemy may occasionally bring them together in some temporal tactical alliances (as we have seen in anticapitalist protests), but this does not extend into the establishment of some general system of equivalence (Guattari 2000) that would point to another "stultifying consensus."

My aim is not to offer a comprehensive or even representative overview of grassroots movements, but rather to capture something of their "movement" of hope in relation to utopianism. My interest is less in the organizational alternatives they represent than in the very possibility of alternatives. They stand as "emblems of the possible" (Guttenplan 2001, 5). By seeking to reclaim control over the conditions of their existence from the "inevitable force of neoliberalism," they are living examples that history has not reached its end, that "there are alternatives."

Putting a Face to the "Inevitable Force of the Market"

If utopianism is about opening up a space for alternatives, it has to shatter any notion of "inevitable" or "natural" forces, particularly the commonly accepted notion that the forces of capitalism and neoliberalism are inescapable (Korten 1995).

Modern organizations efface moral responsibility by distancing actions from effects and by effacing the "face" of those who are made to suffer from these consequences (Desmond 1998). These distancing mechanisms keep the effects and suffering created by organizations invisible. Even when we do see the suffering, we do not see the connections to our actions. We do not know what lever to pull, or we do not feel that any lever is within our reach. These distancing mechanisms create the impression that the "system" is unrolling, independently of our action, and there is nothing to stop it.

Yet some people are saying "No!" (Korten 1995). They are refusing to take their suffering as the products of inevitable forces. Grassroots protest movements are retracing the connections between their suffering and corporate or government actions, choices, and decisions. They are challenging the blind faith in the unstoppable force of neoliberalism and hierarchism.

Through their direct actions, they are demonstrating that whilst global capitalism may run according to a certain logic that drives capital where it can attracts most profit, that relies on and reproduces pockets of poverty and devastation, this logic itself does not impose itself on us of its own volition, without some of us letting it do so.

The power of grassroots protest movements is also about exposing these consequences as the products of actions and decisions, rather than the inevitable force of the market. By putting points of resistance, they are forcing those behind neoliberalism to step up their actions, to show the faces and decisions behind the faceless and distant inevitable force of the market, and to reveal these "decisions" as, by definition, possibly otherwise.

Thus grassroots movements against biopiracy find that their protests do not take them against some faceless force of the market, but into some complex legal regulations formulated by the world leaders behind the General Agreement on Tariffs and Trade (GATT); and that such acts of piracy only become "legalized free trade" if the World Trade Organization (WTO), backed up by multinational corporations and governments, decides so (Shiva 1997). If such acts of appropriation can be exposed as the products of decisions rather than the inevitable force of the market, they can also be overturned, as was successfully demonstrated in the case of the lawsuits launched against the patenting of the nem tree by the Grace corporation (BIJA 1996).

Furthermore, as many women environmentalist movements have suggested, it is not some inescapable logic of the market that dumps toxic waste and builds polluting factories. Such dumping and polluting can only be seen as the product of "economic imperatives," or as contributing to "economic development" (providing "needed economic opportunities," as *The Economist* put it), if we have made certain decisions about what sort of economy we want, if we have decided meeting subsistence needs does not count as "economic development" whilst producing pollution to be cleaned up, or sports equipment from logged forests do (Rocheleau, Thomas-Slayter, and Wangari 1996).

Grassroots protest movements remind us nothing is the product of autonomous, inevitable, faceless "forces." Everything has to be decided. For as J. Derrida (1999) put it, the world is undecidable. His notion of undecidibility is useful to free social reality from the straitjacket of inescapability within which it is held by triumphalist neoliberalism, and to open up choice and possibilities. It suggests reality is always incomplete, containing many latent potentialities. It follows no imperatives and is dictated by no "force" or program.

Undecidibility means we have to decide. If the world follows no inevitable logic, we have to make choices, and to do so without ever being able to resort to absolute standards by which to judge them. We also chose the standards by which we evaluate our choice. With undecidibility and choice comes responsibility (Derrida 1999; Jones, forthcoming). If organizing the economy follows no imperatives, but is the product of (however complex, multiple, dispersed) decisions we take, we cannot hide our responsibility for the devastating effects such organizing creates behind some faceless program, some inevitable logic, of the market or otherwise.

Of course, undecidibility also means that we cannot know for sure that alternatives will be better. We can only hope, take the risk (Young 1996). Utopianism is about grabbing these moments of hope and risk and running with them. It is about embracing undecidibility, as well as the choices and responsibility that go with it.

Inventing Alternative Moral Economies

What alternatives do grassroots movements practice? The idea of self-governance, or self-management and self-determination, is a central principle in articulating the alternative "moral economies" (Bennholdt-Thomsen and Mies 1999) embodied by grassroots movements, from explicitly anticorporate movements, to environmental movements, women's movements, land reforms, and small-farmers movements.

The main idea about self-governance is that decisions are taken by those who will live with the consequences. It foregrounds the ability to make choice about the conditions affecting our lives, but it also (re)connects these choices with responsibility and facing the consequences of our choices. True, we cannot know in advance all the consequences of our actions, but some things we do know. For example, we know if we dump toxic waste somewhere it will in all likelihood impair the health of local people. We know if we pay people less than a living wage, they will find it difficult to survive.

Furthermore, we can also create conditions that may bring the consequences of our action closer to us. In order to create the conditions of possibility for self-governance, economic activity should be organized at the smallest, most local level possible (Bello, Bullard, and Malhotra 2000; Bookchin 1990; Korten 1995). Small local self-organizing groups have been the cornerstones of many grassroots alternatives (Bennholdt-Thomsen and Mies 1999; Starr 2000). However, privileging small, local organizations is not to say that we should all live in autarky, isolated from other communities. In many alternative visions and grassroots movements, these small units are connected through federation, or "municipalities" (Bookchin 1990), which act as networks of exchange.

For example, in the Zapatista movement, self-organizing communities can choose to join municipalities which coordinate an exchange among them to ensure that basic needs are met. A municipality may include between 50 and 100 communities, each delegating one of their members to speak for them in the municipality assemblies, and to report back to them. This system of delegation from below allows decision-making power to remain as close to the grassroots as possible (decisions about the organization of the community remain at that level) and ensures that lines of accountability run from the top down. Thus delegates are given a mandate to represent the views of the group that selected them, and they can be recalled (*Chiapas Revealed* 2001).

Division between Capital and Labor: Reclaiming or Protecting the Commons

Self-governance requires free access to, and control over the means of production, and therefore the elimination of the division between owners of capital (be it land, tools, or raw material) and labor. This involves the abolition of waged labor and a reconceptualization of property rights over capital.

The eradication of the division between labor and capital can take several forms, from the more modest private ownership by either a group of associated workers (worker cooperatives) or a small family/individual enterprise which does not own more capital than the owners can work with, to a more radical vision of communal ownership, where the means of production belong (in the sense of usufruct) to those who work with them (*An Anarchist FAQ Webpage* 2001).

Subsistence and Alternative Forms of Exchange

The separation between consumption and production is one of the distancing mechanisms that enables consumers to either not know or not care for the effects of their consumption (e.g., on those who are slaving away to produce it or on the environment), and reciprocally, for producers to dump harmful products on unsuspecting consumers.

Attempts to break down these distancing mechanisms by drawing toward a subsistence economy (Bennholdt-Thomsen and Mies 1999) or a greater level of "self-reliance" (Bello, Bullard, and Malhotra 2000; Bookchin 1990; Korten 1995) do not have to involve autarky. Throughout the world there are many, maybe less radical attempts to develop exchange systems that tie consumers and producers more closely together, attaching them to the mutual consequences of their acts of production and consumption.

The Organization and Division of Labor

The implications of self-management for the organization of work extend far beyond empowering employees to decide how to reach their targets. It means those who labor can also decide to what end they will deploy their labor and means of production: what they should produce, for whom, and at what cost to themselves. For example, as some rural women's movements have demonstrated, it is about the power to decide that what could be gained by producing crops for the export market would not be worth the loss of domestic crops covering subsistence needs, or the extended journey women would have to make to collect water or firewood (Agarwal 1992).

Self-governance also means challenging the constitution and distribution of knowledge and, in particular, the privileging and sequestrating of "professional knowledge." Privileging expert knowledge has been a powerful device to exclude "ordinary citizens" from decisions and dismiss their protests (Bookchin 1990; Dickens 1996). There is no reason why professional knowledge should be privileged over "citizen science"—knowledge developed and grounded in civil society (Dickens 1996)—or why it should be the preserve of a small groups of scientists or professionals.

This hardly provides us with a blueprint for organizing. It opens endless questions: What counts as "useful product" or "waste in human energy?" How much of such waste should we tolerate? How should it be distributed? This is precisely the point—to open such questions and possibilities to public debate so that we can decide. Self-governance and small self-reliant communes are not an end in themselves, not the answer to all problems: They are only the material conditions under which we can start to open up alternative possibilities to neoliberalism and its devastation.

There is a concern, however, in writing about these alternative grassroots movements because of the tendency of some small, self-reliant communes to align themselves with some spiritual revival (Bahro 1984; Bookchin 1990; Korten 1995). My argument is not about spiritual healing or the recovery of some long-lost moral order. It is about creating the material conditions for the cultivation of possibilities, for (re)claiming control over the ways in which we organize our lives.

Permanent Disruption

If utopianism is about the opening up of possibilities, it requires some mechanisms that will stop it from hardening into *utopia*, some arrested vision of a better society that becomes the only alternative. The grassroots nature of the alternative movements I have been concerned with here provides powerful disruptive mechanisms that make such movements utopian and stops them from degenerating into some tame vision of a third way.

True, grassroots movements have not changed the world. The successful lawsuit against the Grace corporation for biopiracy of the nem tree has not brought GATT, nor Grace, to its knees. The Zapatista movement is still fighting. The refusal of people in Papua New Guinea to sell their collective land in order to repay the country's debt has not made the World Bank or the International Monetary Fund crumble. It has made a difference, however, to those who have resisted, to those who are still fighting against the corporate appropriation of their means of survival.

And of course, there are also many things a grassroots movement cannot do. A grassroot movement cannot run a state (Blaug 1998), let alone the global economy. It cannot produce standardized hamburgers around the world. Isn't this to their credit? Shouldn't we ensure that grassroots movements remain ineffective at running states—that they remain small, spontaneous, and disjointed and that they do not congeal into another unified vision of a better future, another truth, policed by another leader?

If utopianism is about avoiding the closing off of possibilities, it needs multiple breaking points for stirring things up, for stopping the "good life" from hardening into forms of oppressive habits and totalitarian tendencies. It lives in the tension created by the juxtaposition of multiple possibilities. It lives in dissensus, rather than in the search for consensus.

Dissensus, disunity, multiple points—far from diluting the strength of these grassroots movements, these stand as effective weapons against the seduction of closure, the snugness of comfort. The juxtaposition of disconnected grassroots alternatives serves as a reminder that any form of organizing has to establish itself against others, that there are always alternatives.

Summary

Is this all just a fanciful middle-class dream? The significance of utopianism and grassroots movements lies well beyond the alternative organizational forms they create or the local situations they seek to transform. They stand as an emblem of possibility.

By bringing grassroots alternative practices within a discussion of utopianism, I wanted to suggest utopianism is not about escapism, some fanciful middle-class dream, but is eminently practicable and is, in fact, at least for some, a matter of some urgency.

Acknowledgements

I would like to thank Yiannis Gabriel, Mihaela Kelemen, Martin Parker, and Edward Wray-Bliss for their thoughtful and supportive comments on an earlier draft of this chapter. The editor of this volume, Art Shostak, substantially reduced its length, and I urge readers to pursue the original essay as it appears in M. Parker, ed., *Utopia and Organization*. London: Blackwell, 2002.

References

Agarwal, B. "The Gender and Environment Debate: Lessons from India." *Feminist Studies* 18, no. 1 (1992): 119–58.

An Anarchist FAQ Webpage (2001). Version 9.0: http://www.anarchistfaq.org.

Anonymous. "Intellectual Property Rights, Community Rights and Biodiversity." *BIJA* 15/16 (1996): 25.

Bahro, R. *From Red to Green*. London: Verso, 1984.

Bello, W., N. Bullard, and K. Malhotra, eds. *Global Finance: New Thinking on Regulating Speculative Capital Markets*. London: Zed Books, 2000.

Bennholdt-Thomsen V., and M. Mies. *The Subsistence Perspective: Beyond the Globalised Economy*. London: Zed Books, 1999.

Blaug, R. "The Tyranny of the Visible: Problems in the Evaluation of Anti-Institutional Radicalism." *Organization* 6, no. 1 (1998): 33–56.

Bookchin, M. *Post Scarcity Anarchism*. London: Wildwood House, 1971.

———. *Remarking Society: Pathways to a Green Future*. Boston: South End Press, 1990.

Derrida, J. "Hospitality, Justice and Responsibility." In *Questioning Ethics*, edited by R. Kearney and M. Dooley. London: Routledge, 1999.

———. *Specters of Marx: The State of the Debt, the Work of Mourning, and the New International*, translated by Peggy Kamuf. New York: Routledge, 1994.

Desmond, J. "Marketing and Moral Indifference." In *Ethics and Organizations*, edited by M. Parker, 173–96. London: Sage, 1998.

Dickens, P. *Reconstructing Nature: Alienation, Emancipation and the Division of Labour*. London: Routledge, 1996.

Guattari, F. *Three Ecologies*, translated by I. Pindar and P. Sutton. London: Athlone Press, 1989, 2000.

Guttenplan, D. "The Lessons We Can Learn from the 60s." *Guardian Society*, August 29, 2001, p. 5.

Harvey, D. *Spaces of Hope*. Edinburgh: Edinburgh University Press, 2000.

Holloway, J., and E. Pelaez, eds. *Zapatista! Re-inventing Revolution in Mexico*. London: Pluto, 1998.

Jones, C. "Jacques Derrida: Possibilities of Deconstruction." In *Postmodern Organisation Theory*, edited by S. Linstead. London: Sage, forthcoming.

Korten, D. *When Corporations Rule the World*. West Hartford, CT: Kumarian Press, 1995.

Lefebvre, H. "La commune: Dernière fête populaire." In *Images de la Commune*, edited by J. A. Leith, 33–45. Montreal: McGill-Queen's University Press, 1971.

Levitas, Ruth. *The Concept of Utopia*. Hemel Hempstead, England: Allan, 1990.

Marin, L. *Utopics: Spatial Play*. London: Macmillan, 1984.

Monbiot, G. "Market Enforcers," *Guardian*, August 21, 2001, p. 15.

More, Sir Thomas. *Utopia*. Mineda, NY: Dover, 1997 [1510].

Rocheleau, D., B. Thomas-Slayter, and E. Wangari, eds. *Feminist Political Ecology: Global Issues and Local Experiences*. London: Routledge, 1996.

Sargisson, L. *Contemporary Feminist Utopianism*. London: Routledge, 1996.

Shiva, V. *The Plunder of Nature and Knowledge*. Boston, MA: South End, 1997.

Starr, A. *Naming the Enemy: Anti-Corporate Movements Confront Globalization*. London: Zed Books, 2000.

"What Is It That Is Different about the Zapatistas?" *Chiapas Revealed* 1 (2001): 1–24. http://flag.blackened.net/revolt/mexico/comment/andrew_diff_feb01.html.

Young, R. *Intercultural Communication: Pragmatics, Genealogy and Deconstruction*. Clevedon, England: Multilingual Matters, 1996.

Painter Paul Gauguin, writer Robert Louis Stevenson, anthropologist Margaret Mead, various moviemakers, and scores of others have helped us conjure up idyllic fantasies about Pacific Isles as utopias-of-a-sort. We think casually of lush settings, abundant resources, loose morals, and endless beach parties . . . images that have always revealed more about our discontent than about the subject. In reality, the world of the Pacific Islands is increasingly strained. There is trouble in "utopia," and no easy solutions are at hand. Viable utopian ideas are called for and some are cited in the unusual essay below—along with a call for readers to lend a hand (and an idea or two).

35. The Ulithi Project: Can a Traditional Non-Western Culture Survive?

Roger A. Straus and Diane E. Straus

There are big utopias and smallish ones. All are dreams we seek to make real. This is one.

Yap, one of the Federated States of Micronesia, is actually a cluster of small islands jammed together in the far Western South Pacific. The land mass, Yap Proper, was a piece of Southeastern Asia that drifted out to sea on a tectonic plate and ended up about 600 miles east-southeast of Manilla, some 200 miles southwest of Guam. You may have heard of it referred to as the Land of Stone Money. Scuba divers know that it is one of the few places on earth where one can routinely swim with manta rays. It is the least Westernized state of Micronesia.

The people of Yap are determined to keep it that way. That is the utopian connection. There's more—something more than 100 miles off Yap Proper is the outer territory of Ulithi: an atoll of nine islands, four of which are currently inhabited by humans (the rest principally by birds and coconut crabs), which surrounds the world's fourth largest lagoon.

To get to Ulithi, the island of Falalop, specifically, one takes a small prop plane that is run by Pacific Missionary Airlines twice a week or a ship which goes by every fortnight or so. That's it. The end of all supply lines.

Falalop has a population of about 500. Asor, the next island over, has around 200; Mog Mog, the chiefly island, has another 100; another hundred live on a fourth island. So you ask the people where they and their ancestors came from, they will say, "From here." Each island is under the authority of its chief, and there is a chief for the entire atoll, who lives on Mog Mog. Many still have a Men's House, where the menfolk gather in the evenings to discuss the events of the day and plan for tomorrow. Ulithians like to do things in groups. They hang around together chewing betel nut (a mild, habituating buzz), talking and laughing—a lot of laughing. They take their time, but they get done whatever needs to be done.

After puberty, women wear a knee-length skirt, called a *lava-lava*, which they sometimes weave themselves. Men wear a dhoti-like loincloth, called a *thu*, typically a bright, dark blue. Often that is all they wear; many women still go topless, even in church, but they do not ever display their thighs in public. Their thighs are considered to be the sacred "path of life."

Until the 1960s, Ulithians had no reason to consider themselves poor. The lagoon and surrounding sea swarmed with fish and mollusks and other edibles. The people grew breadfruit and taro and got betel nuts to chew from Yap Proper along with various fruits (presumably in trade for fish). Coconuts are everywhere, providing thatch, food, and drink. Coconut sap can be collected and used fresh like sweet molasses or fermented into a moderately alcoholic drink called *tuba*. Skilled artisans made dugout outrigger canoes from the trees. Weavers created baskets, mats, and fans. Nobody had to starve or go without essentials. If betel nuts were in short supply, everyone found something else to chew, like coconut husk.

In the late nineteenth century, Yap and Ulithi intersected the world. A few decades of unpleasant encounters with Westerners decimated the population but had seemingly little effect on the culture. Twentieth-century Japanese occupied Micronesia until they were forced out by the Americans after World War II. Although the Japanese had minimal direct impact on Ulithi, (elsewhere they virtually enslaved the population), they hooked the population on white rice and soya, as well as the custom of wearing zoris (flip-flops). The navy moved the Ulithians onto one island during the war and introduced them to tinned corned beef and other icons of modernity. One village headman told us, "Yes, I know that it's bad for your health, causes hypertension, and is bad for your heart because it is so very salty and fatty—but, once you've gotten the taste. . . ." During this period, traditional arts, crafts, and technologies began falling into decline.

The Catholic Church successfully evangelized Ulithi in the early 1950s, with the positive effect of improving the status of women, but how much else was lost? In the 1960s, a major typhoon smashed through the atoll wrecking all the canoes and leveling the dwellings. So many skills had been lost after World War II that the islanders turned to manufactured boats and galvanized sheeting for their roofs. Suddenly, they found themselves poor. A classic case of (and new spin on the concept of) relative deprivation.

Today, there is an Outer Islands High School at an abandoned U.S. Coast Guard station (students are flown in for the week). The students even have a computer lab and are connected to the Web by satellite. A few students from Ulithi get scholarships to major U.S. universities every year with their flawless English, including Harvard and Yale. Others go to colleges in the United States or Guam. Some learn skilled trades; others join the U.S. armed forces under the Compact of Free Association with Micronesia. Few of these youths ever move back. Those who remain at home become even more marginalized.

These people are neither uneducated nor unintelligent. However, as on Yap Proper, they are bound and determined to maintain their ancient culture in the face of a world cash economy. That is the utopian dream. How can they do that? Ulithi needs some cash to purchase what have now become necessities, ranging from rice to zoris, building materials, water-purification supplies, and equipment. They need to generate electricity. They need medicines and health care supplies—not to mention providers and facilities. They would like to have more cell phones and computers to help connect them with one another and with the outside world.

One way to get such things has been to depend on the kindness of others. Micronesia is one of the last fertile grounds for missionaries, who provide the airplanes, minimal health care, and some contact with the outside world. That doesn't do much, however, to enhance autonomy. Young expatriates may send cash back home from abroad, but the best and brightest are gone.

In 2000 one of the local movers and shakers, John Rulmal, started a small diving resort named the Ulithi Adventure Resort on Falalop. He wanted to provide employment for some of the youth who stay on the atoll and generate a cash flow. John, the deacon of the local Catholic church, managed to convince one chief to allow diving on their reefs and the wearing of Western clothing (which, like alcohol and other aspects of mass culture, have been effectively controlled on the atoll). That's a good start—and it's a lovely place that merits a visit by those interested in diving on a virgin reef or fishing where only locals have fished before.

The challenge is to develop sources of needed income without trading away the peoples' souls and to reduce dependence on imports: for example, setting up solar electricity production to replace the use of diesel generators; weaning people off rice and encouraging the more nutritious breadfruit, taro, and yams; convincing women that breast-feeding is superior to using infant formula, which was successfully marketed to the people as being modern; and training young women and men to be health-care providers, mechanics, and other skilled laborers.

Many of the teachers now are local returnees who obtained their education in Guam or the United States; that project is well under way. There is still the need to systematically teach the ancient culture to children and bring back vanishing skills, such as canoe making—something that is already being attempted on Yap Proper.

It is a tall order—one that has never yet been successfully accomplished. Doing so requires money; solar generating equipment, reverse osmosis equipment, medicines, and other technologies do not come cheap. The object is to avoid trading off the heart of this culture for a stream of cold cash. But that's what a utopian vision is all about—creating something new and worthwhile, even if it is also something ancient and seemingly impossible. This is something we are extremely interested in facilitating, which reveals, I suppose, our utopian hearts.

Reference

Levy, Neil. *Micronesia Handbook*, 6th ed. Emeryville, CA: Avalon Travel Publishing, 1997.

We must stop murdering one another in genocidal conflicts. Every lesson we can extract from relevant peace-promoting efforts merits our careful attention. All the more valuable, therefore, is the cogent identification below of four insights garnered from major national campaigns to keep the peace and protect potential victims of violence. Each connects to viable utopian ideas, and each belongs in the mental (and spiritual) "tool kit" of those who would struggle around the globe to keep us from cruelly or even fatally harming one another.

36. Utopias Discovered: National Policies That Prevent Ethnic Conflict*

Irwin Deutscher

I have run across some solutions to the problem of how powerful national groups often cause great pain and suffering to others in their nation because the others are "different": Nazis and Jews, Turks and Armenians, Croats and Serbs, Serbs and Croats, Serbs and Croats and their cousins who converted to Islam five centuries ago.

Much of this nastiness is avoidable. There are modern countries which have avoided it. Elsewhere I write in detail of at least five major types of national policies have proven effective in preventing intergroup violence.[1] The policies are different from one another, and they achieve their ends under different conditions. I did not invent them. I discovered them in the social science literature and in the daily press. Each works under different conditions, and each is demonstrably effective in preventing intergroup conflict.

I am sure there are other such national policies that curb inter-group violence, and you may come up with a few that I overlooked. But I want to remind you there *are* national policies that succeed in helping people share the same territory *without* hurting each other.

Four Lessons

What can we learn from the existence of violence-curbing policies? First, according to some people, problems cannot be solved by passing a law. In countries where the government takes a law that curbs intergroup violence seriously, and where people are law abiding, sometimes it is possible. It would be nice if the new law changed peoples' attitudes toward each other, but the point is first to make them change their behavior.

Laws, for example, which broke down racial discrimination in the United States following the civil rights movement of the 1950s and 1960s opened up opportunities for African Americans (and others) in such important areas as housing, education, employment, and recreation. American behavior changed. The extent to which white Americans are less prejudiced is not clear. As regrettable as that may be, it is beside the point. The point is that they simply cannot let prejudice dictate behavior as much as they could before the laws were passed.

The second thing to remember is that when the group in power treats with respect the language, religion, traditions, and other differences of the ethnic

---

*Adapted by the editor from a much longer, richer essay.

minorities who live among them, those differences begin to fade. After three or four generations, both the dominant and the minority groups have changed in ways that leave little more than symbolic differences between them.

Mind you, I am not suggesting all facets of minority culture be tolerated. There is emerging in the world today a nearly universal understanding of what constitutes human rights. Some things are intolerable, no matter how sacred and traditional: slavery and human bondage, as well as the mistreatment of and denial of rights to children or women, are examples.

A third thing to remember is there is a certain inevitability about assimilation. Intermarriage, for example, is a very likely development, even for those such as Italians and Greeks whose cultures emphasize their differences. According to the United States Census, a third of Hispanic women marry non-Hispanics, and the rate is 42 percent for Asian American women. The cultures and traditions of all parties blend into something new. (Two of the most popular "American" foods today are nachos and pizzas. Think about that!) The richness of American culture lies in the constant renewal of its diversity.

Finally, a fourth lesson highlights the value of forgiveness. South Africa, for example, taught us much about how to get beyond intergroup violence with its controversial Truth and Reconciliation Commission. Under the leadership of Nelson Mandela, South Africa wrestled with one of the most crucial issues of our time: How might newly liberated citizens deal with the crimes of the past, with the opposing forces of justice versus vengeance?

What we learned from the South African experience is that a full and unimpeachable accounting of the past is required . . . and this, in turn, must be preceded by strong popular support, a will toward creating and respecting democratic institutions, and, perhaps above all, by the quality of leadership provided by the likes of a Desmond Tutu and a Mandela. Thanks largely to all of this, there was no extensive bloodshed in South Africa after the fall of the former, oppressive apartheid regime.

Taken together, the four lessons teach us that we have been, we are now, and we can continue steadily to improve intergroup relations and end any related violence. This is a *very* viable utopian idea.

Note

1. Sweden, the former Czechoslovakia, Canada, Ghana, and South Africa are discussed at length in Irwin Deutscher, *Accommodating Diversity: National Policies That Prevent Ethnic Conflict* (Lanham, MD: Lexington Books, 2002).

References

Deutscher, Irwin. *Accommodating Diversity: National Polices That Prevent Ethnic Conflict*. Lanham, MD: Lexington Books, 2002.

Glazer, Nathan. *We Are All Multiculturalists Now*. Cambridge, MA: Harvard University Press, 1997.

Hayner, Pricilla B. *Unspeakable Truths: Confronting State Terror and Atrocity*. Boston: Routledge, 2002.

Moynihan, Daniel Patrick. *Pandeamonium: Ethnicity in International Politics*. New York: Oxford University Press, 1993.

Schlesinger, Arthur M., Jr. *The Disuniting of America*. New York: W.W. Norton, 1992.

The United Nations is a viable utopian idea realized. Its "blue helmet" peace-keeping forces save lives in battled-marred zones around the globe, and its UNESCO efforts save children and raise hopes everywhere. All the more valuable, therefore, are suggestions for bolstering the UN's global contribution . . . as in the call below for the creation of a UN World Senate and a related UN World Corps Academy. However you come out on the particulars, the general point—that we have in the UN a viable utopian idea well deserving of steady improvement—would seem to warrant support.

37. The World Senate and Academy*

Mitchell Gordon

One problem with the United Nations is that no one is directly elected as a UN representative. When people feel left out of government, they become frustrated with it. Giving even the smallest nation the same say as the largest may work well in the General Assembly, but the absence of a duly elected legislative branch of world government—with more equal divisions between people and land area—is a big gap. What is called for is the creation of a UN World Senate; this is a viable utopian idea.

A World Senate might consist of nine elected members from each of the world's fifteen regions, resulting in a 135-member world body.[1] Elected officials would inspire millions of young people who typically have regarded the UN as just an inner circle of elite, grey-haired appointees. Elections, together with checks and balances, might change public consciousness of the world body and take the principle of federalism (which inspired the United States) to a whole new level.

The World Senate could garner enough support to create great projects, such as, for just one example, a World Corps Academy, which might consist of a training campus, a fleet of mercy sea and air ships, and a few docking

---

*This essay has been drawn by the editor from a much longer, more detailed version available from the writer at mfgordon@excite.com.

and airport service centers. Teachers at the academy would come from a variety of disciplines, including medicine, engineering, planning and architecture, agriculture, and the languages.

Among other things, the UN Senate's World Corps Academy would train young people to carry out mobile emergency life support anywhere in the world, in response to the rampages of nature or man. The full power of technology would be brought into service, everything from cloud seeding to telecommunications, food services, energy, security, transportation, and housing. Trauma therapists and antidisaster technicians would be part of a lightning operation.

Academy vessels would contain operating rooms, a blood bank, a pharmacy, a library, and a food center. Amphibious landing craft and construction vans would also be on board. UN vessels could combine health and engineering services to help renew stability in deteriorated areas. Indeed, the relief ships need not wait for disasters to strike. They could take the offensive in the battles against poverty and pestilence.

U.S. troops, under the aegis of the United Nations, have conducted emergency famine relief operations in the past (Somalia, for instance), so there is a precedent for American participation in a more permanent UN corps of emergency relief workers.

In spite of terrorists who hijack religion, in spite of conservatives who lambaste international organization, in spite of those who fear foreigners and the repercussions of world trade, a new world order *is* emerging. The United States cannot be the world's policeman. A reformed and restructured United Nations, strengthened by the creation of a UN World Senate and an Academy Corps of "comforters," can help show the way.

Note

1. These regions would include the following: 1. Central Asia, including Kazakhstan, Afghanistan, Mongolia, Azerbaijan, Georgia; 2. China: large enough to stand alone; 3. Easternmost Europe and Siberia, including Ukraine, Belarus, Moldova, and Russia; 4. Indian Alliance, including Pakistan and Bangladesh; 5. Middle America, including Mexico, Central America, Cuba, and the Caribbean Islands; 6. Middle East States, including Egypt and Ispajor (Israel, Palestine, Jordan economic union); 7. Northern Africa, including nations above the equator; 8. North America, including Greenland; 9. Oceania, including Australia and islands of the South Pacific; 10. Pacific Rim, including Japan, Korea, Taiwan, and the Philippines; 11. Southern Africa, including Congo; 12. South America–Amazonian States, including Brazil, Uruguay, and Guyana. 13. South America–Andesian States, including Chile, Argentina, Peru, and Colombia; 14. Southeastern Asia, including Indonesia; 15. Western and Central Europe, including Iceland, Poland, Romania, Bulgaria, and Hungary.

XII. The Big Picture: Global Transformation

Tighten your seat belt! The essay below invites you to take a fast-paced trip into a remarkable possible future, one predicated on far-out uses of artificial intelligence and cybernetics in a novel "resource-based economy." Answers are offered to such questions as—What if all the money in the world suddenly disappeared? How might we best react if automation results in the massive loss of familiar jobs? How serious is the threat of a takeover by supersmart machines? Above all, what do we really want in the way of a fulfilling life-style—and what sort of viable utopian ideas best promote that vision?

38. The Future by Design: Beyond Money and Politics

Jacque Fresco and Roxanne Meadows

It is no more possible to design a workable, utopian society than it is to design the optimal television set. Since all things improve, and new technologies are always emerging, any fixed arrangement would prove inappropriate in any emergent society. Even the most intelligent and humane arrangements for viable utopian ideas would fall far short of the requirements of the new and innovative changes that will be forthcoming.

What is needed in the design of viable social arrangements is a flexibility that allows for new and emergent ideas. This must also allow people the ability to accept such changes both intellectually and emotionally.

Today, when we consider viable utopian ideas or alternative social arrangements, they have to include eventually being accomplished on a global scale. Setting up individual utopian communities or nations is insufficient when other surrounding nations are experiencing war, poverty, and deprivation. We must begin to think of our problems globally and consider the solutions in terms of a systems approach for the entire planet.

Here we present a social design that will work toward achieving a global civilization, while maintaining the flexibility to adapt to whatever changes are necessary to protect the environment and the world's people. This vision is what the future can be if we apply what we already know. It calls for a straightforward redesign of our culture in which the age-old inadequacies of war, poverty, hunger, debt, and unnecessary human suffering are viewed not only as avoidable, but also as totally unacceptable. Anything less will result in a continuation of the same catalog of problems inherent in today's world.

Although many of us like to consider ourselves forward thinking, we still cling tenaciously to all the values of the old monetary system, devised centuries ago during ages of scarcity. Most of us accept unthinkingly a system that breeds social inadequacies and actually encourages the creation of planned obsolescence and shortages. Our current practice of rationing resources through monetary methods is irrelevant and counterproductive to the well-being of people.

Today we have access to highly advanced technologies, but our social and economic system has not kept up with the technological capabilities that could easily create a world of abundance, free of servitude and debt for all of earth's peoples. This could be accomplished if we implement a *resource-based economy*.

Resource-Based Economy

Simply stated, a resource-based economy utilizes existing resources rather than money, and it provides an equitable method of distribution in the most humane and efficient manner for the entire population. It is a system in which all natural, man-made, machine-made, and synthetic resources are available without the use of money, credit, barter, or any other form of debt.

In an economy based on resources rather than money, we can easily produce all of the necessities of life and provide a very high standard of living for everyone. In a resource-based economy, all of the world's resources are held as the common heritage of all of earth's people. *This principle is the unifying imperative*. If humankind is to come together toward a mutual prosperity, universal access to resources is essential.

All social systems, regardless of political philosophy, religious beliefs, or social customs, ultimately depend upon natural resources—clean air and water and arable land—and the necessary technology and personnel to maintain a high standard of living. This direction can be accomplished through the intelligent and humane application of science and technology.

Unfortunately, science and technology have been diverted from these ends for reasons of self-interest and monetary gain through planned obsolescence, sometimes referred to as the conscious withdrawal of efficiency. For example, an ironic state of affairs exists when the U.S. Department of Agriculture, whose function it is to conduct research in various ways to achieve higher crop yields per acre, actually pays farmers not to produce at full capacity while many people go hungry.

A resource-based economy considers us all equal shareholders of the earth—and we are all equally responsible both for it and its population and cultures, as well as for the generations to come. In a resource-based society, the human condition is of prime concern, with technology subordinate to it.

To understand the meaning of a resource-based economy, consider this: What if all the money in the world suddenly disappeared? As long as topsoil, factories, and other resources are left intact, we can build anything we choose to build and fulfill any human need. Money is not what people need, but rather freedom of access to the necessities of life without having to appeal to a government bureaucracy or any other agency.

If the thought of eliminating money still troubles you, consider this: If a group of people with gold, diamonds, and money were stranded on an island that had no resources, their wealth would be irrelevant to their survival. Only when resources are scarce can money be used to control their distribution. One could not, for example, sell the air we breathe or the water that abundantly flows down from a mountain stream. Although air and water are valuable, when they are abundant they cannot be sold.

Money is a social convention, an agreement, if you will. It is not a natural resource, nor does it represent one. It is actually no longer necessary or relevant to our survival.

Higher Standard of Living

Even the wealthiest person today would be immensely better off in a high-energy resource-based society. Today the middle classes live better than kings of times past. In a resource-based economy, everyone would live a far better and more meaningful life than the powerful and wealthy of today.

This new social direction is committed to the redesign of our cities, transportation systems, and industrial plants, allowing them to be safe, energy efficient, clean, and convenient in serving the needs of all people. These cities would also support universal health care, and a far more relevant education.

A resource-based economy would use science and technology to overcome scarce resources, and it would involve an all-out effort to develop new, clean, and renewable sources of energy: geothermal, controlled fusion, solar, photovoltaic, heat concentrators, tidal power, and much more. Eventually we would have energy in unlimited quantity sufficient to propel civilization for thousands of years.

In such an economy, production would become fully automated. The concepts of "work" and "earning a living" would be irrelevant. The focus would be on a fulfilling lifestyle.

Accessing Goods and Services

The distribution of goods and services without the use of money or tokens would be accomplished through the establishment of distribution centers. These centers would be similar to public libraries in which anyone can access books, cameras, or any other item along with instructions for their use. For example, if you visited Yellowstone National Park you could check out a camera or camcorder, use it, and then return it to another distribution center or drop-off, eliminating storing and maintenance.

Besides computerized centers throughout the various communities, where products would be displayed, each home would have 3-D, flat-screen imaging capabilities. A desired item could be ordered, and the item would be automatically delivered to your residence. In a global resource-based economy, when people have access to resources, the concept of ownership will be burdensome and serve no useful purpose.

Eliminating Waste

To eliminate the waste from such products as newsprint, books, and magazines, a light-sensitive material printed from a monitor or television would produce a temporary printout of the news of the day or any other relevant information. This material will be capable of holding the information until deleted, and then be reused. This technology would conserve millions of tons of paper. Eventually most paperwork, including the transfer of money, would be eliminated.

As we outgrow the need for professions based on the monetary system, such as lawyers, bankers, insurance agents, advertisers, salespersons, and stockbrokers, an enormous amount of waste will be eliminated. Doing away with the duplication of competitive products, such as tools, eating utensils, pot and pans, vacuum cleaners, and much more, would also save considerable amounts of energy and resources. Instead of hundreds of different manufacturing plants, and all the paperwork and personnel required to turn out similar competing products, only a few items of the highest quality would be needed to serve the entire global population.

Incentive

Some people claim the free-enterprise system and its competition create incentive. This notion is partially true; however, it also perpetuates greed, embezzlement, corruption, crime, stress, economic hardship, and insecurity.

Most of our major developments in science and technology have resulted from the efforts of a few individuals, working independently and often against great opposition: Robert Goddard, Galileo, Charles Darwin, Nikola Tesla, Thomas Edison, Albert Einstein. These individuals were genuinely concerned with solving problems and improving processes, rather than with realizing mere financial gain. Despite our belief that money produces incentive, we often mistrust those whose sole motivation is monetary gain.

The aim of this new social design is to encourage a new incentive system, one that is no longer directed toward the shallow and self-centered goals of wealth, property, and power. These new incentives would encourage people toward self-fulfillment and creativity, both materially and spiritually.

There is always a reason for corruption when someone gets something they consider valuable out of it. Without vested interests or the use of money, there is little to gain by squelching opinion, falsifying information, or taking advantage of anyone. There is no advantage to be gained by limiting the participation of people or restraining the introduction of new ideas. The main objective is full access to information, services, and the resources of the world.

Cybernation

Government and industry will continue to assign more and more responsibility for decision making to artificial intelligence. So many people will be replaced that they will no longer have the purchasing power needed to sustain a monetary-based system. When automation and cybernation are utilized extensively, not only industrial workers, but most professionals will be replaced by artificial intelligence.

Even the most visionary writers and futurists of today find it difficult to accept the possibility of robots replacing surgeons, actors, engineers, top management, airline pilots, and other professionals. Machines may one day write novels or poems, compose music, and eventually replace humans in government and in the management of world affairs. Whether we realize it or not, this process is already well under way.

Nature does not subscribe to human interpretations of good or evil, or hang onto traits of species that are no longer useful. There are no final frontiers or permanent structures in nature, although many human beings would like to believe otherwise, especially when it comes to their own species.

We are rapidly approaching the time when human intelligence will be incapable of assimilating the technological complexities necessary to operate a highly advanced global society. We do not have the capability to process the trillions of bits of information per second necessary to manage efficiently the coming technological civilization.

That is why we urgently advocate a society that utilizes cybernetics not merely as a system of tabulation and measurement, but also as a way to process vital information and channel it for the benefit of all humankind.

Cybernation in a resource-based economy could be regarded as the only real emancipation proclamation for humankind; it could free people for the first time from a highly structured and outwardly imposed routine of repetitive day-by-day activities.

In a cybernated global economy, construction would be vastly different from the method employed today. Mega machines directed by sophisticated artificial intelligence will excavate canals, dig tunnels, and construct bridges, viaducts, and dams—all based on designs that are in perfect accord with ecological concerns. Self-erecting structures would prove most expedient and efficient in the construction of industrial plants, bridges, buildings, and eventually the entire global infrastructure. Human participation will be in the form of selecting the desired ends.

This operation would not create cookie-cutters cities. The notion that large-scale, overall planning implies mass uniformity is absurd. Cities would be uniform only to the degree that they would require far less material, save time and energy, and yet be flexible enough to allow for innovative changes, while maintaining the highest quality possible to support the local ecology—both human and environmental. Utilizing technology in this way would make it possible for a global society to achieve social advancement and worldwide reconstruction in the shortest time possible.

Today, as artificial intelligence develops, machines will be increasingly assigned the task of complex decision making in industrial, military, and governmental affairs. This idea does not imply a takeover by machines. Instead, it is a gradual transfer of decision-making processes to machine intelligence as the next phase of social evolution.

In a resource-based economy, machines will monitor the production and delivery of goods and services, while protecting the environment. They will not monitor people. This would be counterproductive, socially offensive, and serve no useful purpose.

It is not automated technology or machines we should be wary of, but rather the abuse and misuse of this technology by selfish, corporate, and national interests. We can build rockets to explore outer space and to enhance the quality of life on earth, or we can use them to destroy other nations. Ultimately, people decide what ends these inanimate machines will serve.

To make decisions and reach consensus, people must acquire relevant information from appropriate sources and behave accordingly. Unfortunately, in the pursuit of economic advantage, humans acquire and manage information for personal and corporate gain. Cybernated systems, programmed for common concerns, will do much to prevent unchecked executive authority or abuses of power.

In a resource-based cybernated system, decisions will be based upon direct environmental, human, and industrial feedback from all the cities, factories, warehouses, distribution facilities, and transportation networks. All the decisions will be appropriate to the greater needs of society, rather than to those of corporate advantage.

Government and Laws

As for who will govern, the more appropriate question is how will society be governed? The main objective of this new civilization is to surpass the conditions responsible for reliance on laws. For example, in our proposed cities, where people have free access to goods and services without a price tag, this condition would eliminate theft. Another example might be when a car approaches a school district. There will not be a sign that reads 15 mph; instead, the power output to the car's transport unit will be held automatically to 15 mph.

As difficult a concept as this may seem, laws are byproducts of insufficiencies and scarcity. If the free enterprise system does not provide for job security, medical care, and all the other necessities of life to secure the position of each individual, then a wide range of unmanageable human behavior is the result, no matter how many laws are passed.

During the initial planning of a resource-based economy, a current survey of all our available planetary resources and personnel will be needed to ascertain the possible parameters for this new social design. It will also require the management of the population, through education, to coincide with the carrying capacity of earth's resources.

All decisions would be reached and based on this updated comprehensive survey, not on the advantage to be gained by any nation, corporation, or select group of people.

Human Behavior

Too many people today use genes as a scapegoat for many forms of aberrant behavior, when the major influences have been shown to be environmentally determined. Genetic makeup alone cannot fully account for aberrant behavior.

Our most cherished beliefs are influenced by books, motions pictures, television, religions, role models, and environment. Even our notions of good and evil and our concepts of morality are part of our cultural heritage and experiences. This method of control does not require the use of physical force, and it has been so successful that we no longer recognize or feel the manipulation.

The dominant values of any social system rarely come from the people; rather, they represent the views of the established society. Bigotry, racism, nationalism, jealousy, superstition, greed, and self-centered behavior are all learned, and they are all strengthened or reinforced by our culture. These patterns of behavior are not inherited human traits or human nature as most people have been taught to believe. When we come into the world, we arrive with a clean slate as far as our relationship with others is concerned. If the social condition remains unaltered, similar behavior will reoccur.

In the final analysis, then, any judgment regarding undesirable human behavior serves no purpose unless an attempt is made to alter the environment that creates it. In a society that provides for most human needs, people who have difficulty interacting in the community would be helped, rather than imprisoned, and constructive behavior would be reinforced.

Conclusion

Utopian societies in the future will evolve a set of values unique to that period in time, and they may have little or nothing in common with preconceived notions. Research in innovative and new social arrangements must understand that all systems are transitional and are subject to innovative and continuous change.

Of course, no one can really predict the future with precision. There are simply too many variables beyond our comprehension. New inventions, natural and man-made disasters, or new uncontrollable diseases may radically alter the course of civilization. While we cannot confidently predict the future, every action and decision we either do or do not make ripples into the future. We have the capability, the technology, and the knowledge to shape our own future better. If we fail to accept this responsibility, others will do it for us.

Note

The Venus Project—tvp@thevenusproject.com; www.thevenusproject.com—is an organization dedicated to the ideals and direction presented in this essay. We encourage you to become informed about our proposals through our books, videos, and seminars. If you identify with this direction, we welcome you to join with us and work towards its realization.

Getting beyond outmoded mind-sets is indispensable, if also very hard. Achieving desirable out-of-the-box thinking is a goal we must pursue every minute, and practicing the related craft is an essential activity. Help is available from the mind-stretching essay below, as it offers a model of what the writer calls "soft solutions," a viable utopian idea. We are invited to "invent" many more such eclectic solutions, as we must if we are not to make the costly mistake of pouring "good wine" (viable utopian ideas) into tired "old bottles" (existing institutional forms, values, and practices).

39. Our Hard Problems Need Soft Solutions: This Is the Century of Soft Things

Jim Pinto

In year one of the new century, on a date equivalent to an emergency telephone number that will remain forever etched in our minds, the dream of a capitalistic Camelot had a sudden and rude awakening. More than anything else, September 11, 2001, represents a benchmark, a transition to a new century in which the old solutions are no longer applicable.

Hard reality brings the recognition that a new society is emerging—new demographics, institutions, ideologies, and problems. The uneasy realization remains that society has undergone an irreversible change and will never again be the same. The old naiveté has been negated. Both capitalism and democracy need to adapt to the realities of the new age. The problems we face are hard, and they cannot be solved by old, hard solutions that might have been effective in the past. New, soft solutions are needed. The coming century must become a century of soft things.[1]

The Hard Realities of a New Century

Consider this: If the world were a village of 100 people, 1 person would have a college education; of the 67 adults in the village, 37 would be illiterate; about 38 would have access to clean, safe drinking water; 15 people would live in adequate housing and the other 85 people would live in huts and be hungry most of the time; 6 people would control half the wealth; and 3 of the 6 would be Americans; only 7 people would own an automobile (some would own more than one).[2]

The majority of the people on this planet have always been poor, but the situation now is different for three basic reasons: (1) the numbers of poor are increasing exponentially, overloading the carrying capacity of underlying social support systems; (2) the poor now have television access and can see how the wealthy live; and (3) the poor have access to weapons that can produce large-scale destruction.

Anyone who contemplates the future should be concerned about these fundamental trends. They are rapidly growing in significance, and they will collide during the next decade in a way that will very likely make the world a very difficult place in which to live. Each of these problems has no conventional solutions within our present societal paradigms. These are "hard" problems, which cannot be tackled by "hard" solutions.

Soft Solutions for Hard Problems

To stimulate new thinking, let's try to group some of the hard problems and consider four sets of soft solutions.[3]

1) *Ignorance, Misunderstanding, and Needs.* What we need is a new way to think. The words "war" and "crusade" are harmful: "Crusade" reinforces the idea that this is a religious conflict, which it is not. A "war" is supposed to be won or lost, not just endlessly stalemated. We must find effective ways to combine hard power (military might) with soft power (persuasiveness and coalition building) to be successful in this new kind of struggle.

We must evangelize our principles using all the tools at our disposal, including propaganda, advertising, broadcasting, networking, and so on. We must educate the less fortunate so that they are exposed to the freedoms and warmth of our culture. While they subsist with poverty and hunger, vast populations view only those aspects of our culture that are being advertised: our sensational excesses and pornography. The closeness of a global village exacerbates and amplifies the gap, and ignorance compounds the problem. We need to pursue reasonable dialog and global education to understand how others think—to respect other cultures and to achieve healing and closure.

Beyond just guarding against terrorism, we should work to correct the causes. We must find ways and means to turn guns into gifts, bombs into bridges. Instead of waging war against a resentful minority that resorts to terrorism, countries that have a surplus of unsold food, clothing, and other consumer goods could airlift their surplus to needy countries. The malevolence of terrorists is disarmed when the causes of their dissatisfaction are clearly understood and addressed. Terrorism is less destructive when a society is no longer ignorant.

2) *Supporting Non-Democratic Regimes.* In spite of the recent show of force in Afghanistan, the new society will be dominated by brain, not brawn. The world will be borderless for business, with upward mobility for everyone. In a borderless world, democracy will attain a new meaning.

In the United States we espouse democracy, but only within narrow national boundaries. Emerging democracies are difficult to deal with and so, under the guise of noninterference, we collaborate with military dictatorships and royal principalities around the world. On the surface these people cater to our pretensions, but they sneer behind our backs and continue their undemocratic domination of their people.

Democracy is a luxury the poor and starving cannot afford; it works best in an educated society. We must somehow spur democratic governments *and* equitable economic democracy. We must help to create self-reliant, ecological, electronically linked communities (not states). A transformed United Nations could significantly help increase direct democracy.

3) *Vulnerabilities of an Open Society*. The answer to fanaticism cannot be to reduce our openness and increase authoritarianism. We can reduce our vulnerabilities through constructive planning and "soft" technologies. For example, there are several technology solutions, such as visual scanning and biofeedback, which can identify terrorists without penalizing the average citizen or reducing freedom.

Broad-based defenses must become civilian-based defenses. Let ordinary citizens be the first line of defense against terrorists. Without asking everyone to spy on their neighbors, ordinary good people can be expected to provide the equivalent of a "neighborhood watch"—a program that has indeed reduced crime in many neighborhoods. Instead of placing military police on every commercial airline flight, we can train passengers to identify and deal with terrorists. Not everyone can have the heroism of a Todd ("Let's roll!") Beemer, but watchful passengers can indeed make a big difference.

4) *Selfish Capitalism Needs Reform*. Free enterprise is still the best way to make money, but it does not generate value beyond self-enrichment for a few, with questionable trickle-down benefits for the rest. In the closely interconnected global village of a new century, we must recognize that perhaps it is equally important to make the poor less poor. We need to find ways and means to sell the "softness" of capitalism. Employee ownership, for example, has already broadened participation in the fruits of success. We must encourage entrepreneurship at smaller and smaller levels.

Working to Build a Viable Utopia

The opportunities and solutions available today are unlike anything ever available in the history of humankind. In this new century, technology is accelerating to provide miracles no medieval Merlin could ever have delivered at Camelot. Communications at a personal level, the Internet, and media on a national and global scale all bring the concept of an enlightened global village within our grasp.

Let us not dwell on pessimistic probabilities, but rather on the practical possibilities. Let's work together to focus our collective efforts and goodwill to bring about the viable utopia only dreamed about by our forefathers.

Notes

1. I am continuing to work on this new theme: "Soft Solutions for Hard Problems," http://www.jimpinto.com/writings/softsolutions.html. Your inputs, ideas, feedback, commentary, suggestions, and encouragement will be much appreciated. eSpeak to me: jim@jimpinto.com.
2. "The Near Future," Peter Drucker, two-part article, *The Economist*, November 2, 2001. Available at http://www.cfo.com/Article?article=5641; http://www.cfo.com/Article?article=5642.
3. Discussed in "Outlook 2001," November-December 2000 issue of *The Futurist*, journal of the World Future Society: http://www.wfs.org.

Too few of us know enough about the remarkable advances being made in utopian thought outside of the Western tradition. The introductory essay below introduces a leading Indian thinker, Prabhat Ranjan Sarkar. We learn a bit about spiritualism, world government, one world culture, and forecasts from macrohistory. We learn of a plan for ending world poverty, bolstering local cultures, taming capitalism, advancing the "feminine" ethos, and using advances in artificial intelligence and robotics to reduce slavish dependence of waged labor. In other words, we learn to search beyond the Western canon to improve viable utopian ideas.

40. Planetary Social and Spiritual Transformation: P. R. Sarkar's Eutopian Vision of the Future

Sohail Inayatullah

Hailed as a complete Renaissance man, Prabhat Ranjan Sarkar is well known as a social philosopher, political revolutionary, poet, and linguist.[1] He is also significant for his creation of the Progressive Utilization Theory (PROUT) and for his role as a spiritual teacher of the social service and spiritual movement, Ananda Marga.[2]

This essay focuses on Sarkar's contribution to utopian and futures thinking. His interest in the future, however, is not in prediction but, rather, in inspiration—in the creation of a new vision for humanity.[3] His focus is a general critique of the present, along with developing an alternative vision of the future, a eutopia (good place), and social movements to help create this alternative future. Sarkar's works are thus intended to persuade, to transform oppressive social and political structures—to help us envision the world anew.[4]

The root of Sarkar's mission is the spiritual:

not [as] a utopian ideal, but a practical philosophy which can be practiced and realized in day to day life. It stands for evolution and elevation, and not for superstition and pessimism. Spiritual philosophy does not recognize any distinction and differentiation between one human being and another, and stands for universal fraternity.[5]

Progress is possible only in the spiritual realm.

Accordingly, Sarkar's vision of the future is fundamentally different from the predominant Western epistemological (linear, secular, empirical, individualistic, and liberal democratic) tradition. Although he writes that humanity's future is inevitably bright, revolution of any sort—spiritual, economic, cultural, political—is an arduous task. Revolutionaries who desire to transform the numerous pathologies of the present must undergo spiritual transformation; they must suffuse their minds with love, with selflessness, and be prepared to suffer hardships.

The Good Society

The future, then, for Sarkar is part of the larger human story, part of humanity's evolutionary development, or the constant effort of the mind to bridge the gap between the finite and the infinite: It is in the deepest sense of the word, the eventual mystical union between the soul and the Supreme Consciousness.

This is fundamentally different from many thinkers who regard progress primarily in terms of increased economic productivity, a better standard of living; that is, more goods and services and the satisfaction of material needs for a large part of the global population. Certainly, economic growth is important from Sarkar's perspective. His vision of the Good Society is premised on individuals being guaranteed the basic requirements of life (food, clothes, shelter, education, and health). The ultimate purpose of economic growth is to provide physical security, so that women and men can pursue intellectual and spiritual development. It is the unabated accumulation and misuse of wealth that is the central problem, not the goods and services per se.

In Sarkar's eutopia, he sees a more united, globally oriented human society. He hopes that temporary unifying sentiments (but divisive for those not included) such as nationalism, provincialism, and religion are transformed by universalism. In this global society, there will be a world government with centralized powers, for without it capitalistic exploitation will continue. There must be a strong polity, structurally made up of separate executive, judicial, and legislative bodies, within the larger context of a spiritual society.

Sarkar does not believe, nor wish, that a one-world culture will develop. In fact, the key long-term trend will be the decentralization of culture and thus the flourishing of local cultures—languages and economies—a possibility only after the eradication of global capitalism and its necessity to homogenize, commodify, and proleterianize everything. Sarkar's primary social strategy for "transforming" the capitalist system is the development of regional, self-reliant cultural movements based on local languages, local economies, and local geography, in the context of global social, environmental, spiritual, and rights movements—the glocal (global-local) emergent vision.

However, for Sarkar, individual spiritual development must precede any systemic, societal change. In addition, cultural revolution must precede economic change as capitalism works by creating a structure of cultural and economic dependency between centers and peripheries, between empires and colonies. (Communism, based on the materialistic industrial model characterized by the centralization of wealth in the state and the homogenization of culture, created similar oppressive structures.)

PROUT

The principles of Sarkar's good society are developed in his comprehensive theory: the Progressive Utilization Theory, or PROUT.[6] It attempts to balance the need for societies to create wealth and grow with the requirements for distribution. To achieve this balance, an integral part of the PROUTist vision is to create floors under income and ceilings over it, progressively indexed to aggregate economic growth.

Thus, wealth will not be hoarded and thereby underutilized or misutilized, as in the case of global stock markets. However, unlike socialist utopias, which argues for equality, PROUT accepts individual differences and the desire of individuals to own limited property and goods. It also accepts the key role of incentives in spurring technological innovation and economic growth. And, unlike Green perspectives focused solely on equilibrium, PROUT is focused on *prama*, or dynamic balance (progressive sustainability).

The primary economic entity within the ideal PROUT society would be employee-owned and employee-managed cooperatives. These would include producer, banking, legal, health, and other types of cooperatives. However, because of economies of scale, there would remain local small businesses, as well as large regional industries run by quasi-governmental appointed boards. There would thus be three sectors: a government sector, a private sector, and a people's sector.

Sarkar, along with others, has initiated PROUT movements throughout the world. Although these self-reliant, cultural people's movements are still very small, eventually they will reach a critical size and pose a significant challenge to the present world system.

These movements are actively organizing women, students, workers, farmers, and professionals, as well as other groups and classes, against injustices and inequities. Demands, for example, include 100 percent employment for local people; laws against the export of local raw materials; laws against the import of manufactured goods which can be produced locally; primacy of local languages in offices and schools; land reforms; rights for animals, as well as concern for the long-term care of the environment; and support for local music, writing, art, and dance.

In the Philippines, for example, one social movement, Kasama, participated in the ouster of Ferdinand Marcos and in the removal of foreign military bases.[7] In India, Amra Bengali has contested various local elections and has established cooperatives.[8]

Thus, through the creation and legitimation of globally oriented, yet regionally and locally based spiritual, cultural, and economic movements, and through the ensuing dialectical conflict these antisystemic movements will engender as they reconceptualize polities and economies, Sarkar sees the eventual demise of both capitalism and communism.

Methodological Perspective

Sarkar's vision of the future is partly based on intuition and partly based on his analysis of history. He argues that most of us use very little of our mind, geniuses perhaps 10 percent, others not even 1 percent. We remain bounded in the body and the conscious mind. However, through meditation, through the exploration of the deeper layers of the mind, we can develop our creativity and intuition. We can realize perennial truths and thus balance our multidimensional selves.

Equally important is Sarkar's theory of the social cycle—his macrohistory.[9] There are four eras based on four ways of knowing the world: the workers' era, the martial warrior era, the intellectual era, and the capitalist era. Each era is followed by a major transformation, and the cycle begins again. Major revolutions occur throughout the world, largely because in late capitalistic society the exploitation of all, and especially of women, is particularly brutal.

Disgruntled intellectuals and martial-minded individuals bring on the next cycle. The level of violence during transitions between the eras is determined by the aggregate ratio of intellectuals to the martial-minded, and the timing of the revolution is a correlate of the increasing population of these two classes. The question raised by Sarkar is, "Can we fundamentally alter the cycle?" His conclusion is that, although the social cycle follows a natural law and thus will continue, humans can reduce the exploitive phase of the cycle.

The next turn of the cycle can bring on progressively higher levels of human development. Thus, the new martial era, although structurally similar to the historic one, will be qualitatively at a higher level. In addition, the in-between anarchic workers' stage will be short lived, as power will quickly centralize among the intellectual or martial-minded leaders of the workers' movement.

To reduce the exploitive phase of each era, Sarkar argues for the development of declassed individuals who, through their social, spiritual, service (and, if necessary, revolutionary) efforts, bring on the next era.[10] He calls these individuals *sadvipras*. However, unlike present power elites, such as corporate executives or state bureaucrats who are part of the dominant class and ideology that "run the planet," these individuals must be declassed and must have value structures based on love and neo-humanism.[11]

Describing this era, this new future, is difficult. However, we can postulate that government will be centralized, and the world economy will be highly decentralized and cooperative/socialist in nature. Although the world government structure initially will be strengthened by law-framing international agencies, eventually a world polity will develop with executive, legislative, and judicial functions. There will also exist constitutional rights for workers, guaranteed basic necessities for all, and various rights such as world citizenship. Sarkar has also called for a neo–Magna Carta, in which rights for plants and animals (true "deep ecology") are to be guaranteed, spiritual freedom upheld, and linguistic choice honored.

Economic growth will come from ending the global exploitation of workers and others peripheral to the world capitalist system. Through maximum-minimum wealth laws, the world surplus will be redistributed.[12] Through worker involvement in business, labor and capital will become more productive. Intellectual and spiritual resources currently being wasted will become valuable inputs into economic development, moving us to a wisdom economy.[13]

PROUT writer Michael Towsey believes there exists a gender dialectic as well, such that the breakdown of the patriarchal nature of capitalist society will also lead to the incorporation of the mythic "feminine" in the emerging global planetary and martial era. Neither gender will then be commodified.[14]

Science and Technology

This new era is not one that pits spirituality against science. Sarkar believes that technological development controlled by noncapitalists, by humanists, will lead to increased economic growth, intellectual development, and social equality. Technology will come to have "mind" in it, some level of self-awareness, as a result of developments in artificial intelligence as well as through the agency of microvita, what Sarkar posits is the basis of life. (The crudest microvita are similar to viruses; the most subtle have intelligence. They are the stuff of life, functioning as mind and matter, as bottles of energy.)

Once full employment is reached, and once the untapped potential of humans is increasingly realized, instead of massive unemployment because of productivity gains from robotics and informatics, we will simply reduce our workweek, so that:

one day, we may only work five minutes a week. Being not always
engrossed in the anxiety about grains and clothes, there will be no misuse
of mental and spiritual wealth. [We] will be able to devote more time
to sports, literary discourses and spiritual pursuits.[15]

Struggle then will largely be in intellectual and spiritual realms—in the constant effort to reduce the gap between the finite and the infinite, between the
present and the ideal future.

The problem of food will be solved primarily through the cooperative economic structure. Each region will utilize its own raw materials and develop
industries appropriate to the local environment. By encouraging self-
sufficiency and self-reliance, some of the advantages of global trade will be
lost in the short run—the North, in particular, will face a reduction in its
standard of living. However, as regions develop and as economic gains are
redistributed, trade between different regions will flourish. Trade, then, will be
between equals, not centers and peripheries, not the powerful and the emaci-
ated—true globalization can then begin.

In the long run, food tablets will be invented to deal with any temporary
food shortages that may arise. In addition, medical science will increase longevity to perhaps to 150 years, and "in certain fields (we) will even be able
to infuse life in the dead." Sarkar also predicts that by "changing individual
glands, a dishonest person may become . . . an honest one." However, glan-
dular changes will not be able to transform root behavior structures; only
spiritual practices can fundamentally transform the structure of the human
mind. Unlike some futurists who predict that because of revolutions in the life
sciences we are on the threshold of immortality, and that we may soon uncover
"an aging gene," Sarkar believes death cannot be escaped, as brain decay
cannot be postponed.[16]

Nearly forty years prior to the mapping of the human genome, Sarkar fore-
cast that children will be born in "human reproduction laboratories," and parents will choose their characteristics. In the long-term future we will become
primarily intellectual/psychic beings and even lose our reproductive faculties.
We will gradually take on functions now performed by the Cosmic Mind
(loosely, "Nature"). This image should be contrasted with that of other spiritual
visionaries and futurists who believe that technological development should be
severely limited, and we should not tamper with "Nature."[17]

Thus, ultimately, we will become an increasingly technologically developed
society with spirituality as the basis and the goal of life. We will look back at
the days of the nation-state and the great capitalist and totalitarian communist
empires and wonder why it was ever doubted they could not be transformed.
Eventually, we will become primarily psychic beings traveling to other planets
through space technology (the exploration of space will be in the forefront in

the upcoming martial era). We will be able to leave our bodies in one place and travel with our minds. The stars will eventually become our home.

Of course, problems of power and exploitation will not go away. Most likely these will be fought at the mental realm, among ideologies, and perhaps even at the level of psychic warfare. However, neither linear notions of progress (often at the expense of the weak) nor of the cycle (with no possibility of movement forward) will dominate. Rather, the spiral will be in force-progress, with humility.[18]

Conclusion

Sarkar's vision is not a utopia. It does not predict the end of exploitation and struggle. Rather, it is a *eutopia*, a good place, where there will be good actions, but negative ones as well, thus requiring structures and safeguards. Moreover, it is not technological revolutions that will lead to the "death of death," but spiritual practices. And these spiritual practices must be based on rigor, discipline, and selfless service to the Other, not solely on good feelings and the search for spiritual pleasure.

Thus, while love is important—in fact, it is the ground of any lasting social change—so also is the struggle involved in challenging the assumptions and ideas that govern present-day institutions. There exist real global problems that neither cyber nor spiritual utopianism can resolve. Centuries of the misappropriation of wealth and power exercised by nation-states will not be transformed solely by creative visualization.

Sarkar's new era, what he calls *sadvipra samaj*, is about spiritual progress, but also about hard thinking and hard work. Although he is idealistic, he emphasizes the precarious struggle ahead for humanity. He warns of the possibility of a world destroyed by pollution and ravaged by human greed (the desire for endless accumulation) and negative tendencies actions (largely based on misidentification with tribe, race, religion, or nation).

Overall, Sarkar's vision remains optimistic. Although employing a partially deterministic theory of history, he sees women and men, acting courageously, bringing about preferred visions. They must with their intellect develop new scientific possibilities and societal futures, and thereby develop the new human for the new world.

Notes

1. P.R. Sarkar, born in 1921, resided in Calcutta until his death in October 1990. He developed the Progressive Utilization Theory in 1959. He also started the Renaissance Universal Movement—an association of spiritual/socialist oriented intellectuals—that year. He wrote in diverse fields such as health, ethics, devotional literature, fiction, history, political economy, biology, linguistics, and philosophy. PROUT's opposition to Indira Ghandi's government led to Sarkar's being jailed in 1971. He was released

in 1978 when the Janata government created the conditions for an impartial judiciary. See Prabhat Rainjan Sarkar, *Poet, Author, Philosopher*. Corona, NY: Ananda Marga Publications, 1986. See also Sohail Inayatullah, *Understanding Sarkar*. Leiden, Netherlands: Brill, 2002.

2. Ananda Marga is a social service and spiritual movement with centers throughout the world. It teaches meditation and other spiritual practices. The organization is involved in community health and educational development projects. Although its cultural roots are Indian, it is universal in its approach.

3. Throughout this essay, I use the terms *futures studies* and *futurists* in a general sense. Although there are numerous differences among futurists, there is an emerging futures field, which in general accepts the liberal-democratic secular-capitalist tradition (although many do believe this system will undergo massive shocks in the near and long-range future, primarily owing to technological changes). This "continued growth" view is best characterized by the Washington DC–based World Future Society and developed in its journal, *The Futurist*. In contrast is the Hawaii and Europe-based World Future Studies Federation, which is critical of the present global system, its structure, and its ideological underpinnings. Johan Galtung's writings best characterize this perspective.

4. Elise Boulding, "The Imaging Capacity of the West," in *Human Futuristics*, ed. Magoroh Maruyama and James Dator (Honolulu, HI: University of Hawaii Press, SSRI, 1971), p. 30.

5. P. R. Sarkar, *The Supreme Expression*, vol. 2 (Netherlands; Nirvikalpa Press, 1978), p. 161.

6. Books about PROUT by Sarkar's students include the following: Ravi Batra, *The Downfall of Capitalism and Communism* (London: Macmillan Press, 1978); Ravi Batra, *Regular Cycles of Money, Inflation, Regulation, and Depression* (Houston, TX: Venus Books, 1985); and Gary Coyle, *Progressive Socialism* (Sidney, Australia: Proutist Universal Publication, 1984). Also see Acarya Krtashivananda Avadhuta, *PROUT Manifesto* (Copenhagen, Denmark: PROUT Publications, 1981); and Acarya Tadbhavananda Avadhuta, *Samaj* (Calcutta, India: Proutist Universal Publications, 1985).

7. Kasama USA, *Kasama: Six Demands to Strengthen Democracy in the Philippines* (Washington DC: Kasama USA Support Comittee, 1986).

8. See Acarya Tadbhavananda Avadhuta and Jayanta Kumar, *The New Wave* (Calcutta, India: Proutist Universal Publications, 1985), p. 135.

9. P. R. Sarkar, *The Human Society* (Calcutta, India: Ananda Marga Publications, 1984).

10. P. R. Sarkar, *Problem of the Day* (Ananda Nagar, India: Ananda Marga Publications, 1959), p. 3.

11. Tim Anderson, *The Liberation of Class: P.R. Sarkar's Theory of Class and History* (Calcutta, India: Proutist Universal Publication, 1985), pp. 14–15. These ages are also related to different distinct mentalities. The worker is dominated by the environment. The martial type attempts to dominate the environment and the other classes through physical strength. The intellectual attempts to control the environment and the other classes through the mind or by ideology. The capitalist attempts to control the environment and the other classes through the ownership of the means of production. We are warned not to confuse these categories with the old Indian caste system, which are purely psychological types.

12. P. R. Sarkar, *Idea and Ideology* (Ananda Nagar, India: Ananda Marga Publications, 1967), p. 85.

13. P. R. Sarkar, *The Liberation of Intellect—Neo Humanism* (Calcutta, India: Ananda Marga Publications, 1982).

14. Michael Towsey, *Eternal Dance of Macrocosm* (Copenhagen, Denmark: Proutist Publications, 1986).

15. Sarkar, *The Liberation*.

16. See F. M. Esfandiary, *Optimism One* (New York: W.W. Norton, 1970); see also Sohail Inayatullah, "The Future of Death and Dying," *Futurics* 5, no. 2 (1981).

17. See, for example, Jeremy Rifken, *Declaration of a Heretic* (Boston: Routledge and Kegan Paul, 1985). Rifken is the best critic of the new biology (genetic engineering, brain drugs, and the host of other emerging fields which promise radically to change human nature).

18. See James Dator, "The Futures of Cultures or Cultures of the Future," in *Perspectives on Cross Cultural Psychology*, ed. Anthony Marsella (New York: Academic Press, 1979), pp. 376–88.

Cautionary notes are welcomed by all eager to understand more completely what we mean deep down and with exactitude by the term "utopia." One thing, of course, is not to leave any assumption unexamined, as, for example, the assumption that the State is the best instrument for keeping order and is the only agency for punishing offenders. The mind-stretching essay below challenges this and related assumptions and urges us to give fresh attention to an alternative model, one rich in viable utopian ideas, which just might help us secure a far safer and saner world than the one we know.

41. When Can the Just Society Use Force? A Proposal for Radical Tolerance

Adrienne Redd

Just as the first principle of medicine is do no harm, the first principle of practical utopian thought should be to weigh the benefits of a top-down, wholesale approach to solving social problems against the price in human suffering resulting from such an approach.

My search for practical lessons in utopian literature grew out of teaching social problems, a discipline in which one identifies disorder and suffering in society, considers the causes of such difficulties, and seeks solutions. Utopias, whether philosophical, literary, or attempted (as in the case of Findhorn, the Paris Commune, or the many Protestant experiments on North American soil in the nineteenth century) are an attempt to solve *all* social problems.

The Big Idea

In addressing all social problems, the single characteristic that defines utopias (and dystopias) is that they emerge from what I call, irreverently, a "big idea."

In Plato's *Republic*, the basic ideological foundation is that wise and selfless leadership will create a just society, and no sacrifice on the part of individual leaders is too great to serve that just society. In Edward Bellamy's *Looking Backward* (1888), the big idea is that all members of society will share all resources through a system of equal distribution. In Aldous Huxley's classic dystopia *Brave New World* (1932), the big idea is that individuals who are bred and conditioned for their jobs will constitute a perfectly stable society, although they must never be allowed to experience any passion or existential angst that would disrupt that stability.

The big idea of my practical utopian suggestion is that the totalization of every utopia and every dystopia, without exception, cause unjustifiable suffering. In both attempted and literary utopias (and dystopias) they extinguish the spark of individuality, even humanity, even life itself. The golden guardians of *The Republic* of Plato can never love a partner, never have a family, never have private lives. Isn't this too high a price to demand that the philosopher-rulers relinquish everything that makes our own lives fulfilling?

In the collectivist state of *Looking Backward*, given one brief mention, like the hidden and suffering child of Ursula Leguin's "The Ones Who Walk Away from Omelas," is the dark secret of Bellamy's future society. People who refuse to participate in the mandatory workforce are detained, subsisting on bread and water, until they are willing to toil beside everyone else. One cannot sail around the world, take a sabbatical, or live like Jack Kerouac if one so chooses. Autonomy and internal motivation—tremendous sources of vitality and regeneration in our own society—are denied because of the universal work requirement.

In dystopias, such as George Orwell's *1984*, (1949), *Brave New World*, Ayn Rand's *Anthem* (1938), and Kurt Vonnegut's "Harrison Bergeron" (1968), the suffering of the nonconformists reaches tragic dimensions. Revealingly, in *Anthem* and "Harrison Bergeron," individual talent and excellence are actually regarded as deviant behaviors for which the protagonists are punished. Even in the most successful of actual utopian societies, the requirement for cultural homogeneity and the treatment of deviance are the downfall. The most noble and long-lived of all attempted utopian communities, the Shakers, ultimately died out because such a strict, celibate life was simply too difficult to maintain.

We can observe the big idea run amok in Nicolae Ceauşescu's Romania, Pol Pot's Cambodia, and the Chinese Cultural Revolution. Even Sweden, the supposed model of benign socialism, has skeletons of brutality in its closet of cultural homogeneity. Between 1934 and 1974, 62,000 Swedes were involuntarily sterilized as part of a national program grounded in the science of racial biology. And the state lobotomized as many as 4,500 "undesirables," in some cases without the consent of their families.

An even more horrible outcome of intolerance growing out of a single, monolithic ideology is the senseless destruction of life. On September 11,

2001, more than 3,000 lives were extinquished, in part as an act of protest against our commercial, secular, and wildly diverse society.

The central challenge for utopia is how to treat the person who thinks differently, acts differently, or cannot manage to bounce the ball in unison with the other children. If the big idea solves all or most of the problems of the citizen, but crushes the misfit, how just or wise is that big idea? To paraphrase Hubert Humphrey, how we treat misfits and nonconformists is the moral test of a government.

Against Isolated Utopias

A related error of literary and attempted utopias is their isolation. Cultural quarantine is unworkable in the age of global trade and instantaneous communication. It is logistically impossible to propose an ideal society that walls itself off from the rest of the world to implement its big idea. The genius of the American idea of opportunity and the pursuit of happiness is that it is open, if imperfectly, to outsiders and immigrants. Sir Thomas More's "General Utopus" may have been able to isolate his peninsular nation physically, but today's social architects cannot do the same.

Since we cannot isolate ourselves, we need to ask what forms of deviance in our open society *actually hurt* other members of society. What forms of deviance warrant the use of force, and what forms are to be tolerated, even if uneasily? Our traditional utopian thinking has taken us in the wrong direction. The social problems traditionally addressed by utopian thought are problems of deprivation at the lowest socioeconomic stratum, and a proposed social safety net for this underclass.

A more promising option for utopian thought might be to dismantle unnecessary laws. Citizens should only be chased, detained, or physically punished for the crimes of theft, fraud, assault, or violence against other persons, the destruction of or violence against property, or the credible threat of such violence. The gravity of such violence should be measured by the severity and irreversibility of the violent actions. This would lead to what I would like to call *radical tolerance*, an experiment in a society where no detainment or force is inflicted on any member of society for mere nuisances or vices, no matter how annoying or offensive or self-degrading.

In such a society, based upon radical tolerance, pornography, prostitution, and other consensual sexual acts, the use of currently illegal drugs, and ownership of weapons would be legal. No *force* of the state would be directed against citizens for engaging in these vices. Why? Because punishing vices with force is much more destructive. (However, the simple ownership of weapons can cross the line into an implicit credible threat of violence. Thus, private ownership of weapons of mass destruction would not be allowed. Private ownership of light arms would probably be allowed.)

Proposing the withdrawal of state force against vices is not to suggest that fines, opprobrium, and disapproval could or should not be imposed upon a member of society—only that the state would not detain that citizen for smoking or selling marijuana or other drugs, owning an object that could be used as a weapon, selling sexual favors, or publishing pictures considered obscene. Of course, if pictures are taken of nonconsensual acts (including those of children who are by definition not capable of consent), they would be evidence of criminal acts.

There is another powerful argument for not criminalizing victimless vice and deviance. It is clear that laws against vices are selectively enforced, often with nonwhites and the most disempowered members of society bearing the brunt of penal power. One example is that of Timothy Thomas, a nineteen-year-old black man shot and killed in April 2001 by a white Cincinnati police officer. He was running away because he had eleven outstanding parking and traffic tickets, and he had been fined for a number of other safety and public nuisance violations. These included playing music loudly, having the windows of his 1978 Chevrolet tinted too darkly, not wearing a seat belt (six counts), disregarding a traffic signal, and not placing a child in a safety seat. Not one of these was a violent offense, and not 1,000 or even 10,000 counts of such offenses would justify gunning down this young man in the street.

Our utopian vision should reconstruct moral authority so that deadly force will *never again* be abused in this way. It is obvious that Mr. Thomas was pulled over (so that he could be cited six times for not wearing his seat belt) because he was "driving while black"—a colloquial expression for what is known as "racial profiling." This racist and selectively enforced authority is the price we pay for thousands and thousands of laws to "help" people live their lives more responsibly.

There are negative and unintended consequences of our extensive set of "quality of life" and safety laws. The quality of the lives of Cincinnatians was not helped by the ordinances enforced against Thomas; their lives were disrupted by the race riots that raged through that city after the policeman who gunned him down was exonerated.

How Society Benefits from Radical Tolerance

We cannot deem just a society that makes criminals of its citizens who hurt themselves, offend others, or march to a different drummer. Furthermore, it is worth exploring how society at large would benefit from radical tolerance of deviation from established norms. We, as moral beings, will benefit by learning to tell the difference between what directly affects us and what merely offends us. There was a time when people were socialized to be offended by seeing a mixed-race couple, a pregnant woman in public, or a physically handicapped person. We have socially evolved to tolerate what were once deviant behaviors and to realize that we are enriched by having such examples of difference in our midst. There is room for us to grow even more.

Just as we are morally and spiritually better for accepting deviant people and behaviors, we are culturally stronger for doing so. In agriculture, monoculture is a vulnerable state. Though appealing to the misguided, monoculture in human society is as debilitating as it is in botany. A world of only blue-eyed people is weaker—biologically, culturally, artistically, and morally—than a world including brown-eyed, gray-eyed, and green-eyed people too. Diversity, whether genetic or cultural, gives strength. A group trying to solve a problem has more success when differing points of view are considered. New York City, or any of the other great global cities, harbors chaos, crime, and disorder, but also tolerance of difference and the strength and magnificent vitality that come from that diversity. The strongest society is not the one that isolates its fragile prosperity and ideological purity, but the one that is open to creativity, experimentation, and risk.

Guidelines for Socially Positive Behavior

I am not suggesting that we eliminate all laws not dealing with physical harm, but rather that we as a society never use force, particularly deadly force, against a citizen who has not defrauded or stolen from another adult, physically or psychologically hurt another adult, or who is imminently about to do so. This proposal for radical tolerance can never solve all the problems of society; however, if we pare the crimes that are potentially punishable by force to a brief list, this will allow society to focus on the best way to mete out that punishment, which may ultimately involve compassion, rehabilitation, and restorative justice; not force or brutal dehumanizing incarceration.

Paring the crimes punishable by force to a short list similarly does not prevent us from offering guidelines for moral and socially positive behavior— guidelines such as be empathetic, tolerate people who are different from you, be charitable, strive to understand the world so you can act responsibly, and so on.

If we implement radical tolerance, how can we ensure that citizens will act justly, wisely, and charitably? The simple answer is we cannot. But we *can* begin to engender a culture of responsibility, wisdom, compassion, and charity. With fewer laws en*forced* (quite literally), people might take the remaining laws more seriously. Citizens might have more moral and mental energy to consider what is ethical when legislation does not intrusively tell us.

There are still more problems to solve. How will this program of radical tolerance prevent and punish sexual abuse of children? In this limited space, I submit merely that there is a problem with defining crimes against children the same way we define crime against adults. We have to balance intrusion into private families against harm of children. We need to walk the line between allowing children to be raped by their parents or other guardians, and the devastating harm possible if the state regulates and enforces daily vitamins or routine bedtime.

Furthermore, it is a mistake to equate children with adults. In the normal course of parenting, it is necessary to inflict disciplines equivalent to assault, imprisonment, and involuntary servitude. I propose the following calculus: Can we say we want to prevent a child's being deprived of his *future* liberty, health, and happiness? By this criterion, guardians can send a child to bed without dinner and not destroy her ability to function when she becomes an adult. They cannot, however, touch her genitalia in an inappropriate manner without leaving some psychological scars. Similarly, they can spank her, but not repeatedly break her bones.

Social Power

This proposal will not eliminate the nuisances, abuses, and pathologies that exist in any society. However, governmental authorities whose resources are freed up from chasing pot smokers and window tinters can direct more attention to punishing and treating thieves, murderers, rapists, and pedophiles.

What we need to do is to stay morally engaged with one another as citizens, but loosen that grip a little so we can walk side by side, but not in lockstep. Restricting ourselves to using force only in specific cases would eliminate enormous injustices. Governmental resources would be freed to address the most destructive and urgent problems, and individual moral sense could focus on what is the most appropriate and charitable behavior in order to build a more just society.

References

Bellamy, Edward. *Looking Backward 2000–1887*. Boston: Ticknor, 1888.
Dieteman, David. "Sweden and the Myth of Benevolent Socialism," http://www.lewrockwell.com/dieteman/dieteman33.html, 2001. Accessed March 6, 2002.
Huxley, Aldous. *Brave New World*. London: Chatto and Windus, 1932.
Le Guin, Ursula. "The Ones Who Walk Away from Omelas," in *The Wind's Twelve Quarters* (1975). Full text available at <http://lavka.cityonline.ru/text/hugo/Omelas_.htm>.
More, Thomas. *Utopia*. Translated by Paul Turner. New York: Penguin Classics, 1516, 1965.
Orwell, George. *Nineteen Eighty-Four*. London: Martin Secker and Warburg, 1949.
Plato. *The Republic*, translated by Allan Bloom. New York: Basic Books, 1968.
Rand, Ayn. *Anthem*. London: Cassell, 1938.
Vonnegut, Kurt. "Harrison Bergeron," in *Welcome to the Monkey House*. New York: Delacorte Press, 1968. Full text available at http://www.house-of-poetry.com/stories/classics/cs3.html.

XIII. Looking Forward

When Americans think of pro-utopian possibilities we commonly think of them only or primarily in relation to America. This self-centered view sorely handicaps us, and it is vital that we soon grasp the larger picture. Helpful here is the account below from an activist monk in Brazil. He mentions an ally we may underestimate, the annual World Social Forum, and he discusses its link to three leading forces for change in his country. We learn a bit about liberation theology, Progressive Liberation Theory, and other matters of which we commonly know far too little (see the related essays in this volume by Valerie Fournier and by Sohail Inayatullah). Note especially the emphasis placed in closing on the strategic value of patience, persistence, and hope.

42. Living the Dream, "Another World Is Possible": Combining a Spiritual Perspective with Social Action in the Developing World

Dada Maheshvarananda

I am a revolutionary and a monk. This may seem paradoxical, but moved by the terrible tragedy of the Vietnam War, I decided to dedicate myself to revolutionary change based on love. I wear robes of the ancient saffron color, which signifies service, sacrifice, and renunciation. I teach the practical techniques of meditation and demonstrate how a yogic lifestyle can calm one's emotions and channel the natural human propensities in a positive direction toward optimum physical, mental, and spiritual growth.

These ancient practices offer me the most powerful vision of a new future for myself and the world. I am convinced personal development is essential for activists. People do not want to follow angry or bitter politicians. Of what use is a science fiction vision of the future if the actors are driven by emotions of greed, jealousy, and selfishness? I believe the world needs wise women and men who are strong and selfless by nature: saint-like, Christ-like.

I worked for fourteen years in Southeast Asia, and I have lived in Brazil for ten years. I see myself as a teacher because I try to awaken a revolutionary consciousness in people. In the 1960s there was a phrase—"Teaching is the most subversive activity." Through personal example, I try to show that the key to infinite happiness lies within us, not in material objects. Selfless service to others makes one great—not wealth, power, fame, or external beauty. All languages and cultures of the world are rich and must be preserved—they hold the secrets to self-esteem and inner strength for people.

Neo-ethics based on universal principles of morality should be the base of economic activity and global peace. For example, the ancient yogic principle of *aparigraha* is an ecological ideal of simple living, not accumulating unnecessary things. On the personal level it encourages the adoption of a humble lifestyle and donating extra wealth to charity. On the social level it is the basis of creating a ceiling on salaries and wealth which are robbing the planet of the resources God gave to humanity.

Self-realization and service to the universe are universal goals all people can be encouraged to adopt. Service work is both purifying and humbling. Bo and Sita Lozoff's wonderful Prison-Ashram Project of the Human Kindness Foundation in the United States is an incredible example of teaching ancient yoga techniques and sharing correspondence of love with more than 50,000 prisoners around the world (http://www.humankindness.org).

Inspired by their example, for the last four years I have been teaching weekly yoga and meditation classes in prisons, helping men and women transform their lives. The warden of a large prison where I teach told a reporter from the *Jornal do Brasil* national newspaper, "Great changes among the prisoners that do meditation have been noticed. The most important is the decrease of aggression" (http://amps.org/amnews/brazilprisyoga.htm).

Spirituality is deeply important to me, but I do not teach organized religion. It is only by taking the best from the East and the West, and by honoring the spiritual treasure at the heart of every religious tradition, that we can make a better future. At the same time, we must reject dogmas and fight against injustice and exploitation wherever they are found.

Forces for Change in Brazil

A democratic counterforce has begun to rise. The first World Social Forum was organized in Porto Alegre, Brazil, in January 2001, in opposition to the

World Economic Forum of the rich nations held at the same time. Twenty thousand people came to that event with the theme, "Another world is possible." Three times as many attended the following year: 67,000 participants from 131 countries, speaking 186 different languages and representing 5,000 different organizations. The power of this annual event is the shared dream: that it *is* possible to construct another world with justice for all.

The strength of the World Social Forum is its diversity: people from different classes, races, and countries joined together. Hundreds of poorly educated activists from the Brazilian landless people's movement stayed in gymnasiums and community halls, along with more than 600 indigenous people from different tribes. Forty conferences and 800 workshops tackled different themes, analyzing the effects of economic globalization, and struggling to clarify viable alternatives (www.forumsocialmundial.org.br).

At the youth camp, more than 18,000 slept in tents and shared music and laughter. They proved the truth spoken by Kevin Danaher of Global Exchange regarding the new protests against global capitalism: "The young people today are redefining the political party, making a REAL party with singing, dancing, drum circles, chants, giant puppets, and street theater!"

In addition to this coalition of nongovernment organizations, Brazil, with its population of 170 million, has three major progressive movements today interlinked with counterparts in other Latin America countries.

The first is the Landless People's Movement (Movimento dos Trabalhadores Sem Terra, or MST). Less than 2 percent of landowners hold 60 percent of the arable land, and just 342 farm properties cover 183,397 square miles, an area larger than California. Most of this property is cleared to create pasture for the beef industry, which requires very few employees. At the same time, millions of unemployed farm laborers have no land to cultivate in order to meet their basic needs.

The MST has mobilized these landless workers by constructing large camps of activists pressing for land reform. The government continues to stall on redistributing large, vacant land holdings, and so the MST occupies huge unutilized plantations. When the police come to evict them, they leave and then return. Fifteen million people are staying in their camps who otherwise would be living in city slums with their children on the streets. The MST continually organizes demonstrations, marches, and protest rallies to mobilize these masses.

The second large movement is the Workers Party (Partido dos Trabalhadores, or PT). Formed twenty years ago as an alternative to traditionally corrupt politics, this party maintains a reputation for honesty, and it prioritizes the social welfare of the common people. More than 100 cities in Brazil are now run by PT mayors, including the largest, São Paulo. The PT candidate for president, Luís Inácio Lula da Silva, has come in second place in the last three elections. [*Editor's Note*: He was elected in 2002.]

The third progressive force in Brazil is part of the Catholic Church, the main religion of South America since the Spanish and Portuguese conquerors arrived 500 years ago. It is said that there are actually two churches, one of the rich and one of the poor. The church hierarchy, controlled by the Pope from the Vatican in Rome, is very conservative, and it is the religion of the rich landowners and elites.

Liberation theology, a radical blend of socialism and Christianity, is led by ex-priest Leonardo Boff and the monk Frei Betto, among others. It has inspired some priests and nuns to work with the poor and take courageous stands against exploitation and torture. They started the extensive system of ecclesiastical base communities (CEBs) to serve the poorest, most excluded sections of society, and also to radicalize their participants.

These three popular democratic movements are growing in strength among the lower and middle classes, and they advocate a radical transformation of society. All three work directly or indirectly with the World Social Forum. The shared dream, that "Another world is possible," begs the question: What kind of utopia do we want? These groups clearly want a future more democratic, and plural, one that includes everyone in the country's development. Yet they lack a clear alternative economic model to capitalism and communism.

The Progressive Utilization Theory (PROUT) is a utopian blueprint for how to reorganize society and the economy for the welfare of everyone. Holistic and vast in detail (P.R. Sarkar's writings on PROUT total nearly 1,500 pages), it is well outlined in the insightful essay by Sohail Inayatullah in this very book. PROUT is now being seriously studied and discussed by the national leaders of all three of these progressive movements as an alternative, postcapitalist model for Brazil (www.prout.org).

The most frequently asked question about PROUT concerns where it has been put into practice. Whereas PROUT cooperatives and communities exist in various countries and on every continent, until an entire state or country opts to try it, the world will be unable to see how this model of cooperatives, key industries, agriculture, manufacturing, and banks, all working together, can enrich everyone's living standard and quality of life.

To change a society is difficult. To create a total transformation that will benefit all people as well as the planet, what Sarkar calls a "nuclear revolution," requires much more effort. However, the greatest things are achieved only with great effort and struggle. Our most important mission, I believe, is to offer hope that we *can* change the world and construct a viable utopian-like society based on the welfare and happiness of all.

"The fire next time," or so we have been warned. Not again a flood that we might survive, but this time . . . possibly a thermonuclear holocaust of our own making, followed by Nature's retribution in the form of a nuclear winter. Nightmares of this sort, aided by post-9/11 fears of more terrorist attacks, explain the urgency with which we must heed much that is discussed in the instructive essay below.

Viable utopian ideas have a large part to play in securing, holding, and refining the peace. For example, we must weigh the pros and cons of campaigning anew for a cabinet-level Department of Peace. We must assess a call for the establishment of a worldwide network of citizen study circles. Above all, we must keep alive the vision of an ancient utopian prescription—a time when swords shall be beat into plowshares, and men shall not learn war anymore.

43. Peacemaking: From Talk to Action

Robert J. Merikangas

Let's visualize world peace. We need to take action, but we need to talk before, during, and after the action, because we need to reach agreements on our agendas for replacing war and violence with peace and moving to a more peaceful world. There is nothing wrong with our random acts of kindness, but they are not enough.

We cannot leave the talking to the ruling elites, and their diplomats, and their admirals and generals, because we need to imagine steps to a world that lies outside their mental maps. They are unable to lead us from here to there; we have to lead. We need to talk here, where we are now, on the margins and on the periphery, and then move our conversations to the halls of power.

A basic framework for making a change in the way in which the U.S. government does things in relation to war and peace would be the creation of a Department of Peace, as proposed by Congressman Dennis Kucinich of Ohio. The first day of each year, January 1, will be designated as Peace Day in the United States, and all citizens will be encouraged to observe and celebrate the blessings of peace and endeavor to create peace in the coming year. A cabinet-level department in the executive branch of the federal government will be established and dedicated to peacemaking and to the study of conditions conducive to both domestic and international peace. The department will be headed by a secretary of peace, appointed by the president, with the advice and consent of the Senate. [Further information on the Kucinich proposal is available at http://www. house.gov/~kucinich/action/peace_legis_summary.htm.]

The department will hold peace as an organizing principle. It will endeavor to promote justice and democratic principles to expand human rights, to strengthen nonmilitary means of peacemaking, to promote the development of human potential, and to work toward creating peace, preventing violence, diverting from armed conflict, and developing new structures in nonviolent dispute resolution.

To buttress all of this, the new department will create and establish a Peace Academy, modeled after the military service academies. It will provide a four-year concentration in peace education, and graduates will be required to serve five years in public service in programs dedicated to domestic or international nonviolent conflict resolution.[1]

Perhaps this viable utopian idea of Kucinich and others will have been put into effect by the time this book is on the shelf. If not, there is much here to discuss.

What I will now outline are some beginning points for our conversations, which I imagine taking place, first, in people's study circles, in every community. We will use as a model the study circles in Sweden (Oliver 1987) and those already in operation in the United States (see the Study Circles website and Linda Stout's Spirit in Action initiative). We will provide resources for our conversations on the web, along with training materials for our facilitators. Our study circles will create regional and national networks and make videos for use on the mass media.

Specifically, one of the primary manifestations of the control of the U.S. government by corporate interests is the size of the military budget. We need to talk about this military-industrial complex, and what has been called the permanent war economy, using data from the Center for Defense Information and other resources outside the Pentagon, in order to form free judgments.

(This large topic can only be mentioned now, but our talk about peacemaking will undercut the support for nuclear weapons, missile defense shields, and space weapons along with huge artillery weapons. It will replace funding for weapons with funding for peacemaking, peacekeeping organizations, and interventions).

The study circles would make maximum use of the free newsletters and reports of the United States Institute of Peace and other resources. If Congress and the Executive Office of the president do not use them, at least the people and the peace community can and will.

Dialogues in the study circles will need to take the time to go into the foundations of people's judgments about the ethics of killing. We have centuries of complex legal codes, specifying when killing another person is permissible and when it is not. There are rules of war, who may be killed and when, using what kinds of weapons. We recognize the rights of military personnel to refuse orders to carry out killings that are not right. What do we think of these rules? What about the U.S. rule against assassination of a foreign leader?

What do religious teachers say about killing? Limit it, or not do it? In our conversations we need to ask spokespersons for religions whether and how they justify killing by members of their faiths. We may inquire into the genocide committed by Christians in Rwanda, and the reluctance of other Christians to intervene to stop it. Islamic scholars have provided interpretations of the messages of peace in their tradition, and some have criticized sponsors of Terrorism and suicide bombings.

What could have a tremendous impact on the position of many people on the ethics of killing is the growing interpretation of the meaning of the death of Jesus on the cross. Some now see it as a sign of nonretaliatory nonviolence, intended to be a model for all his followers. The refusal to respond to violence with violence, and taking the side of victims against oppressors in every case, would be a sea change in a Christian religion in which leaders have often justified military violence, notably during the Crusades. In a more comprehensive context, nonretaliation may be seen as a fundamental grounding of all universal human rights programs and campaigns.

Even for those who are not prepared to take a position for nonviolence, reflection on war and violence usually leads to the desire to reduce its incidence, so we need to talk about what Chris Gray calls postmodern war (1997): "Some say war can never be abolished, but the same was said about slavery. It [too] was a very old discourse, and yet now it is almost totally discredited. Abolition of war is possible. Lately, it has even seemed very possible in the abstract, but not in practice" (p. 252).

It is not enough for us to talk about the horrors of war, since many who find it horrible also call it necessary or inevitable. So we need to talk on two levels about ways to go beyond war. The first higher level is that one in which we refuse to participate in war. This has been worked out in various methods of civilian resistance. We have seen some examples of success in Eastern Europe, the Philippines, and South Africa. We are moved to ask—Suppose they gave a war and nobody came?

Of course, antiwar warriors will have to risk their lives as do soldiers. Gray notes this situation:

> Many peace activists around the world, even in Western countries, have had friends murdered by the state; they have seen people killed; they have been chased by cars, trucks, police, soldiers; and they have been captured, beaten, and locked up. These nonviolent activists have seen more violence than most military people. (1997, p. 240)

The next level for an antiwar movement may seem more immediately practical, for it is prevention. A masterful report on *Preventing Deadly Conflict* by the Carnegie Commission on Preventing Deadly Conflict was made available in free copies and on the Web in 1997. We have no excuse if we have not talked about it and have not yet moved to the actions it recommends. The commission used a public health model and outlined operational and structural strategies for the leaders of governments and organizations.

For a number of years, even decades, many observers and scholars have seen that the necessary next stage in world history is the move to a system of international governance, taking the formation of the United Nations as the first step, and moving beyond to a more complete system. In a new global system, order would be kept by an international police force, not as in the past by military campaigns by the armies of nation-states and empires, such as the British Empire.

To move to the next stage, citizens everywhere must move faster than their governments. Citizens must reach transnational agreements on a cosmopolitan or world citizenship, with correspondingly higher loyalty for everyone. One way to talk about this move is to imagine becoming civil servants of international organizations, such as the UN.

Finally, some might be skeptical of the significance of the rise and use of study circles. Once networked as committees of correspondence, they have been known to lead to large-scale resistance and even aid the move to independence and a new government. Four score and ten years from now such a viable utopian step would be remembered with praise and gratitude.

Note

1. The idea for a Peace Academy is not a new one. Some of us worked for it more than twenty years ago, and peace studies programs have been instituted in some public and private universities over the years. Such an academy was recommended by a commission, chaired by Senator Spark Matsunaga, which delivered a powerful report, *To Establish the United States Academy of Peace* (1981). The Academy of Peace did not happen, though eventually the U.S. Institute of Peace was created, and it has struggled along, with little funding and little visibility.

References

Bailie, Gil. *Violence Unveiled: Humanity at the Crossroads*. New York: Crossroads, 1995.

Carnegie Commission on Preventing Deadly Conflict. *Preventing Deadly Conflict*. Final Report with Executive Summary. New York: Carnegie Corporation of New York, 1997: www.ccpdc.org.

Center for Defense Information: www.cdi.org.

Department of Peace Proposal: www.house.gov/kucinich/action/peace.htm.

Gray, Chris Hables. *Postmodern War: The New Politics of Conflict*. New York: Guilford Press, 1997.

International Decade for a Culture of Peace and Non-violence for the Children of the World: www3.unesco.org/iycp/uk/uk_sum_decade.htm.

Kavanaugh, John F. *Who Count as Persons? Human Identity and the Ethics of Killing*. Washington, DC: Georgetown University Press, 2001.

King-Hall, Stephen. *Power Politics in the Nuclear Age: A Policy for Britain*. London: Victor Gollancz, 1962.

Langer, William L., ed. and comp. *An Encyclopedia of World History*. Boston: Houghton Mifflin, 1952.

Oliver, Leonard P. *Study Circles: Coming Together for Personal Growth and Social Change*. Washington, DC: Seven Locks Press, 1987.

Stout, Linda. *Bridging the Class Divide: And Other Lessons for Grassroots Organizing*. Boston: Beacon Press, 1996. Available online at: www.spiritinaction.net/ Study Circles: www.studycircles.org. *To Establish the United States Academy of Peace: Report of the Commission on Proposals for the National Academy of Peace and Conflict Resolution to the President of the United States and the Senate and House of Representatives of the United States Congress*. Washington, DC: U.S. Government Printing Office, 1981.

In crafting viable utopian ideas, it is vital that we "walk the talk." An inspiring example below recounts how Hal Pepinsky, an experienced college teacher, speaks in class about, and tries to demonstrate with his actions there the value of a "peacemaking" approach to life. We can help get this approach far more widely employed—especially throughout all the years of our classroom-based education. As life in school can be a critical testing ground for better-than-ever ways of being, we can not reinvent schooling fast enough . . . schooling in the service of peacemaking.

44. Our Safety Is Within Our Grasp

Hal Pepinsky

My mother taught me that "utopia" means "no place"—somewhere that does not exist, fantasy by definition. The late capital criminal Sir Thomas More, before being beheaded in 1535, coined the term *utopia* for his vision of an ideal society.

I am a criminologist, heavily battle-scarred over the last thirty years in the midst of the U.S. war on crime. I divide the attitude with which we approach creation of social order into two fundamental categories that I call "warmaking" and "peacemaking."

As I work with others to build an attitude toward responding to crime and violence I call peacemaking, I focus on what we want from our relations with others. What does it take for us to feel personally safer? To help others to feel likewise? To become more honest in our relations? To trust one another more? To become more responsible and responsive in all our relations? To feel more valued and more respected in each other's company?

I consider relations that help us feel safer, rather than putting us in greater fear of each other, to be heaven on earth. As I see it, heaven is at hand right here on earth. In the midst of globally escalating violence, I find globally spreading peacemaking.

Not long ago, in 2001, I posted a "book" of my criminological findings under the title "A Criminologist's Quest for Peace," for free use and comment at http://www.critcrim.org/critpapers/pepinsky-book.htm. Here, in this brief essay, I summarize my findings on how one makes one's own and others' lives safer rather than more violent.

At social levels higher and farther away from you yourself, noticeable cultural, political, and economic progress may take many, many generations longer than our lifetimes. On the other hand, we can gain safety in our own lives and with those whose lives we touch in daily moments, and in the process, contribute all that human will can contribute to larger social change. That is my faith. Below I describe the process by which I find peace being made, one act of human will at a time.

Distinguishing Whether We Perpetuate Fear

Do you feel safer in the wake of U.S. public response to the events of 9/11? Innocent Afghanis of all ages do not. Innocent Iraqis do not. Only a handful of people I meet in the U.S. heartland feel safer. Here instead, even behind the lines of those with the biggest guns, U.S. politicians and journalists warn us to become more cautious.

For once I am not deviant. I, too, feel more vigilant than I would have had no official action whatsoever followed 9/11. I conclude that all that has been done militarily to retaliate for 9/11 has given more people reason for murderous revenge against innocent people.

A friend and I discovered that in decades past we had had a fascination for the logic of guerrilla warfare. Attack where the enemy is weak, retreat where the enemy is strong. By this logic, security measures are like closing the barn door after the cow has escaped. They feed fear. They do terrorists' work of spreading terror.

The guerrilla logic of resistance to warfare, including resistance to 9/11 and the war on terrorism as a package, is to let the hype pass and attend instead to building community among ourselves as we can do and do do. I've imagined bumper stickers: "Better to Invest in Friendship than in Wall Street" or "Better to Carry a Friend than a Gun."

. . . Or Promote Security

The sophomore class I teach, Alternative Social Control Systems, P202, is available on the Web. Please click on http://oncourse.iu.edu/bl. Under Find a Course on the log-in page, click on Advanced Search. Pick a semester. Type in Pepinsky under instructor. Click on a course. At the announcements page that comes up, scroll to the bottom of the page and Click to Continue. Click on tabs that come up including Syllabus to see about the course.

I tell people peacemaking is the alternative social control system I will offer for my part this semester, to warmaking, as in making wars on crime and drugs and terrorism. Peacemaking and warmaking are attitudes. My peacemaking premise is that, as you become aware you can choose your own attitude, moment to daily moment, you gain control. You become safer. You are able to let down your guard and have fun with those you daily encounter first and foremost. This is the climate in which people let go of wars and other violence.

The challenge of peacemaking is to figure out how to transform our daily encounters with violence—personal and systemic—into zones of honest, nonhierarchical friendship.

Bring It All Home

I meet hundreds of students and greet new associate instructors each semester. We meet in a horrendously designed amphitheater, where I feel like a gladiator in a Roman circus. I am a paid public official. I represent the state. The course is required for criminal justice majors, and hence I can make or break students as freely as I choose, as long as I use the grading system proposed in my syllabus.

And so in the classroom where I, in theory, have incredible power, I have a laboratory in which my challenge is to make peacemaking principles work. I tell the students I am immensely aware of my power position as their professor, and that like the first peoples of the U.S. Northwest and the Canadian Southwest, I aim to make our time together a potlatch. I want to give away my power until we strike a balance among the ways we hear from one another.

I also intend to share "my" time not only with the associate instructors, but also with people who fall into groups that are talked about—convicted murderers, gang leaders, drug dealers, drug enforcement officers, self-reported survivors of childhood violence, their supporters, and also those who believe the reports false, and so forth. They are talked about more than the people in these groups are allowed to speak for themselves.

So on one hand we look at alternative attitudes in practice in criminal justice arenas—at "restorative justice" even in murder cases, on down to my own experience as a victim-offender mediator; on the other hand I invite others to join me in examining their own relations to the subject.

More and more concretely and periodically, I am able to affirm how I learn from other class members. For years I have announced up front that my primary criterion for the success or failure of any class of mine is how much I have learned from class members. Ever since, my student evaluations have become less angry and more effusive.

Case Study: Course Grading System

The principal axis of my attempts at transforming warmaking education into a peacemaking attitude in my classes has been my attempts, continually, to reengineer my grading system.

During my first time in front of a class, in January 1971, an introductory criminology class of 250, I announced that everyone would receive an automatic A because I did not believe in grades. I was the product of an ungraded high school education, where each grade/homeroom would vote on what it would study and write about each school term.

As a recently minted, Harvard-trained lawyer, I was naively optimistic my teaching would be well received by students and colleagues alike. I went before a departmental curriculum committee asking that all my courses be listed as pass/fail. I think that visit sealed my departure from that first teaching job.

I have since experimented with grading systems, trying in consultation with associate instructors to refine them semester by semester. If you look at the Indiana University OnCourse Web site for P202 as I suggest above, you will find a tab for the syllabus. I have written long and short syllabi over the years as I struggled to introduce myself to enrollees. The grading section appears at the end of every syllabus. By that I mean to imply that grading is for me subordinated to the larger objective of opening honest, critical dialogue among ourselves in class. Still, designing my grading response to the graded education around me turns out to be most significant in whether I learn during our time together.

Here, briefly, is the system that appears in my recent P202 syllabi: The grade rests on journal entries turned in, in hard copy, in associate instructors' discussion sections, weekly. To get a point toward the final grade, you have to write at least 200 substantive words of response to each of two topics I post for each "lecture"; ditto for two topics from your associate instructor in "discussion section"; with up to two "bonus" points each week for a variety of other contributions, from introducing Web sites to class, to response to other class members on OnCourse mail. The associate instructors and I post our responses to journals there as part of what enrollees might write about for a bonus.

Among recent refinements have been associate instructors passing around attendance sheets (which rarely would count for anything), setting a two-week limit for an appeal over an associate instructor's miscounting of points, and putting an A-ceiling on points toward the final grade until the last two weeks of class, to encourage attendance at a time when the associate instructors and I wrap up the semester and take student evaluations.

Even I, who have struggled so long to transform grading into a peace-building instrument, am awed by how rewarding class has become to me and to students alike. It takes the equivalent of a minimum of thirty satisfactory double-spaced pages of a journal to earn an A in the class. Not everyone makes it, although there are a remarkable number of A+'s, including people who have written more than 150 pages.

The associate instructors help, too. They can't resist making marginal comments, even though I ask them only to keep a running total of points. A long-held dream of mine has come true—in that associate instructors and I really interact and guide each other on what to do next.

That's all there is to the grading system. After more than thirty years of teaching criminology full-time, this grading system is like newfound gold to me. Time and again, in concrete terms, students affirm they have learned as much or more in this class than in any other they have taken. In my peace-making beliefs, this is because they have been given room to learn honestly about themselves.

At the beginning and end of class, I express the hope that the journals will become among the students' most prized college texts. Time and again, career paths change. Recently, this has included someone turning from law to clinical work in child development. At such times, I feel more than amply rewarded for my efforts.

One other change in attitude falls out. People in class become more critical of mainstream rhetoric about the need to punish our enemies. They discover they have hearts, as they discover that their hearts matter. I most recently concluded my semester with them by saying, "You are change, go in peace."

Peace works. You don't have to wait for another lifetime or an afterlife to enjoy it. The Iroquois, who provided a model for the U.S. Constitution, believed fundamentally that we all have a duty to enjoy life. Wherever you are, whatever the structure of your daily relations, may you seek and find enjoyment and security.

XIV. Drawing It Together— and Moving On

We return with this essay to the fundamental question with which the book opened—Should we? That is, should we consider being utopians, whatever we now take that concept to mean? Should we help create, adapt, assess, and ceaselessly improve viable utopian ideas? The sage essay below invites us to ponder links among lessons from our history as a species, from our responsibility to export democracy, from "green" ethics, and from the remarkable specialness of spiritualism ("spiritual consciousness and awe in the face of beauty"). We are gently urged to nurture viable utopian ideas on behalf of all ideas that will long honor us all.

45. Our Future As a Species: A View from Biological Anthropology

Melvin Konner

I have set myself a difficult challenge. I am not an optimist by nature, and the facts are not on our side at this point in history. Yet I know that little purpose is served by spreading doom and gloom, so I'll do that only at the outset. The bad news is the problems are huge. The good news is our species has solved worse problems. We are not just the upright ape; we are also by far the best and most successful ape. We wouldn't be here and, ironically, we wouldn't be facing the problems we face, except for our tremendous success.

The Bible says, "Be fruitful and multiply, and replenish the earth." Evolution says something similar, and indeed that is what we have done. We have dominion over the birds of the air and the fish in the sea and over every living thing that crawls upon the earth. In fact we have dominion over every living thing except ourselves.

What do I mean by that? Consider our history. Our lineage began some five to seven million years ago as a weak small ape acquired, over thousands of generations, a tendency to walk upright. It took several million more years before we even began our brain expansion, or the toolmaking that turned around and helped make us. We created culture, and it created us. The Bible's authors recognized this was what made us different, and what in time would give us complete dominion. What they could not have known, and what even we have trouble seeing, is that this in itself would prove our gravest threat.

Not just for a few million years, but for a thousand times longer the imperative shaping us was that of reproduction. And oh, did we do it. We don't look so great compared to bacteria or insects—there are a lot more of them whether measured in numbers or biomass. But compared to any other mammal we are incredibly successful.

Most of our runaway reproductive success came in the last few thousand years—in evolution's terms, the blink of an eye. What led to it was not just the evolution of Homo sapiens, but a series of social and cultural transformations after our species came into being. Our first big advance as a species was a spiritual one, about 40,000 years ago, when our ancestors began to create great art on the walls of their caves. This put them in touch with some of the highest ideals human beings can aspire to, both religiously and artistically.

Then about 10,000 years ago, in several parts of the planet, our ancestors began to plant seeds and herd animals for a living. Why did this begin after millions of years of hunting and gathering? Population pressure may have come first, forcing our ancestors to use knowledge they probably already had, or people may simply have developed a new attachment to land that expressed itself in farming.

Either way, the consequences were huge. Population growth certainly followed, and the new need to defend a piece of cultivated land intensified our tendency toward war. Towns emerged, then cities, always the heart of empires. This means they were always the products of conquest and taxation, the control of surrounding weaker peoples by dominant ones: Control of water for irrigation, control of cultivated land and its produce, control of labor, and control of hearts and minds.

The first three came from armed force, and the last from organized religion. Every ancient empire was ruled by a three-part elite consisting of an armed nobility, a priesthood, and a merchant class. Together they were irresistible to the common man or woman. Also crucial was the threat empires posed to each other. If you were a farmer on the edge of an empire you knew, you might be brutally taxed and even enslaved, but at least you were alive. If the empire next door sent its army into your village, all bets were off.

So in a sense what we call *civilization* was a protection racket. Violence was its hallmark, not poetry or sculpture. They were beautiful, of course, but incidental. It was once said of capitalism that it emerged from the mud with blood oozing from every pore. This may not be true of capitalism, but it certainly was true of ancient civilization: the mud of irrigated soil soaked with the blood of conquest.

So why these ancient stories in an essay about the future? Because basically little has changed since then. The social structure of our world is based on the legacy of that ancient one. Empires much vaster than those vie for control of resources—some the same, like land, food, and water; some new, like oil and information. Weapons of unspeakable force have replaced the swords and chariots, but the principle is the same, and our lives are at least equally precarious.

The threat of nuclear annihilation, begun at Hiroshima and Nagasaki, exemplifies the use of weapons of mass destruction in the course of conventional war. The genocides perpetrated against civilians such as the Jews of Europe, the Kurds of Iraq, and the Tutsi of Rwanda are another approach to mass extermination familiar from the ancient world, but now much more efficient. And the attacks of September 11, 2001, show us how the very technology we are so proud of can be turned against us without mercy.

Population studies project that the human species will increase to "only" about ten billion. Some calculations suggest there will be enough food to feed them, so all will be well. This assumption is naive.

First, we are degrading the environment so fast the earth's future food supply may be lower, not higher, and the evidence for the declining productivity of wheat and rice is already at hand. Second, near-future fights will not be over food, but over oil and, especially, fresh water. People as different as United Nations leader Kofi Annan, former Soviet Premier Mikhail Gorbachev, and former U.S. Secretary of State Madeline Albright agree this century could be dominated by wars over water. All this is before we mention global warming, the destruction of the ozone layer, relentless deforestation, mass extinction, and other ominous environmental trends. Finally, as September 11 taught us, our lifestyle inspires jealousy that can turn into hatred.

At a minimum, it inspires people throughout the world to want it. But if the whole world should get even a minimal American lifestyle—a small car, a modest apartment with the usual amenities—the planet's destruction will be accelerated because it simply cannot support ten billion people with that lifestyle, and no one with any knowledge thinks it can.

With this description as background, it would indeed seem only a utopian idea could save us, but there is another way to look at it. We are at a turning, or what some call a tipping point. We can proceed to disaster, which seems where we are headed, or we can do a sort of historical judo flip that uses the weight of the disaster against it. Humans unite against terrible threats, and this one is bad enough to unify our sadly divided species, but only if we understand the threat. So knowledge is the first step, but only the first. The second is will.

The disconnect between knowledge and will was exemplified today—intriguingly, the anniversary of the bombing of Hiroshima—by a news item that appeared as I was writing this essay. A U.S. government department, the Environmental Protection Agency, in consultation with advisors appointed by the White House, issued a report warning that human activity is producing climate change that will dramatically harm the environment and, of course, us. President George W. Bush said, "I read the report put out by the bureaucracy," and he went on to say he would not sign the famous Kyoto Treaty, already agreed to by the nations of Europe and ratified by Japan today.

One positive thing that needs to be done is that someone needs to wake up President Bush. This is most likely to be the same people who woke up previous governments about segregation and the Vietnam War: the young. They have vision and energy, they are open-minded, and they are neither committed to the status quo nor complacent about its dangers. They are the key to the tipping point process. Due to the bulge of births sometimes called the echo-boom—the baby-boomers' babies—there are more people in their late teens and twenties every year. For the near future, the world depends on them.

What should they do? Well, they must begin by shaping the consciousness of their elders, and the experience of the 1960s proves it can be done. And of course, they have to imagine a new world. Fortunately, that is not difficult.

Imagine if in the wake of September 11, in addition to everything else he did, President Bush had announced a $100 billion program to end America's dependency on oil through conservation and energy innovation.

Imagine if he had said today, "My daughters and nieces and nephews convinced me I should sign the Kyoto Treaty," putting us on the road to ending global warming.

Imagine if a $1 million prize was offered every year for the best new idea about how to take the salt out of seawater.

Imagine if as much money was put into diplomacy and exchange programs and the Voice of America and the Peace Corps and supervising elections in developing countries as is put into the Air Force, Army, and Navy—or half as much.

Imagine if, besides the United Nations, there was a parallel international organization consisting only of democracies—an exclusive club others would aspire and change to be admitted to, each new member another beacon to the world.

Imagine that international agreements on the environment were not prevented by religious fundamentalists from mentioning family planning and population control.

Imagine if women throughout the world had equal rights with men and—

as other liberated women have done—invigorated their societies, protected the health of their families, educated their children, and reduced their family size.

Imagine if the Kyoto Agreement, the Nuclear Nonproliferation Pact, the World Court, and the worldwide battle against AIDS became the models for scores, then hundreds of agreements that would move the world inch by inch toward international governance.

Imagine if an effective ban existed against dictatorship, racism, oppression of women, torture, terrorism, and war.

Why should anyone with half a brain think this is possible? Because our species' successes in the past show we can do big things that once seemed undoable.

Slavery was once accepted throughout the world, then only in some countries, then banned. Even the Bible took it for granted. Yes, it still exists, but it is on the run, reduced to pockets of renegade provincial life in very backward countries. With will and luck, we will erase it from the planet soon.

Democracy was once just a well-meaning experiment. In 1776 it was pretty much a joke told about a bunch of dreamy rubes in a far-off savage land who had the gall to think they could become more than a colony. Ha-ha. Now the descendants of the Europeans who laughed have followed the American lead, and they are helping to spread the democratic message and method across the world. Democracy is built not over years but over generations, yet it is already widespread enough that we can believe it will one day be everywhere.

Communism seemed for over a century to be a viable alternative to capitalism. No longer. It collapsed of its own dead weight because it defied human nature, which becomes expansive and energized when the spirit of entrepreneurship—alright, controlled greed—is able to function freely, so that people who work for themselves and their families move the world forward. On this the world now agrees, and communism is dead.

And there have been successes on other fronts. Smallpox was erased from the world by an international effort, and polio will soon join it in the history books. In 1998 fewer babies were born than in the previous year, probably for the first time in the history of the species. Population growth is slowing, and although it is still a grave threat, in another half century or so it will peak and slowly start to decline—not soon enough, but in cosmic terms, soon.

An international agreement banning chlorofluorohydrocarbons (CFCs), which still threaten the ozone, included even the environmentally benighted United States, and it has stuck. Although enough are still around to continue the damage, no more are being made, and that represents the first successful planetwide environmental agreement. In the realm of weapons, mustard gas was a method of choice in World War I, but the results were so terrible that— although Adolf Hitler and Saddam Hussein used them against civilians—gas-attacks have not been used in a major war since.

All these experiences suggest our species can leave bad things behind and embrace new and good ones. What can the individual do? Sermonize your minister, priest, imam, or rabbi. Ask your teachers hard questions. Talk to your parents, siblings, children. Write and call and e-mail your politicians again and again. Light your corner, and help others light theirs. If you don't see a movement, get together with a few friends and shoot the breeze until you see a path to change. Anthropologist Margaret Mead once said, "Never doubt that a small group of thoughtful, committed citizens can change the world. Indeed, it is the only thing that ever has."[1] Often that small group has begun with one person.

It isn't a sure thing, not by a long shot. It's a tipping point, and that means it can go either way. Which side will you be on—the side of complacency and ladder-climbing and piling up stuff, or the side of world changing, bold imagination, and action?

It is a race against time, really. Within fifty years—within the lifetimes of many reading this—we will add four billion people: over 200,000 a day, 80 million a year, a country the size of India in little more than a decade. Four billion new mouths to feed, four billion thirsty throats, four billion legitimate dreams of comfort and happiness.

It is actually even worse than that, because the disadvantaged part of the species will grow much faster than we will, and a growing population is inevitably young. The four billion will include a disproportionate number of poor young men and women. Will they have jobs so that they have some hope of living their dreams? If they don't, how frustrated and angry will they be? What will they do with their anger?

Giving up what we have and turning it over to them will not be an answer because it won't go nearly far enough and it soon will be gone again. We do have to use less, waste less, pollute less. That is our charge, and we had better be up to it.

But the world's poor billions have a job to do too. They must imagine effort, make change, exercise reproductive restraint, employ tolerance, and adopt democracy. And we must give them the tools—not the fish, but the fishing rod. We must find the best, most forward-looking people in those countries—every country has them—and strengthen their hand. We must get over the simpleminded cultural relativism and the absurd, morally bankrupt postmodernism that would condemn those people to be forever separated from their dreams.

Unfortunately, force has a role. It must be used judiciously, but it cannot be foregone. We have seen it work to positive effect in the Persian Gulf, the Balkans, and Afghanistan. We have seen it unite disparate nations and peoples in a common effort against truly bad men with savagely harmful ideas. We saw it half a century ago too, when Germany and Japan rose from the rubble of their justly shattered dictatorships to become two of the strongest and freest democracies in the world.

But to rely only on force is to drift backward in history toward that bad old time when might made right. If, as I believe, our way of life and especially of government is superior, then most people will not have to be forced to adopt it, especially in this age of instant worldwide communication.

Why is it superior? Because it accepts the human differences others try to abolish. Because it respects individuality, while providing an architecture for more or less rational and fair collective action. Because it accepts the inevitability of disagreement and enlists the very energy of conflict to forge new human possibilities. With the right kinds of citizens, democracy is utopia.

Of course, it malfunctions in many ways, and we constantly fall short of our own ideals. Nevertheless, we are capable of getting steadily closer, and the best hope for improving democracy is democracy itself. Indeed, bad as it is, it is not just the best form of government, it is the only form that expresses human nature. That is why, for the human species to last, democracy must spread throughout the world.

But the very freedom we have includes the freedom to destroy the world. When we pridefully refuse to consider changes in our way of life—the over-consumption, the waste, the garbage, the ostentatious displays of wealth—we place ourselves on a path toward destruction from which democracy alone cannot save us. To survive we must somehow combine freedom with self-restraint. This will be something new in human evolution, and it requires a spiritual transformation.

We evolved in face-to-face groups of close relatives, and now we must view the whole world as family. We battled nature to survive, but now to survive we must protect it. The stranger over the next dune or beyond our patch of forest was clearly and simply a threat to be fought, but now that ancient view is too simple and dangerous. For almost all our history, we solved problems day to day or at most year to year, but now we must think ahead centuries. For 10,000 years we tilled the family farm and cherished it, but now the family farm is the earth itself.

Technology is part of the key, and thank goodness for it. We need new ways to produce food and energy, create fresh water, subdue diseases old and new. We need the very best science just to understand what we are doing wrong. Technology, however, is also a threat in more ways than one, not just because of the physical damage it does, but because spiritually it can undermine our grasp of our situation.

The sequencing of the genome is a wonderful thing, and someday it will lead to an understanding of the best and worst in human nature. Perhaps we will even use genes to change human nature, but that possibility is very far off. We must solve our current problems with the genes we have now. Similarly, the manned voyage to Mars is a bold move, but if it undermines our resolve to save the earth because we think we can get off it, it is devastatingly dangerous and should be put off for a hundred years. In the time frame that matters, we are stuck on this planet, and we'd better make the most of it.

In DNA sequence, we are almost 99 percent chimpanzee. In five million years, we first walked upright, then expanded our brains and made tools to master nature. We came out of Africa twice and filled the earth with our ambitious selves. Then one day, after countless adventures, after endless joys and sorrows and bravery and fear, we stood in a torch-lit cave in awe of the exquisite paintings made by our kind, and we knew at last that we were really special—not just in technology, but in spirit.

Now we must draw on that quality, unique in the animal world, of spiritual consciousness and awe in the face of beauty. We must cultivate the loftiest possible vision of our future on this small, lovely planet, and pass through this time of trial with that vision intact. Awareness, responsibility, resolve, courage, compassion, fairness—these have always been part of our nature even when they were submerged in fear and selfishness. Really, now, we must save the world. The good news is, we can. Will we? Time is running out. In the words of a distinguished environmentalist, it is God's last offer.

Note

Evidence for the claims made in this essay may be found in a revised edition of the author's book, *The Tangled Wing: Biological Constraints on the Human Spirit* (New York: Henry Holt, 2002). References are on the World Wide Web at http://www.henryholt.com/tangledwing. Those pertaining to human evolution are mainly the ones for Chapter 3, "The Crucible"; those pertaining to the environment and the future are mainly the ones for pages 463–81. See also *God's Last Offer: Negotiating for a Sustainable Future*, by Ed Ayres (New York: Four Walls Eight Windows, 1999).

1. The quote I have tentatively attributed to Margaret Mead has been attributed to her many times, but no one has found it in her writings. It may be a valid oral tradition, but no one can be sure. Whoever said it, it is provocative and wise.

Imagine—a utopia where some have the ability to live outside of the shadow of death. Would it really be utopian for them? Or for others who still live then as we do, obliged to come to terms with our own mortal fate? How plausible is the prospect of life eternal, an ancient dream of anxious mortals? What unprecedented problems might follow if science soon offered some humans life eternal? How do radical advances in the biosciences bear on this? What, in the last analysis, is the relationship of our fear of death to our musings about a more perfect life . . . and how well have we really thought through this complex matter? Considerable help is offered by the unusual brow raising essay below.

46. Immortality: Closer Than You Think*

Stanley Shostak

What if some of us could live forever? What might immortals be like, and what might life be like in a world shared with immortals?

Immortal human beings would resemble preadolescent human beings of about eleven years of age, with an individual appearance (phenotype) acquired through the interaction of hereditary material (genotype) with a physico-psycho-social structure known as the "environment." Indeed, the only physical difference between mortal preadolescents and immortals would be that the immortals would be of different chronological ages. Because the immortals' tissues, organs, and systems would be maintained and repaired eternally through the differentiation of self-renewing, pluripotential exotic stem (es) cells released by an internal generator, immortals would not mature or age.

The principles for making *Homo sapiens* forma *immortalis* are well established in canonical biology.[1] This science prescribes that an individual organism, such as any one of us, consists of two parts: the germplasm, or nuclear genes, made of heredity units, and the somatoplasm, made of cytoplasm, including organelles. Germplasm flows immortally from generation to generation through germ lines of eggs and spermatozoa, while somatoplasm branches off the germ line at nodes of fertilization or points of recombination, forming somatic lines, or cell lineages that constitute mortal individuals.

From the point of view of biologists, achieving immortality depends simply on reversing these roles, creating an endless flow in the somatic line at the expense of the germ line. The problem for making immortal human beings is that nothing in our Darwinian evolution or normal course of development offers the remotest possibility of performing the sea change of somatic and germ lines.[2]

Prospects for Immortalization

Biological change, however, is not limited to evolution and development, and a window of opportunity would seem to be open in preadolescence for stabilizing individuals around the positive process of life. At that stage of development, degenerative changes would not yet have taken the upper hand in the balance with growth, differentiation, and sculpturing.

Ways of affecting the desired sea change are suggested by the exceptional

---

*Adapted by the editor from a much longer, richer epilogue in Stanley Shostak, *Becoming Immortal: Combining Cloning and Stem-Cell Therapy* (Albany, NY: SUNY Press, 2002).

changes thought to have occurred in early life-forms[3] Early life on earth may have produced cells with nuclei (eukaryotes), sex, death, and multicellular organisms through devolution, the fusion and/or fission of life-forms. A new organ, the generator, might be engineered by mimicking these devolutionary processes.

The generator would begin as a cloned blastocyst, and turn into a perpetual source of immunologically and genetically compatible es cells dwelling within the organism. The generator would wholly replace gonads, and es cells would permanently supplant the germ line, hence juvenilize the human being forever.

Only two questions remain: What are the realistic prospects for immortalization? What adjustments will be required for life among and with immortals?

Not on the Agenda, But . . .

The realistic prospects for immortality are hard to judge simply because immortality research is not currently on the agenda of any national agency, nonprofit enterprise, or even biotech startup company. Rather, "human-machine synthesis is seen as the next stage of human evolution" and the avant-garde of research devotes itself to work on cyborgified longevity.[4]

I expect the cyborgification of human beings will continue, since it is profitable and efficacious in many circumstances. My guess is cyborgian replacement therapy will become the mode for mortal human beings, and the human-machine synthesis will be enhanced only if mortals ever attempt to compete in longevity with truly immortal beings.

The human-machine lobby will probably attempt to dampen enthusiasm for immortality, but the growth of an immortality lobby will ultimately overwhelm resistance. I imagine such a lobby will emerge rapidly once the first immortal mammals are produced. These mammals, probably sheep to begin with, will undoubtedly be generated for all the same reasons clones are currently being generated—to perpetuate organisms with unique and valuable qualities.

If, for example, one would like to have a clone of sheep producing human clotting factor IX, one would like to have such sheep producing the factor in perpetuity. Inevitably, it will be cheaper to produce one or another factor from immortal animals than suffer the uncertainty and expense of producing mortal animals. I predict the same commercial forces now encouraging research on cloning will shortly be promoting research on immortality.

Frankly, I cannot imagine the successful immortalization of other mammals will not be followed swiftly by pleas for the immortalization of human beings. The frustrations precipitated by the inevitability of death currently confronting mortals will not go away, and they will be exacerbated by the immortality of other animals—our cousins.

Adjustments Required by Immortalization

No mortal today can have any idea of what life will be like for the immortals, the kind of social life the immortals will establish, or the society mortals and immortals will create. One can be sure, however, that initially the immortals' problems will seem endless.

Some problems can be anticipated and should be met with adequate prophylaxis. The genome of immortals would initially encompass a small part of the human genetic pool, a fraction of the biodiversity represented by human beings. Such a pool should be expanded as quickly as possible to offset the possibility of new diseases spreading rapidly among immortals. In the absence of adequate countermeasures, new diseases might wipe out the first immortals in a single pandemic.

Other problems will be unforeseeable. Will the immortals bond together? Will they identify with each other as a group? Will they seek their own protection and mutual advantage in clans? Would the immortals perform the same sorts of antisocial behavior performed by mortals? Would the death penalty have to be invoked to "deter" murder by immortals? How would immortals deal with the death of mortal loved ones? Denied the comfort of going to paradise themselves, where loved ones are reunited, what comfort could be offered to immortals doomed to live forever bereft of parents, mortal siblings, and friends—even immortals killed by accident?

Moreover, how will ordinary mortals react to immortals? Will mortals grant them "minority status" and attempt to suppress them? Will mortals objectify immortals and tend to place them in the category of artifact, "something manufactured" rather than a "natural human being" entitled to all the protections granted by law and permitted by fair play?

Contemplating Immortal Life

I may be worrying needlessly. Chances are the immortals' problems will not be that different from ours. For example, pressure on traditional families and kinship structures will certainly continue following immortalization.

Immortal children will outlive their parents, and the problems of immortality will move on to the kinds of adjustments immortals and mortals will have to make to each other. Will this world of the immortals be recognizable to extant mortals? I have only a faint idea of just how different it will be and can only offer conjectures about what mortals, like ourselves, will learn from this new world—about ourselves and about immortals.

Probably, in much the same way children have adjusted to talking toys and reasoning computers, immortal human beings will adjust to their situation and find new and novel ways to cope with their reality. My guess is the immortals will make an adjustment to immortal life, but mortals will find it too cyborgian for comfort.

The World of Immortals

I should say something about what I think the world may look like to immortals. I approach this task with trepidation, not only because I appreciate how utterly speculative my opinion must be, but because I feel uncomfortable in the immortals' world as I see it.

I imagine the most glaring difference in the world of immortals in contrast to my world will be the experience of time in the sense of past, present, and future. Everything about life as I know it, having lived my life in a modern, developed, and still developing Western culture, is predicated on this sense of time, and it is precisely this sense that will be radically different for people who live forever.

Instead of "living by the clock," time will be immaterial for the immortals. It will be infinitely accessible, neither running down nor running out. The difference will not be how an infinity of time affects an immortal's values— whether the immortals will be lazy by today's standards (I imagine they will acquire a work ethic through nurture and will be as interested in completing tasks as we are)—but how an infinity of time will affect everything about perception and the experience of life.

In Western culture, time is ubiquitous. It permeates everything. Even language, our chief means of communicating, requires conjugation, and one can hardly conceive of a sentence in any European language (certainly English) that does not have time already built into it. For the immortals, however, time will be replaced by infinite duration, the present expanded to eternity. Even familiar terms, such as *lifetime*, will cease to have their familiar meaning. Rather than a finite duration, or a period before death, a lifetime will stretch outward forever from the beginning of consciousness.

Ordinarily, one believes one lives in the present because the transition of future and past passes through it without any bump. This passage will make no sense for the immortals. For the immortals, an infinite present will rupture the transition of future and past, or, put another way, the present will spread infinitely into the past and future.

What about time's creations: mortal life and experience? Of course, the sun will rise on immortals just as it does on mortals, and immortals and mortals will feel its warmth. They will share the same admiration for a beautiful, bright day, and they will experience the same joy at the coming of a verdant springtime. But the immortal's sun will not be the same as the mortal's sun, nor will anything else perceived by the immortals be the same as that perceived by mortals.

What is crucial to the difference in perception is that the senses will not define the present for the immortals. The senses will identify moments, and life for the immortals will be a cornucopia of sensory perceptions, but moments will not be recalled in seriatim, akin to the passage of time. When the present is no longer pierced by the arrow of time, by the coming future and the receding past, then perception will implode and time will disintegrate.

Time without End

Here is where the world of the mortals will differ most sharply from the world of the immortals because what a mortal perceives as movement, an immortal will perceive as time. What an immortal perceives as movement, a mortal will perceive as time. Ironically, the same physiology of persistence shared by immortals and mortals will present a barrier to communication and understanding—one that will be overcome only with the utmost difficulty.

The persistence of senses may illuminate another difference between the world of mortals and immortals. For me, as for many others over sixty years of age, time has sped up acutely as it moves toward its one and only end. Memory thus changes, and, occasionally, a persistent remnant of an early experience comes thundering out of the past and back to life. It may even strike with its original force.

But the truth is our present should not be defined as that which is more intense: it is that which acts on us and which makes us act. It is sensory and it is motor—our present is, above all, the state of our body. Our past, on the contrary, is that which acts no longer, but which might act, and will act by inserting itself into a present sensation from which it borrows the vitality.

The immortals will, no doubt, also have memory, but it will not speed up or slow down while life and time stand still. For the immortals, none of the faults and pains of memory that come with age will materialize. Immortality has its compensations.

At What Cost?

It has never been my intention to pretend that immortality could be achieved without sacrifice. Beyond all the problems of communication, the simple pleasures offered by birth, if not death, will be increasingly rare as more and more people enter the population as sterile immortals. Moreover, the preference some of us have for human diversity may not be rewarded as richly as it is today, since some human traits will, no doubt, not be represented among the immortals.

How the immortal humans will look and behave is a matter of conjecture, but some consequences of the indwelling generator would seem inevitable, most conspicuously, the morphological and physiological juvenilization of the immortals. Unquestionably, the immortals will be in unbelievably good physiological shape. They will be ballet dancers, gymnasts, and karate experts with great stamina and grace.

Immortals will not resemble the Eloi envisaged by H. G. Wells in *The Time Machine*—fragile, easily fatigued, of slight stature, "a hairless visage, and the same girlish rotundity of limb."[5] They will appear neither masculine nor feminine, and they will remain sexually immature forever, but these side effects would not be handicaps in a society where everyone lives forever.

Under the new conditions of perfect comfort and security, that restless energy that with us is strength, would become weakness. For such a life, what we should call the weak are as well equipped as the strong, and indeed no longer weak.

Forever prepubescent, the immortals will not suffer from the inevitable, deleterious effects of aging that follow sexual maturity, but unlike the rather dull-witted "five year olds" discovered by the Time Traveler in *Time Machine*, the preadolescent immortals will be in a perpetual "learning mode." They will be capable of acquiring languages flawlessly and without effort. They will never exhaust their mental potential, and they will always be at their peak of poetic and mathematical creativity.

In other words, a world of immortals will be filled with intellectual excitement and dedicated to creative enterprise. Even chronologically older immortals would not lose their intellectual edge, and society might very well return to esteeming the "ancients" without the biting edge of *ressentiment*.

Those spiritual and intellectual values which remain untouched by the process of aging, together with the values of the next stage of life . . . [will no longer have to] compensate for what has been lost. Only if this happens can we cheerfully relive the values of our past in memory, without envy for the young to whom they are still accessible.

Furthermore, although immortals will not exhibit secondary sexual dimorphism, they will be polymorphous and will enjoy uninhibited preadolescent sexuality without the complications of pregnancy. In all likelihood, immortals will quickly evolve socially and spawn a culture without sexism, without homophobia, without stigma attached to sterility, and without the threat of a population explosion resulting from unrestrained sexual reproduction.

On balance, the cost of immortality would seem acceptable, and *Homo sapiens* forma *immortalis* should "live happily ever after." The biggest challenge would be convincing the remaining, adult *Homo sapiens* forma *mortalis* to permit, by and large, the disappearance of that part of their culture built on sexuality and reproduction. If *Homo sapiens* f. *mortalis* cannot be convinced to yield gracefully, I foresee a disastrous schism developing in the species.

Notes

1. Stanley Shostak, *Becoming Immortal: Combining Cloning and Stem-Cell Therapy* (Albany, NY: SUNY Press, 2002), pp. 1–44.

2. Chapter 2, "Why Immortality Cannot Evolve," and Chapter 3, "Why Immortality Cannot Develop," ibid., pp. 45–124.
3. Chapter 4, "Life's Fundamental Feature: Devolution," ibid., pp. 125–64.
4. J.L. Croissant, "Growing Up Cyborg," in *Cyborg Babies*, ed. R. Davis-Floyd and J. Dumit (New York: Rutledge, 1998), p. 285.
5. H. G. Wells, "The Time Machine: An Invention." A critical text of the 1895 London first edition with an introduction and appendices. In *The Annotated H. G. Wells*, ed. Leon Stover (Jefferson, NC: McFarland and Company, 1996), p. 74.

Extraordinary challenges lie ahead in the Space Age, in the settlement of Mars, and in the centuries of space exploration thereafter. We may just have a fresh set of utopian-making possibilities here, complete with the time-honored challenge of defining the Ideal, the Preferable. A remarkably fine guide exists below in the form of a short essay with awesome speculations, a healthy prod to creating the viable utopian ideas we need to get us from here to there . . . from our Earthbound launching pad into permanent residence in Space.

47. The Outward Course: Dystopias and Utopias in Outer Space*

Marilyn Dudley-Rowley and Thomas Gangale

By meeting the challenges of a "wider world," we *change ourselves*. If the ability to cure social ills makes for utopia, then the road to utopia is the high road.

Terrestrial frontiers have stoked utopian dreams, and so it is the same with the Martian frontier or any frontier that is off the planet Earth. The long-duration space flight environment, however, entails psychosocial human problems. A crew of Earth people in such a highly autonomous situation at such a distance, more reliant upon each other than any humans have ever been, may find they are not just strangers to each other in this strange land, but strangers within.

For awhile, it might seem almost utopian to live in a microsociety where people are nice to you, all of you are efficient, and things run smoothly. But, how long can that regimen be mandated? People can stand just about anything for a little while, but in the end they are human. Over the long duration, even in special environments where perhaps the hopes of the world are pinned upon them, a space crew will revert to the needs and costs of being human.

---

*This essay was shortened and slightly altered by the editor—with permission—from a much longer and richer essay available from the writers at md_r@hotmail.com.

However, if we can reasonably design missions that optimize group behaviors for space exploration, then what we learn from them might bring back enlightenment to this world. Psychosocial innovation is like any other kind of innovation: It can spin off into beneficial work team and community processes. It would be a breakthrough if we could just get people to live together safely or eliminate the conditions that make people unhappy.

International cooperation in the pursuit of large capital space projects will likely lead to new social forms which can be turned on the more routine problems of macrosocial life—like war, disease, and hazardous and disastrous events. The many national partners in the International Space Station (ISS) may soon find they are going to have to formulate some sort of formal international commission or panel in the affairs involving the space station and life on orbit.

In addition, they will have to provide a place on such a body for representatives from the ISS crews who will have come to think of themselves as transcending national citizenship in many aspects. That "view from orbit," that "view from the Moon," that "view from Mars" will in time come to erase the things which divide us and let us advance the business of enhancing the human condition.

Over time, populations will become larger in those nonterrestrial places, their social organizations will become more complex, the people living in those places will increase their environmental exploitation and utilization, and their technologies will advance. The extraterrestrialization process that began in the near-Earth and Mars environments will continue and feed back on and affect life on Earth. For example, learning to terraform a planet like Mars will give us the technology to keep the Earth environmentally sound. Even as off-world humans make their worlds more terrestrial, those worlds make Earth-bound humans more extraterrestrial in every aspect of their lives.

Once Mars is settled, Earth people will be changed. They will accept the reality there are people elsewhere in the cosmos. Terrans and Martians will, in time, share a thriving multiworld economy that will promote the expansion of the human ecology. To those of us living now, it might seem almost utopian, these new social forms that fall from the new heights of international (and interplanetary) cooperation necessary to enact large engineering marvels in nonterrestrial environments.

Mars leads to the stars and beyond. Humans on Mars and other extraterrestrial locales in the solar system will have set the stage for the human expansion into the cosmos. It doesn't end with just a few star systems closest to Earth. On our way to becoming a civilization that traverses interstellar distances, we will plant the seeds of a technology that will underpin another type of civilization altogether, one we call Type IV.[1]

The requirements of interstellar travel will lead humans to manipulate processes at cosmic levels. From there, Type IV citizens will be able to exploit the architecture of the universe. The different aspects and dimensions of the cosmos will become like environmental niches for them. If humans can achieve this new sort of civilization, they will have the technology of gods. They might even try to stop the heat death of the universe, assuming that that is the bad thing we now think it is.

There will come a point when Type IV humans must formulate the optimal mix of good and evil in their actions, for their actions have the capability of cosmic consequences. Metaphorically speaking, how many snakes are optimal for the Garden? How many vain angels are optimal for Paradise?

If Type IV extraterrestrialized humans are eventually led or forced to embrace too many dystopian (evil) aspects, they will extinguish themselves and others around them, as did the Jonestowners or the Nazis. Ironically, they might achieve the same result if they are too utopian (good) and fail to act against an aggressor as technologically astute as they. Too few challenges in the environment of a species they are mentoring might result in the stagnation or devolution of that species.

It will be an interesting dilemma for the humans we will have become . . . stewards of the grand environment.

Note

1. The Kardashev types were a classification of possible civilizations in the galaxy based on energy usage. A Type I civilization would control all available energy on a single planet. A Type II civilization would be a spacefaring society which would control all available energy of its sun (for example, through the use of a Dyson sphere). A Type III civilization would control all available energy in an entire galaxy.

Web References

"An Introduction to Martian Time," by Thomas Gangale and Marilyn Dudley-Rowley, *New Mars*, April 2002: http://www.newmars.com/archives/000052. shtml.

"Ten Missions, Two Studies: Crew Composition, Time, and Subjective Experience in Mars-Analog Expeditions," by Marilyn Dudley-Rowley, Patrick Nolan, Sheryl Bishop, Kristin Farry, and Thomas Gangale. Third International Convention of the Mars Society, Toronto, Ontario, 2000: http://pweb.jps.net/~gangale/opsa/TenMissionsTwoStudies/TenMissionsTwoStudiesFrm.htm.

"The National Primary System: A 21st Century Method for Nominating Presidential Candidates," by Thomas Gangale: http://pweb.jps.net/~gangale/primary/index.htm.

"MARSATT: Assured Communication with Mars," by Thomas Gangale and Gail Gangale, MAR 98-051, *Proceedings of the Founding Convention of the*

Mars Society, Univelt, Incorporated, San Diego, 1999: http://pweb.jps.net/~gan gale/mars/marssat/index.htm.

"A Social States Index for Multi-National Crews Co-Contained in the ISS Simulator, Moscow, Russia," by Marilyn Dudley-Rowley, Vadim Gushin, and Tom Gorry. Presented July 12–15, 1999, The 29th International Conference on Environmental Systems (ICES) Conference, NASA-Johnson Space Center's Psychological Services Group Session, Denver, Colorado. SAE Technical Paper Series 1999-01-2101: http://pweb.jps.net/~gangale/opsa/SocialStatesIndex/ SAE_frm.htm.

Epilogue: Getting On with It

*Twenty years from now
you will be more disappointed
by the things that you didn't do
than by the ones you did do.
So throw off the bowlines.
Sail away from the safe harbor.
Catch the trade winds in your sails.
Explore. Dream. Discover.*
—Mark Twain

So much more remains . . . will always remain . . . to ponder, to assess, and to act on.

Roger Kaufman, for example, would have us learn how to define end states in measurable terms. Joseph F. Coates would have us learn how to create inspiring visions "at least as grainy and engaging as the dystopian competitors." Lane Jennings urges us to draw more on poetry; Ross Koppel, on applied sociology; Carroy U. Ferguson, on humanistic psychology; Jacques Fresco and Roxanne Meadows, on cybermetrics; Jim Pinto, on soft solutions; Sohail Inayatullah, on PROUT; Thomas A. Reiner, on planning, and so on.

Michael Marien recommends higher education take up these challenges in a very creative new course in practical utopianism. William McKenna would hasten to add high schools. Disinclined to only wait (and lobby) for this happy development, I suggest we each of us undertake our own "do it" response to the challenge.

One good way of starting is to begin tracing linkages among the book's forty-seven essays. Benjamin Novack, for example, shares intriguing ideas about utopian life in space which resonate with those in Marilyn Dudley-Rowley and Thomas Gangale's essay. Margaret R. Johnston and Claire Keyes have a very creative design for abortion services, as transformative as William Du Bois's blueprint for a youth and community settlement project; Irwin Deutscher's and R. Dean Wright's recommendations for conflict-resolution efforts; Robert J. Merikangas's and Hal Pepinsky's ideas for higher education renewal; grassroots activism, as explained by Valerie Fournier, Dada Maheshvarananda, and Diane Straus and Roger A. Straus; Melvin Konner's call for spiritual consciousness; and the post-Mars vision of Dudley-Rowley and Gangale.

Equally rewarding is assessing the differences—rather than only similarities—among the forty-seven essays. Tsvi Bisk devalues science fiction tales that go out beyond 100 years—much as do two of the book's contributions. David Weinberger appears far more hopeful than does Allan Stegeman about the Web's influence, even as Stephen Downes appears more confident than Adrienne Redd that we may soon opt for a smaller type of government. Jacques Fresco and Roxanne Meadows devalue monetary economics, while David Reynolds prefers a union-aiding scenario designed, in part, to significantly redistribute monetary wealth. Sorting out such intriguing differences is just one of several types of constructive "homework" for any reader who has come this far.

Another sort of homework would have someone soon help remedy—perhaps in a sequel, or better yet, our dedicated Web site—three of the regrettable weaknesses of this volume. First, despite my search for relevant contributors, we offer no viable utopian ideas to help deal with the AIDS epidemic, dying issues (euthanasia), the energy crisis, global warming, health care, the sustainability paradigm, the transportation mess, welfare reform, and scores of other trying challenges . . . all of which would profit from the adroit employ of viable utopian ideas.

Second, we cite many tools for learning, but, inevitably, neglect some, such as motion pictures, which are of special educational value (a variation on the "dream vacationing" that Jennings cites is featured in *Solvent Green*, even as problems that threaten the Type IV civilization of the Dudley-Rowley and Gangale essay are highlighted in *Aliens*, *Gattaca*, and *Outland*. Similarly, the basic question—What *is* the Good Life?—is explored in *Pleasantville*, *The Truman Story*, and many other thoughtful films). New citations of relevant films, documentaries, plays, novels, short stories, and the like, would be a wonderful addition.

Third, while our ranks include essays from a Brazilian, a Britisher, a Canadian, an Israeli, and a South Asian, there were many obvious gaps. Ideas from writers in Africa, Central Europe, Scandinavia, and other underrepresented areas might have added much. While our ranks include administrators, consultants, futurists, a monk, a poet, professors, retirees, and teachers, we do not include any artists, business people, dramatists, journalists, novelists, policy advisers, politicians, or sundry other relevant types.

To help move these improvements along, we have created a Web site (www.UtopianIdeas.net). Please use both to share with us your feedback on the material in the first edition, and your ideas for possible use in forthcoming editions.

So, *much* remains to be accomplished . . . and if the book has been half as successful as we wish, and its forty-seven essays have whet your appetite to help, we should now get on with it . . . the tide runs strong.

Recommended Readings

Below please find a very small sample of the thousands of current, helpful, and reader-friendly books worth looking into as you adapt viable utopian ideas from this book and/or develop your own. Particular reliance in making selections was placed on the May 2002 issue of a unique, annotated bibliographic service, "Future Survey." Every monthly issue features fifty abstracts written by Michael Marien, a contributor to this volume, aided by Lane Jennings, production editor, another contributor. This publication is arguably the single best source for keeping up with the futures literature (and, thereby, viable utopian ideas). (http://www.wfs.org/fsurv.htm).

1. Clampitt, Phillip G., and Robert J. DeKoch. *Embracing Uncertainty: The Essence of Leadership.* Armonk, NY: M.E. Sharpe, 2001. Explores effective ways—the what, why, and how—to employ uncertainty.

2. Courtney, Hugh. *20/20 Foresight: Crafting Strategy in an Uncertain World.* Boston: Harvard Business School Press, 2001. Practical rigorous tools and advice for embracing uncertainty and making tough strategic choices. "All about future studies without using the term." (Michael Marien)

3. Daily, Gretchen C., and Katherine Ellison. *The New Economy of Nature: The Quest to Make Conservation Profitable.* "Much too slowly, yet unmistakably, the world is moving forward with a widening array of efforts to make environmental conservation economically profitable." Major innovations are needed for business plans and policy development to capture the economic value of environmental services.

4. Danziger, Sheldon, and Jane Waldfogel, eds. *Securing the Future: Investing in Children from Birth to College.* New York: Russell Sage Foundation, 2000. Derived from a 1998 conference, the book promotes a new approach, "asset building," which empowers the poor with key human, social, financial, and natural resource assets. "Serious thinking about 'future generations,' not mere generalizations." (Michael Marien)

5. Gunderson, Lance H., and C.S. Holling, eds. *Panarchy: Understanding Transformations in Human and Natural Systems.* Washington, DC: Island Press, 2002. Reports on a three-year project that contends the question is not whether to seek sustainable futures, but how to seek them.

6. Kiuchi, Tachi, and Bill Shireman. *What We Learned in the Rainforest: Business Lessons from Nature. Innovation, Growth, Profit, and Sustainability at 20 of the World's Top Companies.* San Francisco: Berrett-Koehler, 2002. "The highest mission of business is to help fully develop the human ecosystem, sustainably like the rainforest, in all our diversity and complexity. . . . In the emerging economy, businesses excel when they emulate what they once sought to conquer."

7. Pardey, Philip G., ed. *The Future of Food: Biotechnology Markets and Policies in an International Setting.* Washington, DC: International Food Policy Research Institute, 2001. "The ramifications of the market and policy choices taken now regarding agricultural biotechnologies will reverberate for decades to come . . . attempts by wealthy countries, population groups, and advocacy groups to decide for poor farmers and consumers are paternalistic and unethical."

8. Spady, Richard J., and Richard S. Kirby. *The Leadership of Civilization Building: Administrative and Civilization Theory, Symbolic Dialogue, and Citizen Skills for the 21st Century.* Seattle, WA: Forum Foundation, 2002. "Our theme is that a better civilization is not only desirable, but also attainable."

9. Weick, Karl E., and Kathleen M. Sutcliffe. *Managing the Unexpected: Assuring High Performance in an Age of Complexity.* San Francisco: Jossey-Bass, 2001. "If you're uncertain, that's a good sign that you're in touch with reality."

10. Wilson, Edward O. *The Future of Life.* New York: Knopf, 2002. "The race is now on between the technoscientific forces that are destroying the living environment and those that can be harnessed to save it." Asks how we will be remembered in the year 3000. Offers a strategy aimed at protecting most of the remaining ecospecies and species.

Recommended Readings
by Contributors and Allies

Abraham, Ralph. *Chaos, Gaia, Eros*. New York: Harper Collins, 1994. "The history of human history is seen as a dynamic system replete with paradigm shifts. Chaos theory, which studies dynamic systems through fractal representations, is used to study cycles that have happened in the history of humanity, and which can possibly predict future paradigm shifts. Using math to make sense of sociology is a new step for the evolution of consciousness." (Marilyn Dudley-Rowley)

Barber, Benjamin R. *A Place for Us: How to Make Society Civil and Democracy Strong*. New York: Hill and Wang (Division of Farrar, Strauss and Giroux), 1998. "Barber addresses questions concerning the loss of civil society and proposes practical strategies for making civil society real, for civilizing public discourse and promoting civil deliberation. In the process, he helps us consider what it would be to go beyond work and leisure, beyond commerce and bureaucracy to a stronger democracy." (Harris Sokoloff)

Buck-Morss, Susan. *Dreamworld and Catastrophe: The Passing of Mass Utopia in East and West*. Boston: MIT Press, 2000. Argues that with the fall of the Soviet Union, the dream of a "mass utopia" is near extinction. Contends there is nothing wrong with the dream, but its execution went awry, in the West as well as in the East. (Art Shostak)

Clarys, Gregory, and Lyman Tower Sargent, eds. *The Utopia Reader*. New York: New York University Press, 1999. Extensive selections from major utopian texts, both classic and contemporary examples, which demonstrate "how visions of better societies interact with and criticize or improve each other." Barbara Goodwin, University of East Anglia. (Book Jacket)

Dauncey, Guy. *Earth future: Stories from a Sustainable World*. Gabriola Island, British Columbia, Canada: New Society Publishers, 1999. "[W]ith its mix of utopian fiction and reportage of near-reality, *Earthfuture* sows the seeds of an alternative future with such obvious delight that today's fear and loss of hope are allayed, the doom and gloom replaced with optimism." (Book Jacket)

deGraaf, John, David Wann, and Thomas Naylor. *Affluenza—The All-Consuming Epidemic*. San Francisco: Berrett-Koehler, 2001. "Eye-opening, soul-prodding look at the excesses of affluent western societies. If you are uncomfortable about your own ruthless consumption or sigh at the hurried pace of your own life, you may already be ill with 'affluenza'. This is something akin to 'a painful, contagious, socially-transmitted condition of overload, debt, anxiety and waste resulting from the dogged pursuit of more.' It is a powerful virus running rampant in our society, infecting our souls, affecting our wallets and financial well-being, and threatening to destroy not only the environment, but also our families and communities." (Jim Pinto)

de Rosnay, Joel. *The Symbiotic Man—A New Understanding of the Organization of Life and a Vision of the Future*. New York: McGraw Hill, 2000. "A powerful, new scientific methodology promises to dramatically recast our concept of nature and mankinds's place in it. This is Chaos Theory—the sciences of Complexity and Self-organization. Organic chemist, computer scientist, visionary, Joel de Rosnay has been at the forefront of the complexity movement for nearly 30 years." (Jim Pinto)

Drucker, Peter. *Management Challenges for the 21st Century*. New York: Harper Business, Harper Collins, 1999. "Drucker's most recent book includes new and revolutionary ideas and perspectives on the central management issues of the new century by the most important management thinker of our time. At 91 Drucker is more than ever incisive, challenging, and mind-stretching. This new book is forward-looking and forward-thinking. Those who prepare themselves for these challenges today will be the new leaders and will dominate tomorrow." (Jim Pinto)

Etzioni, Amitai. *Next: The Road to the Good Society*. New York: Perseus, 2001. "Argues that our world-leading economy offers more opportunities than ever to end scarcity and break out of a cycle of materialism." (Book Jacket)

Hagerty, Lawrence. *The Spirit of the Internet: Speculations on the Evolution of Global Consciousness*. New York: Matrix Masters, 2000. "The author discusses how much the world is changing and how the Internet has facilitated that. Hagerty believes that as more information becomes available, the more human consciousness will evolve." (Marilyn Dudley-Rowley)

Jacoby, Russell. *The End of Utopia: Politics and Culture in an Age of Apathy*. New York: Basic Books, 1999. "Points to the abandonment of utopian ideals that once sustained dissent and movements of social change; and he calls for writers and critics to reclaim the vision and backbone they are losing." (Book Jacket)

Knoke, William. *Bold New World—The Essential Road Map to the 21st Century*. New York: Kodansha International, 1997 (reprint edition). "Describes economics, communication and relationships in the third millennium. What *Future Shock* was for the 1970s and *Megatrends* for the 1980s, *Bold New World* (1997) sought to be for the late 1990s and the new century. The world will be a placeless society as cyberspace transactions replace the need to be anywhere. Sections of the book begin with vignettes involving individuals in various situations. In audio, these are particularly effective because the voices combine international, generic, sci-fi and high-tech tones. These voices aptly convey the placelessness described in the text." (Jim Pinto)

Kurzweil, Ray. *The Age of Spiritual Machines—When Computers Exceed Human Intelligence*. New York: Viking, Penguin Putnam, 1999. "Imagine a world where the difference between man and machine blurs, where the line between humanity and technology fades, where the soul and the silicon chip unite. This is not science-fiction. This is the 21st century, according to Ray Kurzweil, the 'restless genius' (*Wall Street Journal*) and inventor of the most compelling technology of our era. This book is no mere list of predictions, but a prophetic blueprint for the future. This is the book that started me off in new directions." (Jim Pinto)

Melman, Seymour. *After Capitalism: From Managerialism to Workplace Democracy*. New York: Knopf, 2001. Explores grounds for the hope that aroused white-collarites and New Unions together will soon force radical improvement in the world of work. (Art Shostak)

Mitchell, William J. *E-topia: "Urban Life, Jim—But Not As We Know It."* Cambridge, MA: MIT Press, 2000. "[A]n important way of looking at the future, taking seriously the multiple intersections of the historical, the eternal, and the futuristic." Paul Rosenberg (Book Jacket)

Nozick, Robert. *The Examined Life*. New York: Touchstone, 1989. "Brilliantly renews Socrates' quest to uncover the life that *is* worth living . . . brings philosophy back to its preeminent subject, the things that matter most." (Book Jacket)

Paul, Gregory S., and Earl D. Cox. *Beyond Humanity: CyberEvolution and Future Minds*. Rockland, MA: Charles River Media, 1996. A bold and engaging exploration of the possibility humankind will evolve beyond our present form into pure consciousness, first passing through extraordinary morphing with "smart" information equipment. Far more persuasive than one might expect. (Art Shostak)

Pesce, Mark. *The Playful World: How Technology Is Transforming Our Imagination*. New York: Ballantine, 2002. "Explores how a new kind of knowing and a new way of creating are transforming the culture of our time . . . with incredible speed and power." (Book Jacket)

Reich, Robert. *The Future of Success: Working and Living in the New Economy*. New York: Random House, 2000. "Provocative suggestions for how we might create a more balanced society and more satisfying lives." (Book Jacket)

Rosen, Jonathan. *The Talmud and the Internet: A Journey between Worlds*. New York: Picador, 2000. A sage, gentle, distinctive, and empowering exploration of the desirable and hazardous aspects of the Internet. (Art Shostak)

Tod, Ian, and Michael Wheeler. *Utopia*. New York: Harmony [London: Orbis], 1978. "I used it as a sort of day to day text when I gave my Utopia seminar. It is written very clearly." (Thomes A. Reiner)

Wagar, Warren. *A Short History of the Future* (3d ed.). Chicago: University of Chicago Press, 1999; Wagar, Warren. *The Open Conspiracy: H. G. Wells on World Revolution*, edited and with a critical introduction by W. Warren Wagar, Westport, CT: Praeger Publishers, 2002. "The first title is an imaginary history of the next 200 years, which envisages a global utopia emerging in two stages—initially as a democratic and socialist world commonwealth, and later as a decentralized interplanetary world order experimenting with many different political and social systems. The second title is a re-publication of H.G. Wells's 1928 manifesto on how to build a world state, prefaced by an extensive critical essay of my own, continuing a discussion I began in my *H. G. Wells and the World State*, New Haven, CT: Yale University Press, 1961." (Warren Wagar)

Wallerstein, Immanuel. *Utopistics. Or, Historical Choices of the Twenty-first Century*. New York: The New Press, 1998. "Poses urgent questions for anyone concerned with social change in the next millennium." (Book Jacket)

Walljasper, Jay, et. al. *Visionaries: People & Ideas to Change Your Life*. Gabriola Island, British Columbia, Canada: New Society Publishers, 2001. "We hope this book inspires you to become the visionary you were born to be. . . . Dive into the labyrinth, risk getting lost, and return to your own community with bright ideas that help people see themselves and the world differently." (Eric Utne, ed.)

Wheatley, Margaret J. *Turning to One Another: Simple Conversations to Restore Hope to the Future*. San Francisco: Berrett-Koehler Publishers, 2002. "I believe we can change the world if we start listening to one another again." Her book, both prose and poetry, is intended to spark conversations and dialogue that advances a hopeful future. See www.turningtooneanother.net. (Douglas Bedell)

Williammson, Marianne, ed. *Imagine: What America Could Be in the 21st Century*. New York: Rodale, 2001. Leading futurists, including Deepak Chopra, Stanley Crouch, and bell hooks, address "issues of personal, internal transformation as well as institutional, external change, recognizing that the internal and external are not separate but intertwined." (Book Jacket)

Zander, Benjamin, and Rosamund Stone Zander. *The Art of Possibility: Transforming Professional and Personal Life*. Boston, MA: Harvard Business School Press, 2000. "Offers a set of breakthrough practices for creativity . . . provide[s] us with a deep sense of the powerful role that the notion of possibility can play in every aspect of our lives." (Book Jacket)

Recommended E-Mail Listserves and Web Sites

In addition to those cited after the Introduction:

1. Dan Blatt, Publisher, FUTURECASTS online magazine. Especially good in offering lengthy, informative book reviews: www.futurecasts.com. Mail to: blatt1@futurecasts.com.

2. *Brill Monthly Mentor.* Focuses on creativity and innovation: wbrill@winstonbrill.com.

3. Newsletter from the Copenhagen Institute for Futures Studies: newsletter@iff.dk. Also available in html-format: http://www.cifs.dk/en/nybrev.asp.

4. The Forum Foundation was founded in 1970 to strengthen democratic processes through improved communications: http://www.ForumFoundation.org.

5. *Better Future NEWS* is prepared monthly by John Renesch, a San Francisco writer, business futurist, and consultant/executive coach: John@renesch.com. His latest book is *Getting to the Better Future: A Matter of Conscious Choosing* (see http://www.Renesch.com/TheBetterFuture for a preview).

6. Maintained by Mark Saturn, a radical pragmatist, this web site links to over 100 "21st Century Manifestos," and has annotated links to over 250 "Radical Middle Websites": www.radicalmiddle.com.

Books, Videos, and
Web Sites of Contributors

1. Bell, Wendell. *Foundations of Future Studies.* Vol. 1. *History, Purposes, and Knowledge*; Vol. 2. *Values, Objectivity, and the Good Society.* New Brunswick, NJ: Transaction, 1997. The seminal guide to why futuristics belongs in the "tool kit" of all educated adults. Demonstrates how it can help us imagine alternative futures, including those enriched by viable utopian ideas, "more deliberately and act on them more effectively." (1: xviii)

2. Bisk, Tsvi, coauthor. *Futurizing the Jews.* New York: Praeger/Greenwood, 2003 (in press). A pioneering exploration of one group's probable, possible, preventable, and preferable futures. Thoughtful and demanding. Valuable for seeing beyond the present where such issues of distinctiveness and homogeneity, ethnicity and religiosity, and nationality and globalism are concerned.

3. Coates, Joseph F. *2025: Scenarios of US and Global Society.* Akron, OH: Oakhill Press, 1997. Fifteen diverse chapters on societal components, each of which takes into account the future impact of five drivers of change: infotech, material technology, energy technology, genetics, and environmentalism. Each chapter ends with lists of relevant "Critical Developments, 1990–2025" by year of occurrence and "Unrealized Hopes and Fears."

4. Deutscher, Irwin. *Accommodating Diversity: National Policies That Prevent Ethnic Conflict.* Lanham, MD: Lexington Books, 2002. In-depth exploration of "five national policies which I discovered have succeeded in helping people share the same territory without hurting each other. . . . For me, the most remarkable discovery of this Utopian journey has been that when the group in power treats with respect . . . 'differences' of the ethnic minorities

who live among them, those differences begin to fade, and after three or four generations both the dominant and the minority groups have changed in ways that leave little more than symbolic differences between them." (Irwin Deutscher)

5. Du Bois, William, and R. Dean Wright, eds. *Applying Sociology: Making a Better World.* Boston: Allyn and Bacon, 2001. Twenty-two essays show "how the best sociology applies knowledge to construct programs that benefit people . . . that will spark you to creativity and invention." Four of the essayists in this book are also to be found in this volume.

6. Fresco, Jacque. *The Best That Money Can't Buy: Beyond Politics, Poverty, & War.* Venus, FL: Global Cybevisions, 2002. "Envisions a global civilization in which science and technology are applied with human and environmental concern to secure, protect and encourage a more humane world for all people. It is accompanied by 72 illustrations depicting this alternative direction. 176 pages." Available through the Venus Project, www.TheVenus Project.com.

Cities in the Sea, a video, presents "many variations of ocean structures above and below the sea. It explores the limitless possibilities of this relatively untapped resource to benefit all of Earth's people." Available through The Venus Project, www.TheVenusProject.com.

Self-Erecting Structures, a video, is "about the fantastic future of the intelligent and humane use of AI and cybernation as it constructs our cities, bridges, tunnels, factories, and more while protecting the environment. This video presents the limitless possibilities of the future in a resource-based global economy." Available through The Venus Project, www.TheVenusProject.com (Jacque Fresco and Roxanne Meadows)

Welcome to the Future, a video by Jacque Fresco and Roxanne Meadows, "presents the aims and direction of The Venus Project. It proposes a new social design, one that is directed toward a peaceful and sustainable global civilization in which all of Earth's resources become the common heritage of all of the world's people." Study guide included. Available through The Venus Project, www.TheVenusProject.com.

7. Ferguson, Carroy U. *A New Perspective on Race and Color: Research on an Outer vs Inner Orientation to Anti-Black Disposition.* Lewiston, NY: Edwin Mellen Press, 1997; Ferguson, C., and Kamara, J. *Innovative Approaches To Education And Community Service: Models And Strategies For Change And Empowerment.* Boston: University of Massachusetts, 1993. Two distinct and valuable explorations of challenges and resolutions America must weigh and undertake.

8. Inayatullah, Sohail. *Questioning the Future: Futures Studies, Action Learning and Organizational Transformation*. Tamsui and Taipei, Taiwan: Tamkang University, 2002. "In two parts, the first develops the theory of futures studies (macrohistory, anticipation, alternatives, multi-epistemologies and transformation) and the second is a practical workbook linking futures studies to action learning." (Sohail Inayatullah)

Inayatullah, Sohail. *Situating Sarkar. Tantra, Macrohistory and Alternative Futures*. Maleny, Australia: Gurukul Publications, 1999. "Essays on Indian philosophy, the study of grand patterns of change and futures studies based on the thought of seminal Indian philosopher, P.R. Sarkar." (Sohail Inayatullah)

Inayatullah, Sohail. *Understanding Sarkar: The Indian Episteme, Macrohistory and Transformative Knowledge*. Leiden, Netherlands: Brill, 2002. "Investigates Sarkar's cyclical and spiral theories of history and the future. Sarkar is compared to Ibn Khaldun, Pitirim Sorokin, Oswald Spengler, Hegel, Marx and other macrohistorians." (Sohail Inayatullah)

Inayatullah, Sohail. *The Views of Futurists*. Vol. 4 of The Knowledge Base of Futures Studies (includes vols. 1–3 edited by Richard Slaughter). Brisbane, Australia: Foresight International, 2001. "Over 100 thinkers offer their preferred vision of humanity's future, the methods they use to explore the future, the trends they think will create the future, and the biographical context of their own writings." (Sohail Inayatullah)

Inayatullah, Sohail, and Gail Boxwell. *Islam, Postmodernism and Other Futures. The Contribution of Ziauddin Sardar*. London: Pluto Press, 2002. "Presents the work of muslim and British cultural critic and futurist, Zia Sardar. A compilation of the best of Sardar's work, from multicultural medicine to an analysis of terrorism to Islamic epistemology, and travel tales." (Sohail Inayatullah)

Inayatullah, Sohail, and Jennifer Fitzgerald, eds. *Transcending Boundaries: P.R. Sarkar's Theories of Individual and Social Transformation*. Maleny, Australia: Gurukul Publications, 1999. "Covers the vast range of writings by Sarkar, in areas such as governance, education, silence and communication, food politics, political-economy, bio-psychology and spirituality." (Sohail Inayatullah)

Inayatullah, Sohail, and Jennifer Gidley, eds. *The University in Transformation: Global Perspectives on the Futures of the University*. Westport, CT: Praeger, 2000. "Explores how globalization, virtualization, multiculturalism and democratization are impacting the Academy. Takes a political-economy and futures approach to the subject." (Sohail Inayatullah)

Inayatullah, Sohail, and Susan Leggett, eds. *Transforming Communication: Technology, Sustainability and Future Generations*. Westport, CT: Praeger, 2002. "Explores the futures of communication, focusing on the utopian claims of cyber enthusiasts. Argues for communication futures that are sustainable, participatory and mindful of future generations." (Sohail Inayatullah)

Galtung, Johan, and Sohail Inayatullah, eds. *Macrohistory and Macrohistorians. Perspectives on Individual, Social and Civilization Change*. Westport, CT: Praeger, 1997. "Develops a general theory of macrohistory through an analysis of the theories of social change of twenty macrohistorians from Western, Islamic, Indic, and Sinic civilizations. Includes feminist and gaian macrohistory as well." (Sohail Inayatullah)

Gidley, Jennifer and Sohail Inayatullah, eds. *Youth Futures: Comparative Research and Transformative Visions*. Westport, CT: Praeger, 2002. "Presents empirical research from around the world on how youth imagine the future, which scenarios they prefer and the level of agency they believe they have in creating desired futures. There are also sections on futures studies in education." (Sohail Inayatullah)

9. Jennings, Lane. *Virtual Futures*. Washington, D.C.: OtherWorlds Press, 1996; *Fabrications*. Washington, D.C.: Black Buzzard Press, 1998. Two volumes of poetry.

10. Johnston, Margaret R. *Pregnant? Need help? Pregnancy Options Workbook* (1998, rev. 2002) (www.pregnancyoptions.info). Available from Ferre Institute, 124 Front St., Binghamton, NY 13905.

11. Kaufman, R. *Strategic Thinking: A Guide to Identifying and Solving Problems*. Rev. Arlington, VA: American Society for Training and Development and the International Society for Performance Improvement, 1998; Kaufman, R. *Mega Planning: Practical Tools for Organizational Success*. Thousand Oaks, CA. Sage Publications, 2000; Kaufman, R., R. Watkins, and D. Leigh. *Useful Educational Results: Defining, Prioritizing, Accomplishing*. Lancaster, PA: Proactive Press, 2001. "These recent books identify the 'whys' and 'hows' of 'practical Utopian planning.' They put a measurable focus on the kind of world we, together, want to and will create for tomorrow's child." (Roger Kaufman)

12. Konnor, Melvin. *The Tangled Wing: Biological Constraints on the Human Spirit*. New York: Henry Holt, 2002, rev. ed., 2002. A highly acclaimed exploration of cutting-edge issues in evolutionary and behavioral biology, psychology, and anthropology, enriched by humanistic, philosophical, and spiritual reflections on the complex workings of the mind.

13. Maheshvarananda, Dada. *After Capitalism: PROUT's Vision for a New World*. Washington, D.C.: Proutist Universal Publications, 2002. Foreword by Noam Chomsky, with contributions by Frei Betto, Marcos Arruda, Johan Galtung, Leonardo Boff, Sohail Inayatullah, Ravi Batra, and Mark Friedman. "An introduction to the Progressive Utilization Theory (PROUT), a socio-economic model based on decentralized economic democracy, cooperative enterprise, and the ethics of inclusion." (Dada Maheshvarananda)

14. Porpora, Douglas. *Landscapes of the Soul: The Loss of Moral Meaning in American Life*. New York: Oxford University Press, 2001. "Landscapes is a sociological analysis of what ordinary Americans think about the meaning of life and moral purpose. It finds that while Americans continue to be moral in their dealings with each other, most do not think in terms of the moral purpose of their lives or in terms of any larger moral vision." (Douglas Porpora)

15. Reiner, Thomas. *The Place of the Ideal Community in Urban Planning*. A pioneering exploration of the linkages between utopian thinking and city planning.

16. Reynolds, David B. *Taking the High Road: Communities Organize for Economic Change*. Armonk, NY: M.E. Sharpe, 2002. Presents a vision for far-reaching economic change in America connected to practical grassroots steps. Offers concrete examples, tools, and ideas.

17. Rhines, Jesse. *Black Film/White Money*. New Brunswick, NJ: Rutgers University Press, 1996. "Urges Blacks to aggressively seek independent power and wealth in the film industry in order to take command of the image projected to the world and to augment their position in the global political economy." (Jesse Rhines)

18. Shostak, Arthur. *CyberUnion: Empowering Labor through Computer Technology*. Armonk, NY: M.E. Sharpe, 1999. Explores ongoing efforts made by the largest social movement in the United States to make creative and rewarding use of computer technology. Offers lessons transferable to many comparable movements in wise and foolish approaches to new technological possibilities. Emphasizes the importance of answering the question—What is it you are really after?

Shostak, Arthur. *Private Sociology: Unsparing Reflections/Uncommon Gains*. Dix Hills, NY: General Hall, 1996. A collection of original essays urging the public processing of taboo matters on behalf of finer mental health and stronger social science.

Shostak, Arthur, ed. *Utopian Thinking in Sociology: Creating the Good Society. Syllabi and Other Instructional Materials*. Washington, DC: American

Sociological Association, 2001. Features essays and materials from forty-four contributors, principally academics (including ten students). Contributor Peter C. Bishop, chair of the Graduate Program in Studies of the Future at the University of Houston–Clear Lake cites theories suggesting that "our reality is shaped by our thoughts and attitudes, so why not shape a more positive future by using more positive images of that future."

19. Shostak, Stanley. *Becoming Immortal: Combining Cloning and Stem-Cell Therapy.* Albany: SUNY Press; 2002. This volume is the third in a set of path-breaking explorations of cutting-edge issues in biology (*Death of Life: The Legacy of Molecular Biology*, London: Macmillan, 1998; *The Evolution of Sameness and Difference: Perspectives on the Human Genome Project*, Amsterdam: Harwood Academic, 1999). This volume raises brow-arching questions about the prospect of unlimited life, a matter long thought only an implausible utopian dream, but now closer to achievement . . . and more controversial thereby than ever before.

20. Shumar, Wes. *College for Sale: A Critique of the Commodification of Higher Education.* New York: RoutledgeFalmer Press, 1997. A revealing exploration of much that is amiss in higher education, and what might be required to set it right.

21. Straus, Roger A., ed. *Using Sociology: An Introduction from the Applied and Clinical Perspectives.* Lanham, MD: Rowman and Littlefield, 2002. Twelve essays seek to "communicate how sociology is both personally relevant to the student and generally relevant to the problems of living in an increasingly complex world." Five essayists are also contributors to this volume.

22. Weinberger, David. *The Cluetrain Manifesto: The End of Business as Usual.* Cambridge, MA: Perseus, 2002; *Small Pieces Loosely Joined: A Unified Theory of the Web.* Cambridge, MA: Perseus, 2002. Two highly regarded, original, and engaging explorations of the meaning of Web usage for humankind, now and into the future. While noting risks and hazards, they take a positive view; e.g., the Web "helps to heal our alienation from our own experience" (*Small Pieces*, 180).

Web Site Resources

1. Bisk, Tsvi: http://www.adultdegree.com; site for the Adult Education and Strategic Educational Planning (ST.E.P.) Institute.

2. Coates, Joseph F.: http://www.josephcoates.com (interactive).

3. Fresco, Jacque: http://www.thevenusproject.com (The Venus Project).

4. Glass, John: http://www.familyplace.org. "The mission of The Family Place is to eliminate family violence through intervention and proactive prevention, extensive community education, advocacy and assistance for victims and their families." (John Glass)

5. Pepinsky, Hal: http://www.critcrim.org/critpapers/pepinsky-book.htm. "I have posted a 'book' of my criminological findings under the title *A Criminologist's Quest for Peace* (2001) for free use and comment. It summarize my findings on how one makes one's own and others' lives safer rather than more violent." (Hal Pepinsky)

6. Pinto, Jim: http://www.jimpinto.com/signup.html. Send a blank e-mail message to: Signup@JimPinto.com, with the subject line "sign me up for JimPinto.com E-mail news." See also http://www.JimPinto.com. Focuses on advances in technology and social changes of relevance to futurists; can be custom tailored to your special interests.

7. Salsbury, Patrick: http://reality.sculptors.com/. Many aspects of the floating city as a viable utopian idea are covered in more depth on "the floating-cities mailing list and the Reality Sculptors website—where you can find archives of past discussions, or join in future ones. The essay itself will also be further expanded on the website."

"It's not precisely a book, yet, but my ongoing project to produce an online version of 'The Whole Future Catalog' is up and running on the Reality Sculptors website. It's designed as a group project, so anyone can join in and add submissions of futuristic things they think should be in the catalog. Instructions, details, and the catalog itself can be found at http://reality.sculptors.com/cgi-bin/wiki?WholeFuture. And, of course, the main site at http://reality.sculptors.com/ details many of my forays into trying to create positive futures and utopic solutions to social problems. I highly recommend it for people interested in helping to change the world for the better." (Patrick Salsbury)

8. Shostak, Arthur: http://www.cyberunions.net. A site for posting ideas for advancing the use of computer power by labor unions—ideas transferable to a wide range of social-action organizations and movements.

9. Weinberger, David, ed. JOHO—Journal of the Hyperlinked Organization (self@evident.com). To subscribe, send a blank message to joho-subscribe@topica.com. For the "fully glorious illustrated and hyperlink-saturated online version of JOHO," please visit http://www.hyperorg.com/current/current.html. (See Chapter 11.) (David Weinberger) blog: www.hyperorg.com/blogger cluetrain: http://www.cluetrain.com new book: http://www.smallpieces.com speaking: www.hyperorg.com/speaker. (David Weinberger)

Notes on the Editor
and Contributors

Kyle Bady. "I am a graduate in the class of 2003 at Cheltenham High School. I hope to attend classes at Morehouse University located in Atlanta, Georgia. I will be majoring in psychology and criminal law. I am aspiring to one day become a writer for a magazine or newspaper. I also hope to write a book updating the public on social race relations in America. I can be reached at TAGR3@aol.com."

Douglas Bedell, of Harrisburg, Pennsylvania, has had a career in journalism, public relations, and consulting. A graduate of Allegheny College, in Meadville, Pennsylvania, he was a reporter on the *Philadelphia Bulletin* and the *Wall Street Journal*, and then an editorial writer and assistant editor of the editorial page on the *Bulletin*. In 1980, after the accident at Three Mile Island (TMI) Unit 2, he became TMI's media relations manager and then its communication manager, with responsibility for media, emergency, and employee communications. Following his retirement from GPU Nuclear Corporation in 1994, he launched Resource Relations, a consulting practice in organizational communication. E-mail: dhbedell@mindspring.com.

Wendell Bell is Professor Emeritus of Sociology and Senior Research Scientist, Yale University. He accepted a position at Yale in 1963; before that, he was on the faculties of UCLA, Northwestern University, and Stanford University. During World War II, he served as a naval aviator in the Philippines. He has been a futurist for about four decades, beginning with his research on political change in the new states of the Caribbean. He is the author of nine books and more than 200 articles. His most recent major work is the two-volume *Foundations of Futures Studies*, published in 1997. E-mail: wen-dell.bell@yale.edu.

Tsvi Bisk is an independent Israeli educator, social researcher, and writer. He is the founder and CEO of the adult education website www.adultdegree.com and the Strategic Educational Planning (ST.E.P.) Institute. He is currently coauthoring a book for Praeger/Greenwood Press entitled *Futurizing the Jews*. He can be reached at bisk@adultdegree.com.

Joseph F. Coates has consulted to 45 of the *Fortune* 100 companies, smaller firms, trade, professional, public interest groups, and government. He is the coauthor of four books and author of over 300 articles and papers on the future. He serves on eleven editorial boards. See website: www.josephcoates.com.

Irwin Deutscher is Professor Emeritus at the University of Akron. He has authored over 100 articles and six books. He holds the American Sociological Associations Distinguished Career Award for the Practice of Sociology, and has served as president of the Society for the Study of Social Problems and the Society for Applied Sociology. He can be reached at irwind@juno.com or 4740 Connecticut Avenue NW, #1007, Washington, DC 20008, USA.

Stephen Downes is a senior research officer with the National Research Council of Canada in Moncton, New Brunswick, Canada. "Affiliated with the Council's Institute for Information Technology, I work with the E-Learning Research Group. My principal work involves research and development in e-learning, working with institutions and companies to improve their competitive position in the industry, and outreach through articles, seminars and workshops."

William Du Bois, Ph.D., is coauthor of *Applying Sociology: Making a Better World*. He has taught at several universities and has consulted with a wide variety of organizations including state government, school administrators, chambers of commerce, women's crisis centers, juvenile groups homes, bars and nightclubs, managers, nursing home administrators, and medical staff. E-mail: dubois@itctiel.com.

Marilyn Dudley-Rowley is a lecturer in the Sociology Department at Sonoma State University in California. She edited and prefaced the recently published Russian-language version of *The Case for Mars* by Robert Zubrin and Richard Wagner. She is the only sociologist ever accepted in the NASA Astronaut Mission Specialist Candidate training-eligible files. Her interest in extreme environments began Earthside, however. Between 1981 and 1982, she orchestrated the first mass Afghan refugee airlift, the Kirghiz Afghan rescue. Before that, in 1975, she was the first U.S. Army woman to be trained as an Arctic combat mountaineer. (www.Martiana.org)

Carroy U. Ferguson, Ph.D., is a tenured professor at the College of Public and Community Service, University of Massachusetts/Boston and associate editor of the *Journal of Humanistic Psychology*. His books include *Innovative Approaches to Education and Community Service* (1993) and *A New Perspective on Race and Color* (1997), in addition to chapters in other books and various journal publications. He is cofounder of both Interculture, Inc., and Associates in Human Understanding; is a practicing clinical psychologist, consultant, and workshop leader; and is on the national board of the Association for Humanistic Psychology. His research interests include a focus on the nature and evolution of consciousness, the mind-body-spirit connection, and alternative models of human nature as they apply in practical ways to race relations and social justice. E-mails: carroy.ferguson@umb.edu or cuferguson@aol.com. Mailing address: University of Massachusetts-Boston, CPCS, Human Services, 100 Morrissey Boulevard, Boston, MA 02125-3393; phone: 617-287-7232.

Valerie Fournier is the senior lecturer in organization studies at Keele University, Keele, UK. Her writing so far has been concerned with disciplinary practices, as well as subjectivity and embodiment in organizations. She has been published in a range of sociological and organizational journals, including *Body & Society, Gender, Work & Organization, Organization*, and the *Sociological Review*. Her growing commitment to exploring alternative forms of organizing has directed her interests toward anarchist theory, anticapitalist protest movements, alternative medicine, and women farmers' cooperatives.

Jacque Fresco. His background includes industrial design, engineering, lecturing, and futurist studies. He has invented and patented many different products which have achieved wide commercial acceptance in fields as diverse as the aeronautics, automotive, prefabricated housing, medical, and motion picture industries. His numerous books, videos, and articles about the Venus Project have been published worldwide. His most recent book is *The Best That Money Can't Buy: Beyond Politics, Poverty, & War*, published in 2002. Jacque Fresco can be reached at 21 Valley Lane, Venus, FL 33960; phone: 863-465-0321; e-mail: fresco@thevenusproject.com; Web: www.thevenusproject.com.

Thomas Gangale is an aerospace engineer and a former officer in the U.S. Air Force. While on active duty, he served on the management team of several classified satellite projects at the highest level of national priority, including a Strategic Defense Initiative program and two Space Shuttle payloads. He is the primary writer-thinker today on time measurement in extraterrestrial settings and social implications. His published works over the Internet, in journals, and in newspapers involve Mars during the Ancient and Classical periods, communications systems for Mars missions, reforming the U.S. presidential primary election system, and military topics. E-mail: marcus@martiana.org.

John E. Glass is a sociologist currently working in the field of domestic violence. He "discovered" his male privilege while at work: "It was a humbling experience. Although I take credit for all of the content of my essay, I can neither confirm nor deny any resemblance to the narrator. I am certainly open to discussing the possibility, however." John Glass can be reached at johneglass@yahoo.com.

Mitchell Gordon is a writer and futurist from Philadelphia. He is an urban planning journalist (M.U.P.), a program director for the Philadelphia Chapter of the World Future Society, and vice president of the Philadelphia Area Space Alliance. He also does consultanting work involving copywriting and administrative services. He can be reached at mfgordon@excite.com.

Sohail Inayatullah is a professor at the Center for Future Studies, Tamkang University, Taiwan, and on the faculty of arts and social sciences at the University of the Sunshine Coast in Australia. Inayatullah is an associate editor of *New Renaissance* (www.ru.org) and coeditor of the *Journal of Futures Studies*. He is author/editor of a dozen books on futures studies, macrohistory, and the politics of knowledge. Web: www.metafuture.org.

Lane Jennings has been an editor and reviewer for the World Future Society since 1976. Currently he is the production editor of *Future Survey*. He is also a freelance writer and translator, with a Ph.D. in German and two published books of poetry: *Virtual Futures* (1996) and *Fabrications* (1998). E-mail: lanejen@aol.com.

Margaret R. Johnston, has been providing abortion services to women in upstate New York for over twenty years. She has written extensively on the abortion issue and has created two self-help guides: "Pregnant? Need Help? Pregnancy Options Workbook" and "Abortion: Which Method Is Right for Me?" (www.pregnancyoptions.info). She has been a trainer in abortion counseling for both the National Abortion Federation and the National Coalition of Abortion Providers (NCAP) and is currently the president of NCAP. E-mail: info@pregnancyoptions.info.

Roger Kaufman is a professor and director of the Office for Needs Assessment and Planning at Florida State University where he received a Professorial Excellence award. He is also a research professor of engineering management at the Old Dominion University, Norfolk, Virginia, and director of Roger Kaufman and Associates. Kaufman has published thirty-four books, including *Mega Planning, Strategic Planning Plus*, and *Strategic Thinking-Revised*, and has coauthored *Useful Educational Results: Defining, Prioritizing, and Accomplishing* and *Strategic Planning and Thinking Field Book*, as well as over 200 articles on strategic planning, performance improvement, quality management and continuous improvement, needs assessment, management, and evaluation. E-mail: rkaufman@onap.fsu.edu.

Claire Keyes. "Most of my life's work has been in abortion. Although I have been the Executive Director of Allegheny Reproductive Health Center in Pittsburgh for nearly 25 years, my heart has always been in counseling. For the past decade I have been training counselors; I presented at both the National Abortion Federation and the National Coalition of Abortion Providers, focusing on new paradigms for healing spiritually and emotionally after abortion as well as men's issues. I'd like to hear from anyone who would like to comment." E-mail: arhc1234@aol.com.

Melvin Konner is an anthropologist and nonpracticing M.D. who was educated at Midwood High School and Brooklyn College (CUNY) and trained at Harvard's graduate and medical schools. He is the author of *The Tangled Wing: Biological Constraints on the Human Spirit, Becoming a Doctor, Childhood*, and *Why the Reckless Survive*, among other books. "He spent two formative years among the !Kung Bushmen, then hunter-gatherers of Botswana, and two formative decades raising three children, partly as a single parent. He is the Samuel Candler Dobbs Professor of Anthropology and of Neuroscience and Behavioral Biology at Emory University." E-mail: antmk@emory.edu.

Ross Koppel, Ph.D., sociology, is the president of the Social Research Corporation in Wyncote, Pennsylvania. He conducts research on work, medicine, education, and social policy. The recipient of the William Foote Whyte Award for Distinguished Career Award in the Practice of Sociology, Koppel also teaches in the Department of Sociology at the University of Pennsylvania. He is currently studying the role of hospital culture on the commission of medication errors and the cost of Alzheimer's disease to society. E-mail: rkoppel@sas.upenn.edu.

Dada Maheshvarananda is a monk and activist in Brazil and the author of *After Capitalism: Prout's Vision for a New World*. He can be reached at Proutist Universal, Rua Buarque de Macedo, 35, Floresta, Belo Horizonte-MG 31015-350, Brazil; tel/fax (55-31) 3555-1574; e-mail: maheshvarananda @prout.org.

Michael Marien is the founder and editor of *Future Survey*, published monthly since 1979 by the World Future Society in Bethesda, Maryland (www.wfs.org). *Future Survey* is the authoritative literature review for books, reports, and articles on trends, forecasts, and betterment proposals ranging from the pragmatic to the utopian. Marien holds a Ph.D. in social science and national planning from the Maxwell Graduate School of Citizenship and Public Affairs at Syracuse University. E-mail: mmarien@tweny.rr.com.

William (Thad) McKenna earned a BA in history and education from Gwynedd-Mercy College and an MS in sociology/criminal justice from St. Joseph's University where he was a graduate assistant. He currently teaches sociology, American history, the future, and contemporary issues at Cheltenham High School. He can be reached at 2010 Lodges Lane, Oreland, PA 19075; phone: 215-836-2044; e-mail: wmckenna@cheltenham.org.

Diane McManus runs, writes, and occasionally sees egrets in the Philadelphia area. She received her Ph.D. in English at Temple University and is managing editor of the *Journal of Modern Literature*. Her poem, "Marathon Presence," appeared in the anthology *Body Stories*, edited by Lisa West Smith (2000). She has given presentations on writing and running, and has published poetry and fiction in the *Runner's Gazette*. E-mail: dmcmanus@nimbus.temple.edu.

Roxanne Meadows is an accomplished and well-known technical, medical, and architectural illustrator and model maker. In addition, she is president and founder of Architectural Arts, Inc. For over twenty-five years she has worked toward the realization of the Venus Project. Roxanne can be reached at 21 Valley Lane, Venus, FL 33960; e-mail: meadows@thevenusproject.com; web: www.thevenusproject.com.

Robert J. Merikangas is a retired librarian at the University of Maryland, College Park. He holds a Ph.D. in history from the Catholic University of America. He has published articles on library management and has written a utopia of the University of Maryland. He published an article on wisdom communities in *Futures Research Quarterly*. E-mail: rm30@umail.umd.edu.

James Mitchell teaches architectural engineering at Drexel University using student teams that create their work on the Internet. He received a BA and MS from Harvard University and an MArch from the University of Pennsylvania. Before joining the Drexel faculty, he was a partner in an architectural firm he founded. He believes that "including the lessons one learns from studying humanities are essential to retaining humility and integrity in the face of increasing technological change." He is a registered architect and a published poet. E-mail: mitcheje@Exchange1.drexel.edu.

Benjamin Novack graduated from Cheltenham High School in 2002. He currently attends the University of Pittsburg and is studying to major in computer science. In his spare time, he writes about the past, the present, and—especially—the future. He can be reached via e-mail at bhn3@pitt.edu.

Hal Pepinsky teaches criminal justice at Indiana University, Bloomington. His latest book, *A Criminologist's Quest for Peace*, may be found at http://www.critc.org/critpapers/pepinsky-book.htm. E-mail: pepinsky@indiana.edu.

Jim Pinto is a technology entrepreneur, investor, futurist, writer, and commentator. Born in India, he lived in England for eight years and in the United States since 1968. He was named California Small Business Person of the Year for the State of California in 1980. He has been featured in many books and national journals as a pioneer in participative management. He has traveled widely throughout the world, and has significant experience in the comparative study of American, European, and Japanese business cultures. E-mail him at jim@jimpinto.com. Or look at his poems, prognostications, and predictions on his website: www.JimPinto.com.

Douglas Porpora is a professor of sociology and the head of the Department of Culture and Communication at Drexel University. He is the author of numerous articles and four books, among them *How Holocausts Happen: The US in Central America* (1990) and *Landscapes of the Soul: The Loss of Moral Meaning in American Life* (2001). E-mail: porporad@drexel.edu.

Adrienne Redd teaches sociology and a seminar on utopias at Cabrini College in Radnor, Pennsylvania. She is a contributor to the 2001 publication of the ASA: "Utopian Thinking in Sociology: Creating the Good Society." She holds an MA degree in sociology from Temple University and is pursuing a Ph.D. in human and organizational systems from the Fielding Graduate Institute. She can be reached at adrienne@redd.com.

Thomas A. Reiner is a professor in the Regional Science Program of the University of Pennsylvania. He has also taught in the Department of City and Regional Planning. The author of *The Place of the Ideal Community in Urban Planning* (1963), he has also worked as a planner in the United States and Puerto Rico and has consulted with community, local, national, and international agencies here and abroad.

David Reynolds is a faculty member in the Labor Studies Center at Wayne State University. His recent publications include *Taking the High Road: Communities Organize for Economic Change* (2002); *Living Wage Campaigns: An Activists Guide for Building the Movement for Economic Justice*, and *Democ-*

racy Unbound: Progressive Challenges to the Two Party System (1997). He helped organize several local living wage coalitions in Southeast Michigan, and he served as principal researcher for two studies on the impact of Detroit's 1998 living wage ordinance. He can be reached at aa2589@wayne.edu.

Jesse Rhines is an assistant professor of African American studies at Rutgers University in Newark, New Jersey. He earned his Ph.D. in ethnic studies at UC Berkeley. The second edition of his *Black Film/White Money* was published in 2000. His research interests include black political economy and global ethnic interaction. He is currently writing a book on the subject of African Americans and the utopian imagination. E-mail: jrhines@worldnet .att.net.

Patrick Salsbury is a design scientist living in the San Francisco Bay area. He works on creating solutions for social problems such as traffic congestion, homelessness, poverty, hunger, water shortage, and poor education. He is also the founder of Reality Sculptors: http://reality.sculptors.com/.

Arthur B. Shostak. A sociologist since earning my Ph.D. in 1961, I first taught at the Wharton School of the University of Pennsylvania from 1961 to 1967, and ever since at Drexel University (Philadelphia, PA). My courses include "Futuristics," "Industrial Sociology," "Social Change and Social Planning," and "Introduction to Sociology." As my undergraduate degree is in Industrial and Labor relations, from 1975–2001 I was also an adjunct sociologist at the AFL-CIO George Meany Center for Labor Studies (Silver Springs, MD). An applied sociologist, I have worked over the past 40 years on abortion reform, educational technology, Higher Education, K-12 public schooling, labor union renewal, Planned Community design, and many other challenges. At present I am focused on helping labor unions make more creative use of computer power. An early member of the World Future Society, I helped create its Philadelphia Chapter in the early 1970s, and have headed it since 1980. My 23 books include such titles as *Utopian Thinking in Sociology* (2001); *CyberUnion* (1999); *Private Sociology* (1996); *Robust Unionism* (1991); *Men and Abortion* (1984); and *Modern Social Reforms* (1974). My Web sites are at http://www.Futureshaping/shostak and also http://www.cyberunions.net. I can be reached via e-mail at shostaka@drexel.edu.

Stanley Shostak received his Ph.D. from Brown University in 1964 and, after a postdoctoral year at the Developmental Biology Center at (then) Case Western Reserve, joined the faculty at the University of Pittsburgh's Biology Department (now Department of Biological Sciences) where he has remained ever since. He is the author of numerous articles on the development and evolution of cnidarians, chiefly Hydra, and of several books, most recently, *Death of*

Life: The Legacy of Molecular Biology (1998), *The Evolution of Sameness and Difference: Perspectives on the Human Genome Project* (1999), and *Becoming Immortal: Combining Cloning and Stem-cell Therapy* (2002). E-mail: sshostak+@pitt.edu.

Wesley Shumar is a cultural anthropologist at Drexel University. His research focuses on higher education, virtual community, and ethnographic evaluation in education. He is the author of *College for Sale: A Critique of the Commodification of Higher Education* (1997) and coeditor of *Building Virtual Communities: Learning and Change in Cyberspace* (2002). E-mail: wes@drexel.edu.

Harris Sokoloff is an adjunct associate professor and director of the Center for School Study Councils at the University of Pennsylvania Graduate School of Education. He also directs the Deliberative Democracy Program there. His applied research focuses on issues of developing community strength and community engagement. Major projects involve building a public for public education through deliberative community forums. E-mail: harriss@gse.upenn.edu.

Allan Stegeman is an auxiliary instructor in the Department of Culture and Communication at Drexel University. He has been researching communication technologies since 1980 when he undertook a series of economic analyses of high-definition television. For the past twelve years, he has been teaching a seminar class on the economic, social, and technological aspects of the digital convergence at Drexel. E-mail: allan.stegeman@verizon.net.

Diane E., Straus, R.N., M.S.N., A.P.N., C., is a nurse practitioner and recent president of the Advanced Practice Forum of the New Jersey State Nurses' Association. Both Diane and her husband, Roger, as might be inferred from their essay are avid scuba divers. Diane had the privilege of making house calls on Falalop and having a dive site named after her in Ulithi Atoll. E-mail: dstraus@earthlink.net.

Roger A. Straus, Ph.D., is a clinical sociologist, editor, and senior author of *Using Sociology: An Introduction from the Clinical Applied Perspectives* (2001), *Strategic Self-Hypnosis* (2000), and *Creative Self-Hypnosis* (2000). He currently works as a marketing research consultant. E-mail: roger-straus@earthlink.net.

Jon Van Til is a professor of urban studies and community planning at Rutgers University in Camden. He served for twelve years as editor in chief of the *Nonprofit and Voluntary Sector Quarterly*. He is the author or editor of nine books on social policy and voluntary action, and he holds a career award for distinguished research and service from ARNOVA (the Association for Research on Nonprofit Organization and Voluntary Action). E-mail: vantil@camden.rutgers.edu.

Ernest Vlahos has been a practicing utopian/futurist and futures researcher/writer for more than thirty years. A professional member of the World Future Society and a graduate of the University of Southern Mississippi, he has also been a public schoolteacher and a small business owner. He has devoted years of research to developing and promoting the Resort Circle concept, a modern, futuristic, sustainable, and viable utopia. He can be reached at 2603 Catalpa Avenue, Pascagoula, MS 39567; e-mail: justernest@cableone.net; phone: 228-762-4980.

Marilyn Vlahos has been a teacher of children with special needs for twenty-five years in Pascagoula, Mississippi. She received a BS degree in English and French in 1966 and a M.Ed. degree in special education in 1976 from University of Southern Mississippi. She is occasionally a freelance journalist and always a gardener and concerned citizen. She has been married to utopian/futurist Ernest Vlahos since 1989. Marilyn Vlahos can be reached at justernest@cableone.net or marilynvlahos@mail.mac.com.

David Weinberger is the editor of *JOHO* (*Journal of the Hyperlinked Organization*), an independent web zine on "the sometimes subtle effects of the Web on the way businesses work." The author of two recent innovative books, *The Cluetrain Manifesto* (2000) and *Small Pieces Loosely Joined* (2002), he has written for *WIRED, Smithsonian*, the *New York Times*, and others. David has a Ph.D. in philosophy "that entitles him to affect an air of smug obscurity whenever he chooses . . . and [he] really hates writing about himself, especially in the third person." David Weinberger can be reached at self@evident.com.

Jay Weinstein, a professor of sociology at Eastern Michigan University, is the author of numerous articles and books and has worked as a consultant in the United States and throughout the world. He is the recipient of the 1998 Charles Horton Cooley Award and served as president of the Michigan Sociological Association (1989–1990) and the Society for Applied Sociology (2002–2003). E-mail: Weinst@aol.com.

R. Dean Wright is the Ellis and Nelle Levitt Professor of Sociology at Drake University. He is past president of the Midwest Sociological Society, chair of the Iowa Criminal and Juvenile Justice Council, and chair of the Salvation Army Board of Greater Des Moines. His research interest is in poverty, homelessness, and crime. He and his coauthor, William Du Bois, have recently published *Applying Sociology: Making a Better World* (2001). E-mail: dean.wright@drake.edu.

Index

Books by the Editor

The CyberUnion Handbook: Transforming Labor Through Computer Technology. Armonk, NY: M.E. Sharpe, 2002. Provides practical, how-to information and advice on every aspect of using technology to advance Labor's interests.

CyberUnion: Empowering Labor Through Computer Technology. Armonk, NY: M.E. Sharpe, 1999. A thoroughgoing discussion of the first book to discuss the impact of computerization on the labor movement here and abroad. Offers a typology of three current union models (Cyber Naught, Cyber Drift, Cyber Gain) and outlines a distant and vastly improved model (CyberUnion) for labor's consideration.

Impacts of Changing Employment: If the Good Jobs Go Away. Thousand Oaks, CA: Sage, 1996. An edited collection of fourteen original essays exploring the potential of massive job loss and alternative public policy options before and after such an event.

Private Sociology: Unsparing Reflections, Uncommon Gains. Dix Hills, NY: General Hall, 1996. An edited collection of twenty-three first-person studies of "that which we hesitate to tell," the first such book of its kind in American sociology. Essays cover such topics as childhood sexual victimization, the loss by murder of one's brother, the experience of having one's research stolen, the experience of dying in the aftermath of a medical mistake, the challenge of growing up a minority member, and so on.

For Labor's Sake: Gains and Pains as Told by 28 Creative Inside Reformers. Lanham, MD: University Press of America, 1995. An edited collection of twenty-eight first-person accounts by grassroots activists of ongoing efforts to renew the labor movement.

Guidelines from Gomberg: No-Nonsense Advice for Labor-Management Relations. Philadelphia: Chapel, 1992. An edited collection of six timely essays by an internationally renowned professor of industrial and labor relations, William Gomberg, complete with commentary.

Robust Unionism: Innovations in the Labor Movement. Ithaca, NY: ILR Press, 1991. A scholarly monograph that explores and assesses the state of risk taking and planned change in and by organized labor in this country.

The Air Controllers' Controversy. Coauthored with Dave Skocik. New York: Human Sciences, 1986. An analysis of the 1981 strike of Professional Air Traffic Controllers Organization (PATCO), the firing of 11,400 strikers, and the lessons in this historic event for modern labor-management relations.

Men and Abortion: Lessons, Losses, and Love. Coauthored with Gary McLouth and Lynn Seng. New York: Praeger, 1984. A scholarly exploration of the meaning of the abortion experience for 1,000 men located in the waiting rooms of thirty clinics in eighteen states.

Blue-Collar Stress. Reading, MA: Addison-Wesley, 1980. A scholarly monograph that focuses on work problems and reform possibilities where male manual workers are concerned.

Our Sociological Eye: Personal Essays on Society and Culture. Sherman Oaks, CA: Alfred, 1977. An introductory text and reader. Combines basic concept discussions with illustrative first-person reflexive essays from twenty-four contributors.

Modern Social Reforms: Solving Today's Social Problems. New York: Macmillan, 1974. A scholarly monograph that explores overseas and frontier remedies for long-standing social dilemmas such as alleviating poverty, delivering optimum healthcare, improving educational institutions, and many others.

Privilege in America: An End to Inequality? Coprepared with Jon and Sally Bould Von Til. Englewood Cliffs, NJ: Prentice-Hall, Spectrum Series, 1974.

A scholarly monograph on various aspects of social stratification and social egalitarianism. Includes three chapters by Arthur Shostak on the New Populism, the New Socialism, and the Ethnic Revival.

Putting Sociology to Work: Case Studies in the Application of Sociology to Modern Social Problems. New York: David McKay, 1974. An edited collection of twenty-six original essays exploring off-campus uses of sociology in contemporary social reform projects.

Sociology and Student Life. New York: David McKay, 1972. An edited collection of thirty-two reprinted essays that help illuminate both modern campus issues and the basic concepts of academic sociology.

Blue-Collar Life. New York: Random House, 1968. A scholarly monograph analyzing hundreds of scattered research reports and proposing original reforms for pressing blue-collar problems.

Sociology in Action: Case Studies in Social Problems and Directed Social Change. Homewood, IL: Dorsey Press, 1966. An edited collection of thirty-eight first-person accounts of applied projects (twenty-three original essays).

New Perspectives on Poverty. Coedited with William Gomberg. Englewood Cliffs, NJ: Prentice Hall, 1965. An edited collection of twenty essays (six originals) exploring promising reforms for key aspects of poverty.

Blue-Collar World: Studies of the American Worker. Coedited with William Gomberg. Englewood Cliffs, NJ: Prentice Hall, 1964. An edited collection of sixty-two essays (fifty-five originals) about blue-collar realities.

America's Forgotten Labor Organization: The Role of the Single-Firm Independent Union in American Industry. Princeton, NJ: Industrial Relations Section, 1962. A scholarly monograph drawing on Shostak's 1961 Ph.D. thesis research into unaffiliated so-called "company unions."

DATE DUE

GAYLORD			PRINTED IN U.S.A.